# THE FIRST 50

THE FIRST 50

# THE FIRST 50

## A SAGA OF BACKSEATS, BEDROOMS, LOOKOUT POINTS, AND DIVE BARS

### NATASCIA TORNETTA MALLIN

RARE BIRD BOOKS

LOS ANGELES, CALIF.

THIS IS A GENUINE RARE BIRD BOOK

Rare Bird Books
453 South Spring Street, Suite 302
Los Angeles, CA 90013
rarebirdbooks.com

Set in Dante
Printed in the United States

10 9 8 7 6 5 4 3 2 1

Library of Congress Cataloging-in-Publication Data
Names: Mallin, Natascia Tornetta, author.
Title: The first 50 : a saga of backseats, bedrooms, lookout points, and
dive bars / Natascia Tornetta Mallin.
Other titles: First fifty
Description: Los Angeles : Rare Bird Books, 2021.
Identifiers: LCCN 2021008142 | ISBN 9781644281642 (paperback) |
ISBN 9781644282106 (epub)
Subjects: LCSH: Young women—Sexual behavior—California—Los Angeles. |
Man-woman relationships—California—Los Angeles. | Los Angeles
(Calif.)—Social conditions—20th century.
Classification: LCC HQ27.5 .M2106 2021 | DDC 306.7084/ 22—dc23
LC record available at https://lccn.loc.gov/2021008142

*To Richard Alexander Friedman, and the city of stars below*

# CHAPTER 1

In the beginning there was Ricky. Stories of his wild abandon preceded him. They used to talk about the time that Ricky jumped from the roof. Not even from the roof and into something sensible like a pool. He just drank too much one night and jumped off the roof for fun. Broke his arm or his leg or something, which kept him home while we were out, so I met him first through these stories. My best friend, Dahlia, used to say he was full of zest, but I like to think it was something more primal than Ricky's zest that drew me to him. Something feral. Something hormonal. I was probably fourteen and he was probably nineteen and it was definitely against the law, but we never bothered with such details.

I wrote a poem for Mr. Brown's poetry class senior year about the first time I saw Ricky. And then I recorded myself reading it as part of a multimedia class project we were doing in the AV department. The poem was that sort of over-the-top theatrical, romanticized garbage you'd expect from a teenager, but the thought of that recording being out there in the world today, burned onto a CD that God knows who still has a copy of, makes me wanna puke a little. I wonder if I would have remembered the first time I saw him so vividly had I never recorded that fucking poem.

He was sitting on a brown corduroy recliner in his sister's living room on Sixth and Sunset in Venice. The rest of us were just stopping by on the way to some party, standing around drinking forties, lamping in varying degrees of awkwardness, posing as cool. Not Ricky though. Ricky was totally himself. Totally at ease, like he would have been doing the exact same thing had the house been empty. Even though we didn't speak that night, or really look at each other, I decided then and there that he was mine. I wanted a piece of that unrestrained recklessness, and I didn't care how.

•••

BACK THEN THE NIGHTS always ended north of Montana in David Fox's backyard on Georgina. It was there in the Jacuzzi where we all first learned the erotic art of toe-sucking—which is not a euphemism for anything else. We legitimately sucked toes. All of us. No matter to what corners of the Westside the evening brought us, in the end it was always the backyard on Georgina and a hot, wet orgy of feet.

I remember the first time it happened. Katya was getting a massage from one of the boys and someone dared her to suck David Fox's toes. We all giggled and grimaced, but she just shrugged her shoulders, mumbled something about sterilization and chlorine, and went at it. After the initial shock made its way around the pool, the pure euphoria on David's face became a waterborne virus. Before any of us knew it we all caught fever, mouth deep in toes. Sucking toes was safe and noncommittal—daring enough to be erotic, but innocent enough not to circulate in rumors the next day. No one had to kiss or suck anything else, and everyone was doing it. Girls on boys. Boys on girls. And of course, girls on girls. But never boys on boys. This was Los Angeles in the late nineties and despite being literally surrounded by water, shit just wasn't that fluid back then.

After that first night toe-sucking was a given, like the backyard, or the series of pages and callbacks that eventually led us there. Though to be perfectly frank, I never participated in the latter. I mean, sure, I had a beeper. Everyone had a beeper. And while I could drink and toe-suck with the best of them, I wasn't about to "411, 143, *88 so you know it's me" any of those dudes. It was just too intimate, and like my parents used to love to remind me, I was only fourteen. But as long as I had my girls Isabella and Dahlia by my side, I knew that eventually one of the boys would swoop us.

If David himself were picking us up, we'd pile into his E-Class and I'd wonder about the life that would lead an otherwise unremarkable, kinda nerdy nineteen-year-old boy into his own brand-new luxury sedan. But alas, such were the marvels of the north side of Santa Monica. Million-dollar cottage mansions with pantries stuffed full of name-brand snacks. Driveways with multiple Mercedes, backyards with hot tubs, and whole rooms designated for games. The north side of Santa Monica: where friends were always over and always welcomed to stay for dinner, and where parents were always away on vacation, or "business." I never understood the mechanics of such living, yet I pondered them relentlessly until we pulled into the liquor store. Then it was either a bottle of Bacardi Limon, or as much Natty Ice as all of us could stomach and afford. When Portia was with us, she would always make the boys pay. She was older, sixteen at least, and classier than the lot of us put together. Still, it never felt right to me having the boys buy the booze. The implications terrified me, and I would make a point to show that I could fund my own intoxication. It seemed like the smarter thing to do, and I was just naive enough to imagine I had principles and ignorant enough to imagine that those principles would keep me safe.

Those boys had it made. Hanging out with young girls who would insist on paying for their own booze. Ending up in hot tubs at the end of the night, toes in mouths for nothing. We were all amateurs, really, but I digress.

On this particular night, Ricky's night, we all opted for Natty Ice and snuck onto the polo field at Will Rogers Park to pregame. Dahlia always brought apples for the horses on Will Rogers nights. When we used to go horseback riding every summer at Y Camp in Big Bear, if you could get her to even sit on a horse, she'd be shitting her whole pants with fright. But at Will Rogers with them safely tucked into their stables, trespassing in the dead of night, Dahlia could walk right up, apple in hand, like a damn horse whisperer.

So there we were, pounding can after can of sparkling malted piss-water, and I just knew I had to say something to Ricky. I mustered up the liquid courage to ask if he wanted to race.

"Oh, yeah?" He grinned. "Do you seriously think you can beat me?" His look was all fun and mischief and toothsome possibility.

No one had ever looked at me like that before, and though I was on the verge of disappearing into a thousand glittering bubbles of amber, I managed to squeak out a charm I'm proud of to this day. "I have an older brother. I've been training for this my whole life!"

If there were ever a moment in which Ricky could have loved me back, it would have been right there on the dew-soaked grass of the polo field in the midnight moments before the great race.

We took the field together, eyes locked. Back at the tables someone shouted the countdown. At "GO!" we shot out like cannon fire. I had never felt so alive. Maybe it was the April fog that clung to our clothing, or the intoxicating aroma of the eucalyptus trees that filled our lungs, or the squish of soggy peat under our bare feet as we ran. Or maybe it was the six-pack of malt liquor in my belly that magnetized me to him and propelled me in effervescent fury faster and faster. In any case, I almost beat him. It was practically a tie. I mean, I was never more than a step behind him, and as we crossed the imaginary finish line I grabbed him, and he let me.

That was it. We didn't kiss. We didn't embrace. There was no moment of romantic pause, no climax to that massive crescendo. I just grabbed him and we roared with laughter all the way back to the tables while I wondered if this was what love felt like. And then as we drank some more, we grinned incessantly at each other like you do when you know "this shit is about to be on," except I was fourteen and shit had never been on enough for me to know that the shit was on, so I was just grinning at him like an absolute dummy, mistaking his grinning for genuine interest. Though the laughter and the moment promised infinity, the empty beer cans marked the passing of time and the inevitability of a backyard hot tub. It was time to leave.

Climbing to the street we came upon a taxi driver pulled over at the top of the hill with his overhead lights blaring, dirty magazine in hand. Either at the end of a long night or the beginning of one, this poor dude was just tryna catch a beat. When we caught him scrambling to kill the light, Ricky and I lost it. Like finger-pointing, sidesplitting howls that shattered the stillness of the Palisades after midnight.

Stepping through the gate into David's yard, the memory of the race and the taxi cab, and time eternal still pounded in our chests. All at once a hot tub full of toes seemed a vulgar absurdity. With a glance and a squeeze we stole away into the steam shower upstairs. Engulfed in clandestine embrace, flexing in discovery, fourteen-year-old Natascia dissipated into expensive vapor and the newness of passion. There was no age. No time. No law. There was only Ricky and the beating rapture of zest. Hours went by. A lifetime. I don't know. It could have been forever for all I cared, but eventually the water ran cold, and infinity ended. Ricky wrapped me up in a million-thread count, pre-revolution Egyptian cotton towel and ushered me into David's brother's room and onto David's brother's bed.

In a breath he was inside me, and in the fifteen seconds that followed before I ended up stopping him, two thoughts rang out like church bells at midday: One, I want this, and two, he never even bothered to ask. They kept clanging like that in tandem: I want this. He didn't ask. I WANT THIS. HE DIDN'T ASK. Over and over until my body stiffened with thoughts of virginity, purity, reputation, and absolute ruin. Just like that I was fourteen and Natascia again.

"Wait," I barely managed.

He stopped and asked, "Why?"

I had no reason and every reason. I was attempting to hang onto the imagination of virtue, but it was over just like that. Lying there frozen with him inside of me after an eternity of silence, the angels who watch over underage girls finally took pity on my self-generated confusion, and my friend Kimberly Anderson knocked on the door. I jumped up in triumph.

"That's why!" I grabbed my clothes, ran out the door, and promised myself that as long as I never spoke of it that it didn't have to count and I could manage to hang onto my virginity at least through the summer.

In hindsight, it was a much better origin story than the one I ended up going public with, but I was a melodramatic brooding teenager, and perhaps the passion of that night was just too pure for me to believe in. Touching infinity? Who was I kidding? What followed that steamy night was a four-year, gut-wrenching obsession that culminated in a seven-page letter in which I professed my undying insanity for this boy I hardly knew. From fourteen in a moment with no words to seventeen in a letter with far too many.

I don't know. I suppose I did my best.

We met again when I was just barely twenty-one. He was just barely sober and calling me in a poor attempt at the ninth step. Sort of perfunctory and deficient of any real substance, I choked down the humiliation of his "I'm sorry if I, like, did anything to hurt you or whatever." I remembered all the nights when I would pretend the whiskey on his breath made him taste like tangerines and all the days I'd check my voicemail over and over hoping he would call again. Then I remembered the years I spent fighting between the fantasy of what could be and degradation of what was, and here he was calling me after all this time on the goddamned telephone to tell me that I was on the goddamned list he wrote for his ninth step, and that in order to get fucking better, he had to call and like, "make amends, or whatever."

I don't know. I suppose he did his best too.

But fuck me if I didn't somehow reimagine my own specialness as the object of Ricky's persistent and irresistible charm. He kept calling until I eventually relented. He even took me out a couple of times with the boys and their girlfriends. I pretended it meant something. That he was finally coming around and wanted to be with me...you know, like a normal couple. Slowly, reluctantly, after so many years of working to exorcize the demon of fantasy, I'd be lying if I didn't say she crept back in, gnashing her teeth.

He asked me over for Valentine's Day that year, and I did my very best to talk myself back from the ledge of romantic oblivion in the car ride over. I brought him a kombucha thinking I was being really clever and sweet. The closest thing to a brew without being a brew. I handed it to him, feigning a toast, and half-sarcastically exclaimed, "To your sobriety and your health!" He took it and mansplained something about only drinking a shot glass full at a time for optimal digestion.

I rolled my eyes, but he wasn't looking. "Well, you're welcome," or whatever.

Then it was his iTunes library and stories about his long-distance girlfriend, on the couch, where he quite literally charmed the pants off of me. Which admittedly wasn't very hard to do. But with the ninth step behind us everything had changed. Unpropelled by the ecstasy of whiskey-flavored infinity, he stopped before even starting, looked deep into my eyes, and uttered eleven words I'll never forget: "I want you to know that this is just about sex."

I shrugged, said okay, and let him fuck me. As he did, I realized how wonderful it would be to never see him like this again. He got off and into the shower. I got up and into my car, and that was that. In that one night we finished what we had started seven years earlier, which proved in the end to be nothing at all.

# CHAPTER 2

I WAS PRETTY FUCKING young when I met Pablo. I'd like to think I was at least thirteen, but I could have been twelve. Some of us grew up fast in this city. That's neither a point of pride nor a mark of shame. It is a pure and simple fact.

We were at Dahlia's grandmother's house on Marine. She had given us the place for the night as she babysat Dali's little sister down the street. For all of Granny's pompous morality, it seems ridiculous now. She must have known what we were up to. She certainly knew who her granddaughter was. I think she only ever gave a damn if she could have a part in chastising and condemning after the fact. When she finally died and her reign of emotional terror was over, I tried to be sad. I really did. But all I could think of was the time she read Dali's diary and made fun of her as she feigned concern: "Oh, for Pete's sake! You think Scott really loves you? Oh, Gawd. Don't be an idiot. Well, you shouldn't have left it out if you didn't want anyone reading it!"

Afterward Dahlia printed a hundred pages that said "FUCK YOU FOR READING THIS" in bold red caps. We taped them up all over her room and sat on her bed, arms crossed, waiting. When Granny saw our installation, she snickered, "Oh, Gawd! You're both idiots."

But this was before all that. This was the beginning of the debauchery that ensued over the next five years, and it may also have been the first time I met Felix. So there we were in Granny's house—Dali, Isabella, me—and Dali had invited the group of boys over I'd been hearing so much about. The Drinking Crew. DC. Dahlia and Isabella had spent their entire freshman year latched onto these senior boys. I was in the eighth grade and lived off their stories. I don't remember the details of who else came that night, but I vividly remember the flavor of vodka and orange juice from the tall glasses Felix and Pablo kept pouring me. Later I'd hear the fantastic myriad of rumors that circulated the city about those two, which mostly involved getting young girls loaded and having their way. Sometimes it was psychedelics in the woods and the promise of photography. Sometimes it was just screwdrivers in someone's grandmother's house and seeing how far the night would take them. Honestly, I think I was one of the lucky ones.

I really had no interest in Felix. He and Dahlia had formed a strange nonsexual bond that wasn't strange because it was nonsexual but because it oozed codependence without benefits. I guess the holes in each of them mirrored the other's. Not that Dahlia got my vote of confidence, but I sure as shit never trusted Felix. Rolling around in a primer gray sixty-seven Nova with stacks of pills, caps, and tabs in the trunk and a tattoo across his back with another last name he claimed was his but couldn't really talk about. The man smelled of suspicion at a cellular level.

But this chapter is supposed to be about Pablo, and that night after pouring me another very tall, very warm glass, I remember looking at this gorgeous boy and thinking to myself that this is how bad things happen. We were still on the couch when he asked me what kind of music I listened to. I didn't know how to answer his lame-ass question, but I knew I certainly wasn't going to tell him the truth. *You ever hear of Gilberto Gil? Jorge Ben? Yeah, you know, despite the lukewarm reception it's gotten in the Brazilian crowd, I think Caetano Veloso is killing it with Fina Estampa.* No, there was no way I was going to out myself in front of these cool older boys, so I shrugged. When he asked if I listened to KROQ and The Beat, I just nodded and he nodded right back, like he'd had me pegged from the jump.

"Yeah," he dismissed. "I don't listen to that shit. I'm different. I listen to something called 'classic rock.' You know? The shit they play on Arrow 93.1. Yeah, Led Zeppelin, Pink Floyd. Shit like that."

What kind of girl would go for a line like that, you ask? I'll tell you. A thirteen-year-old girl drowning in room-temperature screwdrivers, that's who. I can barf about it all I want now, but back then I ate that shit up right down the hall into Granny's bedroom, and onto Granny's bed. I had never really been kissed by anyone like that before. There was something altogether serious and final about it, like all the fun had been surgically removed under anesthesia. I knew ephemerally I could say no, but in reality

I couldn't discern between my curiosity and apprehension, and damn it all, I just wanted him to like me.

He unzipped his pants and pushed me down. I had no idea what to do and only a very vague idea of what he wanted, so I pretended we were still kissing. I was a lamb. Pretty soon he tired of my ignorance and did his best to mask the frustration in his tone when he said, "Just suck it." I still didn't know what that meant, and maybe I took him all too literally at first, but with his hand on the back of my head the rhythm finally clicked.

Then the most disgusting thing happened. Flat-out foul. He got up, zipped his pants, and said we should go out separately. I was all, "Whatever, dude. Just go." He snuck back into the hallway while I tried to find anything in the bathroom that would give my poor tongue amnesia.

*Go out separately?* I rolled my eyes and spit. *Like no one knows we snuck off into the only room in this tiny-ass apartment? What a ridiculous suggestion.*

A breath later Felix burst into the bathroom and started peeing right in front of me. "It's cool…I just couldn't wait anymore…I'll be done in a second. So, what were you doing with Pablo?"

"That's none of your business." *You fuck.*

"Damn, girl. Okay. Okay," he said. "Hey, are you okay?"

"Yeah, no. I don't know. I don't think so."

He gave me a hug and the moment I began to relax into it was the very same moment he unzipped his pants, and with the second shock of the night I finally found my voice.

"No, Felix, please. Don't."

"Don't what?"

"Just don't!" I may have started to cry.

He said something very Felix-like, along the lines of "what the fuck? It's okay," or "whatever, you're weird."

*Whatever, indeed.*

*Fine, I'll be weird so long as I can get the fuck out of this bathroom.*

Rocco had thrown up outside and the party was over shortly thereafter. It was months before I ever saw Pablo again. Still every time we went out I looked for him, and thus began my affair with classic rock. You know, Led Zeppelin, Pink Floyd. Shit. Like. That. When I did finally see him again it was always at a party, and it always ended in the same kind of blowjob as it did that first night. I got pretty good at them over the next year or so, and right around the time he told Kimberly Anderson that he would never take my virginity, I stayed with him at Jasper and Liam's house on Thirty-Third and Pico when all the other girls left. He asked me if we could have sex. I didn't want to. I really fucking didn't. But it just felt inevitable. I got my wallet, took out the condom I got in health class, and tossed it at him. He told me he'd never hurt me right before he took me out to the front yard and fucked me doggy-style on the brick wall. Sometimes there's just no way to hold back the river.

I wasn't allowed to feel sorry for myself—and yet. No, I deserved that. It wasn't like Ricky, who still didn't count. He'd asked and I'd said yes, so who was I to feel violated? Still, I spent the next four years in darkness throwing everything at that hole I could get my hands on. Pills, drugs, booze, boys. I didn't care what it was or how it would affect me. I just swallowed and hoped for oblivion.

About seven years later I saw him again at Isabella's Halloween party at the house on Rose. He came right up to me, eager to catch up. Genuinely happy to see me. Maybe I'm dreaming, but I half remember him apologizing, explaining his confusion when he woke up the next morning on the couch and I was gone.

Another "I'm sorry if I did anything to hurt you."

I must have laughed, pushed out a "thanks."

It didn't matter to me anymore, but I'm sure it made him feel better.

# CHAPTER 3

FOR BETTER OR WORSE, Cole sealed his fate at number three. On the one hand, it's easy to look back on him with a faint tenderness, and on the other, he marks the beginning of a landslide into a life I retain very little fondness for. He was always kind, so he oughtta get a prize for that or something. He was also the first of them to call me on the telephone. We even made plans for the crew a couple times. Sometimes he would call me late at night. Just to talk. "You are so young and pure," he'd say. "Life hasn't beaten you down yet."

I was still fourteen and a "virgin" when we first kissed. He was twenty-one. I'd usually initiate it. He usually put up a lot of resistance. I'd get pouty, act fourteen, fold my arms, and eventually win him over. Afterward he'd scold me, tell me that we shouldn't have. I was too young for him. I tried to go down on him one night on Euclid Street near my pop's house, but Cole was nothing like Pablo, and try as I might I wasn't up for the sheer physical challenge in front of me. I might have laughed before giving up. Cole hung his head quietly. It wasn't right; I was turning him into a bad person. That sort of thing.

He didn't talk to me for a week after. I loved him for it though. I really did. So long as he let me lead, I knew I'd be safe—statutory laws be damned. Sure, I'd boast to my friends that he was tall, dark, and handsome. That his voice was the shade of foghorn. That he was studying to become a firefighter. That his figure was chiseled. But I didn't really give a shit about any of that. He was sad, and he was kind, and in the middle of the night when he would call I'd think of his ears and beam. Round and big, they stuck out of his Hollywood smile like they'd been shaped from silly putty. Those ears on that man, soothing me to sleep. Cole could never hurt me. Not with ears like that.

He had a girlfriend at the time that was sort of on-again, off-again. She made up the bulk of his sorrows, but the rest were reserved for his family. Everyone knew the rumor that spread about how his brother and Patrick got arrested. Something about a girl and a broomstick. I never knew Quinton, but Patrick and I became friendly years later when I was dating Skylar. He even stayed at my mom's house while she was out of town and helped us lay some pipes in the back yard. I'd make us salmon sandwiches on challah and he would tell us stories of the work he did in the union, all of the Indian bones they dug up in the Ballona Wetlands to make room for more yuppies. Patrick seemed like a genuinely kind man despite the record and the prison tattoos. I never knew Cole's brother—I hardly knew Patrick, really—and I don't know for certain what happened with that girl. I do know that any one of these assholes could have ended up in prison for the shit they did to young girls. The unlucky ones got locked up, or escaped to Serbian relatives, having to register as sex offenders for the rest of their lives. And the lucky ones could high-five their conquests and land wives and daughters a few years later. Far be it from me to gossip. Who knows where truth and justice really lie?

•••

COLE LIVED WITH HIS mom and his brother in their tiny apartment on Seventh and Michigan. I could see their front door from my desk in Ms. Willow's English/Yoga class, and I'd spend the better part of third and fourth period staring, dreaming, hoping to catch a glimpse. *Can he see me in class from his front porch? Will he call me tonight and pour it all over me? What would he do if I just showed up at lunch? What if it had been Cole and not Pablo?* I wanted to crawl up in his long arms and die. I wanted to be sad together. I never told Cole about Pablo. I never told him I was sad too. I never told him anything. We couldn't both be sad. I was the young and pure one. I couldn't betray him like that.

Still, after Pablo, the hypocrisy of feigning innocence for Cole enveloped me like a vest strapped with explosives. I could lead, but only so far. Cole set the limits. Eventually I tired of the game. Not being able to choose to have sex with Cole was almost as bad as not being able to choose NOT to have sex with Pablo. At Billy's mom's house late in the fall of '99 I sat him down in Billy's little brother's room to set him straight: "I've given it some serious thought and decided that we are going to have sex tonight. You can try to resist all you want, but we both know that in the end I'm going to win."

Parker was in the next room with Billy. She always seemed to be enjoying herself. So carefree. If I could be more like her—if I could choose this and enjoy it—I wouldn't have to be so sad all the damn time. I never really considered the other side of that. The backside with the big red target on it. I forgot about that part of being Parker and focused on how much fun she always seemed to be having. *That could be me. I can have fun.*

But that wasn't the only thing I had forgotten. And if the damned thing hardly fit in my mouth, how in the hell did I imagine I was going to fit it anywhere else? I was still virginish. It really fucking hurt, which made it frightfully hard to "have fun." Delight quickly turned to horror. *Oh, shit, is that my appendix? Can you sprain a spleen? Can you break a vagina?* But I didn't want him to stop. I was going to get through this, and by God, I was going to enjoy myself! *Screams of pain could be masked as screams of pleasure, right? Guys like that sort of pornographic "I love this/I'm going to die" thing, right? I got this.*

Parker started banging on the wall. "Tash, shut the fuck up!" Cole shushed me in my ear. I ignored them both. I was going for it, and I'd be damned if anyone was going to get in my way. In a room littered with WWF action figures, shit got weird and loud, but I gave it my best. The jig was more or less up after that. I wasn't a virgin, and it wasn't his fault. He stopped calling me late at night to be sad.

# CHAPTER 4

Zev Gold was having a party at his parents' house in Brentwood. I was in the throes of hating life, but Genevieve was going to be there, and I loved Genevive so I agreed to come. *Maybe I just need a break from the DC boys. I'll just hang out with kids my age for a while. It'll be fine. I'll get out of the house. Go to a sophomore party. Be normal.*

I drank a lot that night. Alone. When Genevieve finally found me I was sitting under the volleyball net, crying softly. She asked about Pablo.

I lost it. I couldn't even speak. I couldn't even cry anymore. I howled.

Someone at the party yelled, "Tell that drunk girl to shut the fuck up!"

"You shut the fuck up!" she snapped back.

Eventually I slurred out the details and she said she'd kill him. "I'm fine with that," I told her, both of us laughing. Then she held me under the volleyball net and told me everything was going to be all right, and I believed her too. Everything was always all right when Genevieve was there. She'd had that effect on me since the sixth grade. V was too tall and too gorgeous for her age. She looked about ten years older than she was and had the maturity of a college freshman at eleven. She used to call me Little Natascia and would take any opportunity to tearfully remind me that she'd run into a burning building to save me.

"Tash, do you want me to find you a ride home?"

"No, V. If I have to spend another night in my room staring at the yellow paint on my walls, I swear I'll lose it for good."

"I fucking love you, dog." She laughed and held my hand, walked me back into the party, and poured me another drink. Told me she wouldn't leave my side unless I wanted her to. Fifteen-year-old Genevieve was a godsend.

Surrounded by a bunch of Crossroads private school kids I didn't know, I finally began to relax. Hell, maybe I could even have a good time. The scrawny one in the corner said his name was Elvis. I laughed out loud. "Fuck you, no it's not!" I said, and I sat my drunk ass down on his lap.

Then it was Never Have I Ever, and guess who was killing the game? Elvis sheepishly had to admit he was still a virgin.

"It's no big deal really," I teased. "Sex. It's no big deal."

But my reassurances only made his cheeks glow brighter. He didn't believe me.

"So how about it, then? Want me to show you it's no big deal?" I ushered everyone out. Genevieve grabbed my face and penetrated my eyes. "Tash, is this what you really want?"

And for that split second I sobered up. "V, I can't explain it right now, but yes. I need this." She kissed me on the cheek, told me she'd wait for me outside. I shut off the lights, took off his clothes, climbed on top, and a virgin he was no more.

"See?" I said. "No big deal."

# CHAPTER 5

Rocco once told me that you could spot a virgin a mile away. No matter their age, gender, etc. The moment someone has sex their nature visibly changes forever. You can practically see it dripping off their skin if you know what to look for. Well, in general Rocco was absolutely full of shit, but I suppose it was on account of my skin that it suddenly became open season. Where they'd held back in years past, whether they'd heard the rumors or not, the DC boys collectively and actively started coming after me. For once, I hated the attention. Most of them downright repulsed me, and it was always those ones who would bristle in entitlement and rage when I said no. Still, I was growing and learning, and most times I could manage to squeeze out a no. Unless, of course, I was falling over, seeing triple.

That is precisely how he got me. So loaded I couldn't keep upright, and Rocco, all three of him, pulled me out of the bush I'd fallen into and right up to his room. I guess he liked 'em like that, too wasted to stop him. Rocco was a real piece of shit, but I was pretty convinced I was too, so fuck it, right? Match made in garbage-can heaven.

He'd just moved in with Tim on Wilshire and Berkeley in Santa Monica. Tim was Dali's new Felix. She'd let him take nude photographs of her; they'd go on trips together and flirt, but they never touched. Tim was okay, I guess, but I'd hated Rocco since the night he punched Clay in the face. We'd just started branching out to a different group of boys and Clay, for all intents and purposes, was my boyfriend. He and I pulled up one night to Tim and Rocco's to pick up Dahlia. Rocco reached through the driver's window and decked Clay right in the nose. Muttered something about the music being too loud.

I hated going over to Rocco's about as much as I hated Rocco. But with enough of that good medicine I'd stop caring. That suited Rocco just fine.

"You're still a virgin, right?"

"Yeah, yeah. I'm a fucking virgin. Just let me take this tampon out."

When it was over we both sat there in utter disgust. Or maybe that was just me.

"Uh, you were definitely not a virgin."

*Uh, Surprise. Motherfucker.*

# CHAPTER 6

I WISH I COULD SAY that was the end of Rocco. I wish we could have faded out from that moment into the nothing, roll credits. Imagine my teenage disappointment when I awoke the next day to discover my life was not a made-for-TV movie. One low begets another, and so on, and so on.

It was just another night at Billy's mom's. Just another night breaking into liquor cabinets, and fighting over who was going to play the next song on his stepdad's stereo. *Billy's mom's house.* That poor woman. I wonder if she ever knew how much depravity she hosted over the years. If she ever knew who her son was, who his friends were, who all the girls were. All of us, the babies of the baby boomers. All of us together, grasping at the straws of our parents' failed revolution. The poverty and political havoc they'd wreak in our adulthood still the faintest apparition. Us: wanting to stand for something but plagued by the indifference of the truth, suckling on the multicolored psychedelic lie of free love and peace, man. Us: abandoned on the hunt for better versions of themselves. Them: the self-indulgent on a perpetual quest for the meaning of life, true enjoyment, and the obsessive pursuit of enlightenment. The fully mechanized golden praying Buddha. Them: a generation canonized by self-help books. Us: a generation canonized by Saturday morning cartoon jingles, lost in the energetic minutiae of divorce and blame, spoon-fed Adderall and family therapy sessions, choking on corn derivatives pre-packaged to give the illusion of choice. Us: instructed to idolize martyrs of the non-violence movement and Woodstock, apathized in a post COINTEL PRO world of surveillance, Neighborhood Watch, and D.A.R.E. programs. JUST SAY NO like a mantra to oblivion. They always knew better. Theirs was the only music, theirs was true youth, theirs was real revolution. And us? Trading houses three days a week and every other weekend, stuck in front of cable TV and video games, choking on Bagel Bites and Snapple.

We were lazy. We were ungrateful. We didn't know shit.

It was just another night at Billy's mom's. She wasn't there. We drank. I teased Carlo for turning green. "But I'm still standing," he boasted. "I'm still standing! DC for life!" Just another night at Billy's mom's. Mistaking lust for kindness. I was dancing to Steve Miller Band with belligerent fervor. Thanks to Pablo's bullshit line years back I knew all the words to garbage like that. *Look, ma! I'm dancing!* But it was more like falling. And who was there to catch me but good ol' Captain Save-A-Ho. Mm, falling. That ancient seductive dance of the seven veils. Poor Rocco. Who could resist the temptations of the drunken teenage fall? He grabbed me and made me dance for him. A fucking puppet with no strings attached. Caught me and pulled me right into Billy's room like some goddamned sacrilegious fisherman. Dancing, falling, catching, pulling. The first four veils. Just make it quick, I prayed. Make it quick so I can start to forget. Brenda McCaullagh pounded on the door. "I need my jacket, asshole. Tell that drunk slut to get off of you so I can get my jacket." *What in the Lord's fuck did she mean by that?* Me *get off of* him? Rocco ignored her. She gave up. *Get me out of here. God, just finish already.* Prayers finally answered, I lay there alone in the tiniest pool of blood. He always got me like that. Mid-menstruation. The shark and the chum bucket.

I couldn't move for a while. *The train frozen, the station pulling away. What was that? Go slow, Tash. You got this. Just make it to the bathroom. You can make it to the bathroom. Don't worry about going back to the party. Back to cataloging our parents' music. Back to pretending you're okay. Back to the girls who are too busy forgetting themselves to remember you. Back to the boys who don't know who they are without each other. Back to my home, I dare not go.*

I only made it to the bedroom doorway. Skinny legs and all. Some mother's son came by, asked if I was okay. The fifth veil. *We're friends, right?* He had the same name as my childhood dog. We spelled it with an I, I once told him. The dog that ran away. The dog that became a code word. All I had to say was, "Hey, Pop, how's Billi?" and he'd know I was in trouble. *We're friends, right? We've talked about baseball before. You smile and laugh at my jokes. You know the name of my perfume. Angel. Your mom wears it, remember? We're friends, right?*

"Hey. Are you okay?" he asked innocently.

"No. Uh, yeah. No. I don't think so." He held me. "Whoa. Natascia. Is there anything I can do? Do you want me to leave you alone?"

"No. Not that. Just…sit down with me for a minute. Just give me a hug."

My shirt came up over my head. *Please, I can't. Talk. I can't. No. You don't understand. I'm barely here at all. Please don't do this. We like the Dodgers and smoking weed, remember? We're friends. Not like this. Not now. Not now.* When he turned me around I wanted to stop him. *Say something. Anything.* But all I could manage was his name, "Billy." The sixth veil. It came out dull, like a flat line. Billi. I was in trouble, but no one came a-runnin'. "Natascia!" He slapped my ass. *FML. Make it quick. Make it over. Make it stop. So much to forget.*

Blood had soaked through to the mattress. He pulled the sheets off the bed. "I'm sorry," I apologized. The seventh veil. "Don't worry about it." He shrugged. "I have a girlfriend…I know all about this kind of stuff."

# CHAPTER 7

THE FIRST 4/20 I EVER celebrated was in 1999. We woke up early that morning to hike down to Pointe Dume. Johnny Pine was maybe going to be there and that was as good a reason as any to be up at sunrise to "go surfing." I liked the idea of surfing plenty, of some young boy to paddle out with who would show me how to pop up. Smoking joints together at the shoreline, our tan bodies laughing squint-eyed in the Malibu morning sun. Trading puka shell necklaces and shit. Staying at second base till, you know, we were ready. But that morning when we got to the shore and saw the swell, that perfect teenage fantasy faded out. Johnny decided last-minute to sleep in. Pointe Dume is no place for beginners, and no one exactly jumped up to teach me. I just sighed and resigned myself to the scenery. It was just the way things were, and there was no use getting upset about it when the sun was high, the weed was kind, and the boys were smiling—even if they weren't smiling at me.

Genevieve and I stretched out on the cool sand and smoked a couple of joints, daydreaming, gossiping, and relaxing in the mid-April sun. She hated her body. Her shoulders were too broad or her legs too muscular or her feet too big or some other such nonsense. Truth be told this girl had a figure that was about one or two Photoshop clicks away from supermodel. Five foot ten, 130, and a six-pack that she maintained with a strict regimen of sitting on her ass eating doughnuts daily. Fucking bitch. I, on the other hand, was about five foot two, awkwardly beyond double-D, looking perpetually younger than I was, and one or two clicks away from being called curvy. I was obsessed with the idea that I was fat, and for fuck's sake, she was too. She'd pinch the skin from her *Sports Illustrated* stomach as some kind of proof: "See, Tash...I'm disgusting!" I used to think she was just fishing for compliments, but this shit runs deep AF in LA, so don't you dare judge her. In this city, whether you're a picture of strength and beauty like Genevieve, or just a short girl with a perpetually round baby tummy, body dysmorphia is practically our birthright. That morning, justified or not, we both uncomfortably sported bikinis and feigned confidence because that is just what was done. And body dysmorphia, like any other mind fuck, was nothing a few joints couldn't fix.

By the time we got back to Jean Michele's in Venice that afternoon we must have collectively consumed a quarter ounce of ganja. I kept waiting for Johnny to show. The lunch crowd started spilling into the backyard. Between Black and Milds and beers I landed somewhere in the living room. The TV had been on all day. I was staring at it for God knows how long, not really registering what I was seeing. All the channels were stuck on breaking news. Jean Michele walked by. "Yeah," he sighed. "It's a fucking tragedy." "Oh, yeah, man. For sure," I nodded. *What is this dude talking about?* "And on a national holiday," he went on. "It's sacrilegious!" Johnny appeared sarcastic and statuesque on his way to the bathroom. *He's here!* "Isn't it Hitler's birthday, or some shit?" he shrugged as he passed. *He's finally here! Play it cool, Natascia. Play it cool!* I took a deep breath and tried to focus on the TV. *Find something clever to say.* The toilet flushed. *Shit!* He walked past the TV and back to the party in the backyard. *Boys pee so damn fast. Did he even wash his hands? Okay, regroup. Hitler's birthday? You can still salvage the moment, Natascia. Pay attention.*

Security footage—two boys in a cafeteria—assault rifles—pipe bombs—trench coats—9/11 recordings—hysterical parents looking for their kids—helicopter shots—students running from school—eyewitness interviews—fathers shaking their heads—something about gun laws and violence—girls sobbing—everyone at my table was shot—and they were shooting like anyone who had a white hat or played a sport and they didn't care who it was and it was all like close range—everyone around me got shot and I begged him for like ten minutes not to shoot me and he just put the gun in my face and started bleeding everywhere and started laughing and saying that it was all because people were mean to him last year—he killed my best friend—we're trying to find my brother—oh, it was just horrible—the worst experience OF MY LIFE.

I couldn't watch anymore. *It's gotta be past 3:08 p.m. now. School's out. When I sat down I Love Lucy was playing. Where is everyone? Did Johnny leave?*

I stumbled into the backyard. Everyone was laughing, passing blunts. Johnny was sitting in a circle of white plastic lawn chairs. Genevieve was there too. And me, Captain Buzzkill: "Hey, did you guys see the news?" Shit got quiet. "Yeah...it's fucked up," someone answered. Everyone sort of looked down. "Hey," someone shouted. "It's puff, puff, pass, motherfucker!" Laughter again. More ganja. Someone put Legend into the CD player. "Turn that up," was the general consensus. Everyone sang along. *Don't worry / About a thing / 'Cause every little thing / Is gonna be all right.* Johnny sold some weed and left. I eventually walked home. Alone with a powerful hunger for French fries.

•••

TEN YEARS LATER WHEN he was stationed in Iraq, Johnny found me on Facebook. We wrote every day for months. He told me that he had lied in high school. That I was his first. I told him I figured it out a long time ago. When he got back to the States, he called me every day, drunk on his days off. Sometimes the slurring sounded like tears. Stories about IEDs, the moment he realized that he could have died if he'd only been a few feet to the left, how the food was so much better in Iraq than Oklahoma, the moment he realized that targets translate to people, that time he discovered a gun in his friend's room and didn't report it, how the next night that same friend blew his brains out, how he was thinking about reenlisting.

"I just don't get it, Johnny. Why do you do it? You don't seem to like it all that much. And you get out in a few months. Why would you even consider reenlisting?"

"Natascia," he sighed. "I went into the army because I felt like I needed to hit the fucking reset button. I've never been good at anything in my life. I tried college, I tried to become a chef. I've always sucked at school. And there's something kinda cool about having one of the oldest jobs in the world. I know it's fucked up. But they pay me on the first and fifteenth of every month. And there's no fear of losing my job. And I'm sort of well-liked out here. I don't know. I know it's fucked up, but for so long I just wanted to be good at something, you know? Really good. It turns out I'm a really good soldier." He chuckled. "I'm really good at killing people. So fine. I don't love it, but maybe that's just who I'm supposed to be."

•••

BY THE TIME I REACHED the tenth grade Isabella kinda dropped out of school. Dahlia kinda went to Africa for a semester and the better parts of her never really came back. I tried sticking closer to Genevieve, you know, in case the building ever caught fire. V was one of those few people in high school who was friends with everyone. And not just like cool with everyone. Like really friends. In the tenth grade she started spending a lot of time with the eleventh-grade surfers. I went through a dry spell. Boys my age seemed a lot less interested in me. Maybe it was because they knew my brother, but I'd put serious money on the fact that without the huge age difference there was just no novelty. I sort of lost confidence, thought of myself as an ugly piece of shit and didn't want to do much but find someone who would be sad with me.

It was easy to infatuate myself with Johnny. I was taking a break from DC, Billy's mom's house, and boys over eighteen in general. Johnny was quiet, and dark. I could never tell if he was brooding or just high. They called him Dope on account of the fact that he sold weed. It was a stupid nickname, and I was embarrassed on his behalf anytime someone would use it. Genevieve took me to his mom's house on Sunset in the south side of Santa Monica after school one day. We got high on the back deck with a bunch of kids that I knew but didn't really know, and I don't think he said anything to me other than hi, but I had a capital imagination. That first meeting. The salmon sky that surrounded the deck, the view of the golf course below, the boy with a killer smile who was always stoned. I remember looking at his house, seeing his room, smoking his weed, basking in his sunset smile, and thinking, "Yeah, I could get used to this."

Ten years later we'd sit on that same back deck alone together in the midnight air. He'd take my hand and look away. "Wouldn't it be great if my first was my last?" he'd sigh. I'd scoff at the lie of fidelity. He'd propose marriage.

"Uh...Johnny, I ain't the marrying type."

"Just think about it, Natascia. Just think about it."

•••

IT HAPPENED THE WAY most things happen in high school. Indirectly and without much discussion. We were high, for sure, I remember that. Another smoked lunch. I remember rolling my eyes when he put on the *Chronic 2001*.

"Xxplosive." West Coast shit. My heart like thunder in my ears. *God, I hope he can't hear it over Dre's beat.* The lunchtime light shining through his dark bedroom window. His mom's house on the south side was set against the south side of the hill (probably still is). His bedroom window was below the front porch. He tried to have sex with me before fifth period but couldn't quite bring himself to do it, blamed it on the weed. Asked me not to tell anyone. "Sure thing, and it's actually pretty common, and don't feel bad." And then, I don't know. We just sort of lay there on his bed like that until we had to go back to class. Him feeling embarrassed and me, I don't know. Satisfied, unsatisfied? Was there a difference? We had a secret. That was enough for me. I relished in the perceived closeness. I could've spent an eternity supine under the lunchtime light of his window.

Even with V there was no keeping away from DC altogether. One night I ended up at Billy's dad's house. Not quite his mom's, but too close for comfort. I cornered Genevieve in the bathroom. I couldn't bring myself to tell her why but begged her to help me get out of there. She wasn't quite ready to leave. "Do you want me to call Johnny for you?" she asked. "I know he'll pick you up."

He came in his mom's blue Volvo station wagon and we drove all the way to his bedroom. We started kissing under the window, the streetlight pouring in. He asked point-blank if we could have sex. I choked down a laugh in the face of his blunt intention. "Have you ever done this before?" He nodded, but I knew he hadn't. You can spot a virgin from a mile away. When we fell asleep together it didn't feel like I'd imagined it would. It was a first for me, falling asleep beside a lover. My "I could get used to this" morphed into a grotesque "fuck fuck fuck, get me out of here." He slept like a rock. I spent most of the night waiting for dawn through that window. When dawn finally came she brought a zit on my nose the size of Malibu.

Months later, when we had a past, when he'd landed himself a blonde, when I became a cinch to ignore, I sat in lotus on the standardized polyester blue carpet in English / Yoga class. We had a substitute teacher that day. One of Ms. Willow's friends. She couldn't have been more than twenty-three, twenty-five. Under other circumstances we might have been sharing beer from the same keg at the same party. Me in shocking youth, her feeling old already. Me passing her a joint, her thinking twice before taking it. Us having a laugh. Fuck it, right? It's all illusion.

*Hardy har har.*

"Today we are just going to breathe," she says. "Close your eyes and just breathe. Focus on one thing. Anything. Without judgment, without worry. Just dedicate yourself to focus. Concentrate on your breath. Inhale deeply, exhale deeper—that's it. The next time you hear my voice will be in fifteen minutes."

I remembered the window in Johnny's room. The smell of gym socks and Cool Water and male youth engulfed me. Blindingly dull. Glaring and dizzy. The light, the window, the boy. The light, the window, the boy. Fifteen minutes. Chest rising and falling in cascading breath. My skin an electric goose. The light, the window, the boy. I broke out into a sweat, thunder in the back of my ears, the blood rushing through my chakras and shit. Third eye, root. Third eye, root. Third eye, rooooooooooooooot. My body shuddered. Her voice broke through, "Slowly, slowly. And whenever you are ready, open your eyes. Gently." Fifteen minutes was all it took...who needs boys? The class got up, shuffled to their desks. I moved gingerly, my cheeks still red-hot, my knees suddenly made of spaghetti. She came over to me on the carpet. "Hey, I was watching you. Your energy took over the whole room. You really went somewhere, didn't you?"

"Meh," I shrugged. "I guess so."

•••

BY THE TIME JOHNNY was a senior, fate saw fit to land us in the same Spanish class. He saw it as an opportunity to try his luck again, or something. I saw it as an opportunity to hand him one of those long letters I used to solve all my problems back then. I took about two and a half pages to spell out the precise ways in which he could go fuck himself. He transferred out the next day. The night Johnny graduated some folks from his class threw a party at the Doubletree Inn next to the football field and he cornered me in the bathroom as I was peeing. Gave me the whole "I'm sorry if I ever hurt you" spiel.

"Oh, you know. I'm totally over it. It's all good."

•••

THE LAST TIME I SAW Johnny was nine years later, New Year's morning, 2010. He'd already reenlisted and was headed off to Afghanistan by way of Hawaii the next day. I zipped up my pale pink tutu party dress with the black satin sash, kissed him on his stale whiskey lips, and with three-inch heels in hand I waded through the two-foot perimeter of empty bottles that perpetually surrounded his bed at his mom's house whenever he was on leave. I took one last look at that window and walked out through the front door, past the blue Volvo station wagon, and down the hill to the golf course. Barefooted, curls messy and losing their bounce to the whistles and cheers from the old men who woke up early for a few holes in the New Year. I was not ashamed of shit. I threw my arms up, a heel in each hand, and gave them a curtsy fit for the stage. They exploded in standing ovation, golf clubs and all.

We kept in touch for a couple weeks after he moved to Hawaii, you know, before he went AWOL. He'd call me blathering about our wedding plans by the fountain at the Bellagio. It just killed me when he did that. I had no intention of hitching my ride to that painted wagon. I didn't want someone to be sad with anymore. Still, I felt responsible for him somehow and would always answer the phone when he called. Until there was only silence. Months passed. When he turned himself in to a detox center in March, the army demoted him, but so long as he enrolled in an alcohol treatment program and went to AA weekly, Uncle Sam saw fit to deploy him once more. By May he was married to a blonde and flew off to Afghanistan with a baby on the way. When his tour ended a year later and he finally got to meet his son, the calls started again, and so did the drinking. That was just before his wife contacted me and told me to leave their family alone, and after writing back a fifteen-hundred-word essay on the precise ways in which their family could go fuck themselves, I was happy to oblige.

# CHAPTER 8

I'VE HAD FOUR FIRST boyfriends.

The first first one was Angelo DePalma, in the seventh grade. He was the first one I ever called boyfriend. We made it a whole two weeks talking on the phone and being too shy to do anything in person except for that one time in the hall outside of detention. No one was around, and we sort of grazed the corners of each other's mouths as we said goodbye. It wasn't quite a kiss, but it was enough to take my eleven-year-old breath away. We broke up the next Monday in an epic showdown on the quad. He'd sorta heard that I was going to do it, and I'd sorta heard that he was going to do it, and we marched right up to one another, his friends behind him, mine behind me. It was a draw.

In the eighth grade I had my second first boyfriend. Adam Perry was the first boy I would ever love. The first love letter I'd ever write. The first truly erotic encounter I would have. This was no first kiss at the point of the bottle, no dare in a darkened closet. It was the summer going into freshman year. We had wanted each other since the beginning of the eighth grade. We even went out briefly that year, which amounted to nothing more than the quiet exchange of letters. I confessed my undying love for him, an eternity of well-wishes and gratitude. He confessed guilt for his heart's infidelity: his continuing crush on Rachel Weiser (I still haven't forgiven her). He signed it with a proclamation that we were only thirteen and had our whole lives ahead of us, for God's sake!

We made a plan to meet at Justin Busch's house that summer going into high school. Justin and I used to talk all night wondering if life was pointless after youth, if there was any joy to be had after thirty. If it made artistic sense to commit suicide before the fall like Marilyn or Cobain. We made a pact to marry each other if we were still single at thirty. Justin and I didn't talk much after the age of sixteen and he married at twenty-five. I'm thirty-something now, and for all intents and purposes, still alive. Justin knew the extent of my love for Adam and set up a double date so Adam and I could be together without having to be alone.

I bathed for about two hours that morning at my pop's apartment in Santa Monica and took another two picking out my clothes. Surrounded by piles of nothing to wear I finally got the courage to break out the shit I'd poached from the leftover wardrobe box Mom had from her work as a director at Playboy TV. I guess they didn't need the white lace front clasp bra with matching thong for *Sexy Girl Next Door*, so I put those on first. Then came the white negligee top with blue roses. I rounded it off with my favorite faded denim bell-bottoms and bobby-pinned my hair back, wondering if the smell of ginseng orange shampoo was strong enough to be noticeably subtle. I gave myself one final look in the mirror, one final pass of watermelon lip balm and strapped on my black Reefs to meet Emily Sato at the bus stop on Fourteenth and Wilshire.

Emily and Justin disappeared into his mom's room immediately. Adam and I sat on the couch in the living room across from Justin's drum set. Staring at each other. Looking away. Staring at our hands. Smiling. Sweating. Whispering. Adam Perry had courage, grace, and intelligence. I was a bumbling idiot. "I'm going to move closer to you," he decided after about an hour. We stared into each other's eyes for another forty-five minutes. I kept picturing it. Leaning in to kiss him. How much easier it would be to continue once we got started. *It's just like jumping into a cold swimming pool, Tash. Don't be a little bitch. You're courageous. Bold. Daring. You got this. One, two, three. Come on! Get a running start.* But I was frozen. Paralyzed. I kept inching up and stopping short. Adam kept waiting. I don't remember what pushed me over the edge, what finally got me to jump. I just remember landing. How easily we navigated tongue and teeth. Slowly, softly. We had our whole lives ahead of us, for God's sake!

Adam Perry took my hand and led me to Justin's room, to his mattress on the floor. He lay down beside me, staring into my eyes and smiling. He told me that the female body has seven erogenous zones. He was always doing shit like that. Knowing more about being alive than anyone else his age. Even if he was just getting it from watching *Friends*, you have to have real balls as a fourteen-year-old boy to drop a line like that. But don't let me give you the wrong impression. Adam Perry was no heartbreaker or anything like that. Dude played the trumpet and wanted to start a nineties ska band called the Testostertones. He listened to Big Bad Voodoo Daddy and The Aquabats and shit. I'm not saying he was a dork, I'm just not saying he wasn't a dork. Then he named the seven zones as he softly kissed them all. Well, almost all. We were only thirteen and we had our whole lives ahead of us, for God's sake!

Later, the four of us went up to the rooftop to smoke cigarettes and watch the sunset. I told Adam about the tumor they'd biopsied from my gums, all the tests they were running on me. He held my hand and told me we'd get through this. And I knew it was true. With Adam Perry by my side, I would get through anything.

The last time I saw him he was sixteen. It was the summer again. His parents had let him out for the afternoon and everyone came to my house to play *Mario Kart* and get high in my tiny bedroom. We started talking about all the things we'd do when night came; all of the things Adam couldn't do anymore. He was wearing a baseball cap to cover what was left of his hair. His cane leaning on my bed next to him. He looked like he was in his thirties. I wanted everyone to go home. I wanted to hold him and cry and tell him we'd get through this. But I just froze, and he just looked at me with his famous closed-mouth smile. He died a month later while I was in Spain. No one even bothered to write. He was only sixteen. I had my whole life ahead of me, for God's sake!

But this chapter is about Clay. Clay was my third first. Alas, between Adam and Clay, I'm not sure I'll be able to lighten the mood, and if I could skip writing this chapter I would. I don't want to write about Clay. I don't want to relive any of it. I don't want to do all that just to get to the inevitable end of chapter eight. So I'm just going to start with it, because if I skip Clay he'll haunt me for the rest of my days. Clay died on January 6, 2013. Two months after his birthday. Two days after Adam Perry's birthday. Adam would have been twenty-nine. Clay had just turned thirty-two.

The circumstances surrounding his death are somewhat suspect. No one but Clay, and The Great Mystery, knows what truly happened. All us mere mortals know for certain is that sometime after midnight on Sunset Boulevard, right next to Amoeba Records, Clay plummeted to his eventual death. After exchanging messages on his birthday in November we decided to give our friendship another go. As the third first, Clay holds the place for being my first relationship. We broke up and got back together about as many times as years we knew each other. It was like breathing for us, and in so many ways, because he always looked for the best in me while I insisted on giving him my worst, Clay knew me better than any of the others.

I was a fourteen-year-old virgin when we met and started dating. It was an odd, out-of-place crossing of friends that could only have been brought about by the randomness that was Kimberly Anderson. They had graduated Uni High and were all up in the Thursday frat nights at UCLA. Though of all of those boys, only Ryan actually attended school there. I don't know how she knew them. I don't know how Kimberly Anderson knew anyone outside of Santa Monica, but Clay had a car, and that was more or less all she needed to hang out: something useful to her.

In a high school heartbeat we were always together. Going to parties or getting picked up from them. It didn't take long before I'd be the last to be dropped off. Clay would drive me up to some beautiful hill in Malibu or some secret lookout in the Hollywood Hills and we'd make out in the back of the black Honda Accord all night, the city of stars below us.

I'd put bougainvilleas in my hair, and I still wore bell-bottoms. "Fucking hippie," he'd call me. "So what, you believe in peace and free love, right? Very original." He had an eyebrow piercing, wore raver pants, and listened to Depeche Mode.

"At least I'm not a dirty raver," I'd say. "I'm sure the music you listen to will stand the test of time and shit."

We'd drive around Westwood listening to "Californication." At least we could agree on that. He liked me so much. *Too much?* I didn't know his last name for the first three months. He didn't know mine. We thought it was funny that we could feel so close without knowing them and giggled as we swapped surnames one night outside of his dad's house on Ophir Drive. "Hold on, I have something for you," he said shyly as he ran inside. He was blushing when he returned holding a cheap print of "The Dream" by Picasso. "I saw it and it instantly made me think of you." I still don't get it. I've stared at it for years now. Searching for the secret of how he saw me. Just a woman blissfully pleasuring herself? I don't get it, but it's hung in my bedroom ever since.

The day that I bought my first ounce of weed, he picked me up and showed me how to roll a joint with a dollar. "I can't believe I'm dating a drug dealer," he laughed like he'd struck gold. *We're dating?* I wanted to like him from the start, but no one else seemed to. I didn't get it. I didn't know what I was missing that everyone else saw, but it seemed that all of Santa Monica clicked their tongues at this boy. A better woman wouldn't have let that stop her, but I was no woman. And I'd be lying if I didn't say that their perception tainted it for me.

After Rocco busted his nose and my brother chased him down our block, I had a hard time feeling at ease bringing him around. Our relationship went underground. Clay was always a long drive on a dark night. We'd smoke cigarettes and go to Kenter Canyon or the top of Chautauqua or some secret gate in the Hollywood Hills with a killer view. One night we cut through the Bel Air Beach Club to a private clearing on the Cliffside no bigger than our two bodies.

"Random, Clay. What is this place?"

"I don't know, maybe it's just where the valets take their breaks."

"But how did you find it?"

He grabbed a blanket from his trunk and told me about the night he took too much LSD and sat there with that same blanket wrapped around his body. I told him how sometimes I felt like I was the only human in a world of robots. How I'd always know it in my soul, but no matter how hard I'd try to confirm it, and no matter how close I got to another robot they'd never be able to tell me. It wasn't in their programming.

"Huh. Is that it?"

"What do you mean, Clay? Yeah, that's it."

"I don't know. Seems pretty basic. I was expecting more from you."

It was always like that. Just the two of us alone in the dark somewhere, expecting more from each other. One night behind inspiration point, right around Adelaide Drive on the north side, we pulled over in the black Honda Accord, got into the back seat, and made out. For a very long time. Long enough for me to notice that he wasn't trying anything. Didn't try putting his hand up my shirt, or down my pants. Didn't try putting my hand anywhere. It was intensely uncomfortable. I stopped kissing him.

"What is it?" he asked.

"Can I take my shirt off?"

He shrugged. "If you want to."

He didn't stare at them. Didn't touch them. Didn't put his mouth all over them. We just kept kissing the same way we had before. None of it made sense.

"Umm. Is everything okay?" he asked.

"Yeah, I'm going to put my shirt back on. It's just…it's cold."

"I told you I'm not going to try to have sex with you unless you're ready. Don't be mad."

"I'm not mad. It's fine. I'm not mad." I didn't answer his calls for three weeks.

He wanted to know me. He asked detailed questions, challenged my answers for truths I had reserved only for myself. We'd talk about what books we were reading, compare authors. I gave him a copy of *The Tribes of Palos Verdes*. He gave me a copy of *The Beach*. I wrote him a story about a kiwi tree. He gave me a poem about a boy in a dark mirror. He told me about his time in Egypt. His trip up the Nile. How men walked down the streets holding hands. "There's more to life than this godforsaken city!" I'd nod and tell him about Italy, and how the peaches there put Georgia to shame. How easy it is to wake up in that country. To wake up and to fall asleep. You wouldn't believe how restful life could be.

"So what about you, Naughty?" I fucking hated that nickname, which, of course only encouraged it. "You gonna be stuck in this bullshit city for the rest of your life?"

"Nah, I'm gonna travel the world. I'm gonna be a writer."

"You'd fucking better be."

If it were just me and Clay alone forever maybe I could have truly loved him. But at fifteen it couldn't be. Dahlia thought he was a piece of shit because he'd kissed her first, and immediately lost interest. I'd never been more interesting than her to any boy, and she couldn't stand the idea. Any chance she'd get to tell me that Clay was an asshole, she'd practically sing it.

It wasn't just Dahlia, either. Any time I'd bring him up, Genevieve, or Parker, or Isabella had some shitty thing to insert about him. "Ugh, Clay? You're still fucking with that dude? He's weird. Yeah, something's off with him." Then Kimberly Anderson would chime in, "Whatever, maybe she can get him to pick us up if the party is lame." After that night with Rocco, the boys talked endless shit too. "Don't be bringing bitch-ass dudes around anymore, Tash." And if I had to hear my brother call him that "Dylan McCay, *90210*-looking motherfucker" one more time I'd lock myself in my yellow bedroom and never come out.

All my life I've been terrified that one day I'd find out that everything I know to be true is just some bullshit fantastic version of the truth I'd invented in some desperate attempt to maintain my own sanity and everyone has more or less just been humoring me: I'd wake up one morning, the bubble would burst, and I'd see myself the way they actually saw me. Delusional. Pompous. Infernally irritating and terrifyingly fragile. In that moment it wouldn't matter what was on the other side of thirty. All that would matter was me, the cliff, and the will to jump.

On my fifteenth birthday Clay bought me a copy of *The Catcher in the Rye* and wrote me a poem about a kiwi tree and a rose. We dropped Ecstasy and went to Parker's house with Isabella. Parker's brother Cameron was back from military school or rehab or whatever the place is called where they grab you out of bed in the middle of the night, throw you into a van, drive you far away, lock you in a room, and beat the shit out of you if you resist.

Cameron was that dude who always had some lockbox filled with psychedelics and dough. Cameron was the guy who could talk for hours about the differences between LSD and mushrooms, who knew what Mescaline felt like. Who knew the precise effect, duration, and chemical composition of every drug known to man. How long it was traceable in the blood and the urine. How to beat a surprise drug test. Each week the discussion of another conspiracy. Another way they were tapping the phones, the house, the ether. Sometimes he would make shit up about the law, or the government, just to see if he could get you to believe him. A Y2K Hunter S. Thompson.

Cameron wasn't for everyone. If you hadn't been his little sister's best friend since the sixth grade you'd be hard pressed to see through the thick mist of ginger hair that spun psychedelic webs of speculation and deceit. More still, if for some reason you decided to drop in and tune out with this dude, he'd take you for your wits and your Benjamins just for the pure sport of it. One time my brother went to the north side to sell him some weed and ended up eating a few mushrooms. Within an hour of coming up he found himself in Venice in only his boxers, his car still running on the corner of Lincoln and Washington.

"What happened?" I asked him the next day after he got his car from the impound.

"I don't know, Tash. We ate some mushrooms, and cuz got mad weird and started locking the doors and shit. Then he started going on about the CIA and the phones being tapped. Cuz is into some weird shit. All I knew was that I had to get as far away from that fool as I possibly could. I tried to drive back home, but just gave up around Washington. Nothing made sense anymore. Fuck Cameron."

Cameron got along well with Clay, which was never a good sign. When Clay, Isabella, and I got to Cameron and Parker's house the night of my fifteenth birthday, Cameron passed me a couple of mushroom caps to top off the E I'd dropped an hour earlier. Just when I started coming up he put on the *Trainspotting* soundtrack. Lou Reed sang "Perfect Day." Clay and I were sitting beside one another on the loveseat. Cameron stood above us conducting the melody in the mystic swirling air. Tripping balls, I kept mistaking the lyrics. *What is he singing? Just a perfect age? Wait. What? Why is Cameron standing above us like that? Is he trying to tell me something? Something about Clay? Does he know something about him that I don't? Did Clay tell him something about me? Our age difference? Does he just like me because I'm young? Oh, my God! Is he just like the rest of them? Is that why nobody likes him? The books? The poems? The late-night conversations at Top of The World? Is it all just to fuck me?* I looked up at Cameron and he just smiled and nodded. Then he produced a bright red carnival ticket from his goddamned pocket that had the words *Admit One* written on it, and handed it to me with an all-knowing look. "Happy birthday, Tash."

I lost my shit. "I have to go." I turned to Clay. "Now. Take me home! Now!" I didn't talk to Clay for the next three months. Please understand that that fool is my roll dog for life, but in that moment I was all, *Fuck Cameron*.

That was the first time I went ghost on Clay. Once in their basement Parker, Cameron, and I were comparing the virtues of Lennon and McCartney. Clay said something about the Beatles being overrated. About Led Zeppelin being a better band and about how Page and Plant knew more about making music then Lennon or McCartney ever did. "You're fucking kidding me, right?" I burst into tears. Broke up with him on the spot. Three more months passed. He never asked for an explanation. Always gave me second chances. Third chances. Chances enough for the fourteen years

I knew him. He'd just pick me up in his black Honda Accord in whatever corner of Los Angeles, at whatever hour of the night, and let me promise I wouldn't leave him again. That this time it would be different. I'd mean it, too, when I said it. I'd mean it right up until the morning when I'd tiptoe out of his house, through the sliding glass door of his bedroom, cursing every creak and moan of the floorboards, and running through the cemented walkway to the open anonymity of the Westwood dawn. He'd be asleep, I'd be free, and more months would go by. Sometimes years. We carried on like that for damn near a decade and a half.

The first time we lay in his bed together it'd been months since we had seen each other. I was almost sixteen. Riddled with longing and guilt, I relented and finally called him back. He picked me up in his black Honda Accord. It had one of those stereo systems where you had to pop the face off and hide it so folks wouldn't have a reason to break into your shitty early nineties Japanese car. We drove through the streets of Westwood and he played "Goin' to California" on the stereo with the flashing blue neon lights. "This song really got me through after you left," he confessed. I rolled my eyes at him but listened to the lyrics with every part of me. Some point between Olympic and Selby, when the sea was red and the sky was gray, I realized where we were.

"Pull over. This is my elementary school. It's so small now."

He held my hand. "Oh, come on, Naughty. That's the most clichéd thing I've ever heard you say."

"Fuck you, Clay! Don't ruin the moment."

"Look, I'll stand here with you all night holding your hand in silence as you reminisce on being a little girl, but this school is not smaller. You're bigger. Everyone goes through this."

I dropped his hand. "Whatever. Never mind. Let's just get out of here."

Back in the black Honda Accord with the flashing blue neon lights, "Enjoy the Silence" came on the radio. He took my hand back and wouldn't let go. Sang every word, staring at me through every stop sign. When we got to his house, through the sliding glass door to his bedroom, I was first to take all of my clothes off. He followed suit and we held each other like that, nude in the light of the midnight moon. He kept sighing. "What's wrong, Clay?" He got up and sat on the futon with his head in his hands. I stayed on the bed lying on my stomach, chin in my palms. It was the first time I felt comfortable being naked around anyone. Beautiful, even.

"Is it me?" I asked. "Genevieve says I'm too intimidating."

"No, it's not you, and I don't give a shit what Genevieve says. I was just so nervous to see you tonight. I didn't want you to think I just wanted to fuck you, so I masturbated before picking you up. I'm really fucking embarrassed and feel fucking stupid. I'm sorry. It's not you. Believe me. It's not you."

I'd been playing with my necklace as he spoke. Looking down and fidgeting with the tiny wooden gecko on a hemp chain until its tail eventually broke. "Oh, no!"

"What? What's wrong?"

"His tail broke."

"Oh, no! I'm so sorry. Maybe we can fix it."

"Meh," I shrugged. "Maybe it'll grow back."

"Jesus fucking Christ, Naughty! That's it right there! That is why I love you."

I love you. I got up, sat beside him, and cradled his body in mine. "It's okay, Clay. Really, it is. We don't have to have sex, I'm just happy to be here with you. Alone like this." When he took me home that night he parked across from my mom's house.

"Will you call me this time, Naughty?"

"Yeah, sure." But staring at the porch light on my front door I already knew I wouldn't.

He grabbed my hand. "You're not just saying that, are you? You won't disappear again?"

*Be brave, Natascia. Be truthful.* I wanted to tell him I'd try. That I'd think about it every day, but in the end I wouldn't call. I wanted to explain what happens to me the moment I leave him. How my body fills with this sickening inexcusable dread and suspicion. I wanted to tell him I'm not who he thinks I am. That I'm not deep, or beautiful, or strong. That I'm just a weak teenage girl who can't stand up to her friends. That I'd probably love him more than I could take if I knew what the hell love was and wasn't afraid it would send me to my death. Instead I just sat there in the black Honda Accord with the flashing blue neon lights preparing myself for the crushing months of guilt ahead, and said something stupid, like, "Of course I'll call you this time. I promise."

The last time we slept together was ten years later. I got up from his bed, nude in the afternoon sun, and confessed I had a boyfriend, sort of. That he'd asked me to marry him, sort of. "He's in the army. It's complicated. I feel bad. I can't do this."

He got up naked, sat on the futon, and looked up at me. "Why do you do this to yourself?"

"Why do I do what, Clay?"

"Naughty, I've been watching you do this for years. You deliberately do things to make yourself feel bad about having sex with people. We haven't seen each other in over five years, and today we had a great afternoon together. Then we decided to have sex. That's it. There's nothing to feel bad about. But you wait until after to tell me you have a boyfriend (sort of), who wants to marry you (sort of), and now you feel bad? When are you going to stop this shit?"

"Fuck you, Clay. You don't know me."

He nearly choked on his laughter. "Oh, I don't know you?"

I stood there naked with my arms crossed in front of my chest. He kept on laughing. We both knew I was full of shit, but I was still too vain to admit it, so I left through the sliding glass door like I always did.

In a bid to show him I had changed, that I wouldn't just disappear again, I called him a few days later, made plans to have lunch with him and Isabella. *Remember her? Look, I'm normal. I can hang out with you and other people.* But I totally clammed up over sushi when they started swapping stories about me like they were old friends. Back at his house on the futon through the sliding glass door they shared a joint and had a good laugh at my expense.

"Isabella, did she tell you that she waited until after we slept together to tell me she was seeing someone?"

"Hahahah. Of course she did!"

"Yeah, then I called her on it and she told me to fuck myself. That I didn't know her. Hahahahahhaha."

"Fuck you guys. I'm standing right here."

"Whatever, Tash. Clay, you still coming to Taco Tuesday?"

"Look at her, Iz. She doesn't want me there."

"Whatever. Come anyway. She'll get over it."

"Hahahahahahahahhaha!"

Fucking. Hilarious.

He brought his friend Val to Don Antonio's that night. They sat at a different table because ours was full of people I didn't give a shit about. Just like old times.

"Look, Tash—Clay is here."

"Fuck you, Izzy."

She scoffed as I turned into a fifteen-year-old again. Ignored him. It was pathetic. He and Val drank beers and had a good time anyway. Ate their tacos and laughed. Whenever he caught me looking over he'd raise his bottle and smile. Without judgment. Clay always took me at my worst while I took him for granted until the day he died.

•••

*I FOUND OUT IN the most pedestrian way possible. Just back from Fiji. I'd been waiting for the trip to end to set up a date with you. To try again. I was at work scrolling through Facebook, the kids I nannied napping upstairs. In the end the only mutual friend we had coincidentally was also named Clay. When I asked him how he knew you he said something vague about the Hollywood club scene. Bullshit, I thought. That stinks of anonymity. Clayton Bowler was the Godfather of recovery on the Westside, and after your last two DUIs you two were bound to meet. He'd written something cryptic about having just talked to you the day before on your Facebook page, which confused the hell out of me until I kept scrolling. I'd already missed the funeral. You would have hated that. I didn't know what to do. I had no one to call. You were my only real link to you. I sent Clayton Blowler a Facebook message looking for answers. Posted a cry for help on your page. Wept on my boss's shoulder. Took the rest of the day off. Drove all over the city. Went to the church where they'd held the services. Spoke to the pastor. He had one program left over. He made me a Xerox copy. Your picture in black and white. Clayton Alexander Freed. November 5, 1981–January 6, 2013. He said it was packed. The church was packed. People standing in the back. In the aisles. Even with such short notice. Your dad buried you four days after you were pronounced dead. You would have hated that too. Months later people were still posting on your Facebook page that they'd just found out, but four days after they took your heart and gave it to another man, you could still fill a church.*

*Nine days later I was back at your house on Ophir. Your friend Toby saw my Facebook plea on your wall and took pity on me. I met her by the Veteran's memorial. We went to your house together. Your hipster friends had a party for you there. I wasn't allowed through the sliding glass door to your room. No one really was. You would have hated that too. Everyone was drinking. Smoking. There was a DJ. Photographers. People were in the pool. Your dad gave a speech about how your musical tastes were unrivaled. You would have loved that. I sat at a table with*

45

*your friends from the old days. Ryan was there. He was the only one who recognized me. "Naughty," he called out. I hadn't heard that nickname in years. Never would again. "He still talked about you," he said. "The one that got away."*

*We went to your mom's house that night. She had an intimate dinner catered. I sat around the table with your brother, your best friends, and with Blair, who kept leaving through the front door and coming back. We went up to your childhood room. Your brother showed us where you used to stash your drugs. We went back down to the dining room table, and your mom brought out the old photo albums with coffee and dessert. We took pictures of the pictures with our phones. I told your mom that I was glad to finally meet her. That I didn't even know that she was in LA. That you'd told me she moved to Tennessee. Why would he say that about me? I didn't know. Your brother had nothing but the best things to say about you, and hung his head low remembering the times growing up when he was mean. "He was such a great person, how could anyone be mean to him?"*

*"I was mean to him," I confessed at your mother's dinner table. It got quiet and I became the focal point. Blair stared at me with daggers.*

*"Why?" your brother asked. "Why were you mean to him?"*

*I shrugged. "I don't know. I was just a kid."*

# CHAPTER 9

"WHAT'S THAT, NATASCIA?"

"No, forget it, Robert Michael. It's embarrassing. It doesn't matter."

"No, I want to hear it. What's your theory on pain?"

"Well, I don't know. It's stupid."

"Yeah, come on, Natascia. What could you possibly know about pain?"

"No, Julian, it's really nothing."

"Oh, come on already!"

"Fine. It's just something I've been wondering about. I don't know. Maybe we all get dealt the same amount of pain in life. Like, all humans get the same amount to handle over the course of their lifetime. And maybe some folks get most of it all at once, and so it feels like a lot, and it feels like more than everyone else, and they get all 'why me?' about the world. But maybe what they don't see is that everyone else is dealing with the same kind of pain, just more often, and in smaller degrees. And if that's true then who could really say whose pain is harder or more important? Maybe it's all exactly the same pain, in exactly the same amount. And maybe for some people the pain comes out like the slow leak of a faucet. You know, like, it feels like no big deal, really. Like, it's not going to flood your house if you don't fix it, or anything. But after an hour, or a week, or a lifetime of hearing the slow drip, you can't hear anything else. And you feel like you are gonna just fucking kill yourself if you have to hear one more drip. And everyone around you keeps telling you to just get over it, and it's not that bad, and you should be grateful because some people have it worse, and it gets better, and shit, but all you hear is *drip, drip, drip, drip, drip drip, drip.*"

Robert Michael, whose red-headed mother sat beside us on the couch smoking ganja through a crack pipe, nodded. "Huh. I never thought about it like that. Yeah...maybe."

But Julian, whose mother walked into the ocean one night when he was a boy and never came out, looked at me and scoffed. "Yeah, you don't know shit about pain." He shut the door to his bedroom and didn't come out for the rest of the night.

•••

I wasn't sure if I wanted to be her friend or not. Something always rubbed me the wrong way about her. Something that was altogether suspiciously attractive. But, she kinda looked like me, and had a toughness to her that I still hadn't decided was total bullshit.

Yasmin was loosely affiliated with folks I knew in the walk-down-the-hall-and-say-what's-up kinda way, but she was still right on the precipice of being invited to everything on her own, so she was cool but still too far removed to be a safe bet. She was the only girl in my grade with a car, however, and that's not nothing. She had this phantom-rich Persian father that seemed to constantly dangle material wealth in front of her to make up for his absence. Always going to get her new clothes, or a new car, or something that he'd never quite follow through on. She took me to the Ford dealership on Santa Monica Boulevard after school one day when the Harley Davidson edition of the F-150 came out. We bobbled in, threw our backpacks in the bed of the truck, and hopped into the front seats. There was a little button on the roof of the truck that recorded memos. I pushed it and giggled at Yaz, "What should we say?"

"We're 'bout to get this shit," she boomed and threw up non-affiliated nonsense gang signs. *Kook.* The salesman came over. "My daddy said he'd get this for me," she smiled, and batted the old lash as they chatted about things like credit and down payments. But her daddy never did get her that truck.

Yaz was connected to people in the South Bay. Redondo Beach, Palos Verdes, and beyond. Phantom places and phantom people in an anonymous world that suited me just fine. We were sort of flirting with the possibility of friendship at a time when I was full throttle to my own destruction, and one night I let her convince me to spend the night at her mom's apartment on Fifteenth in Santa Monica. I was never really hot on sleepovers in strange places. The inevitability of being up all night uncomfortably listening to someone else sleep. The seeping regret of the twelve-hour sigh fest on foreign surfaces. Was it going to be a problem if I flushed the toilet in the middle of the night? How long after sunrise did I have to stay before it stopped being weird to leave? Did she even have a spare bed? I hemmed and hawed until she laid the old "I just got a new puppy! You've gotta come see her" routine on me.

I'm only human. We went over after school and I played with the miniature terrier puppy with sharp puppy teeth well into the evening as Yaz busied herself on the phone with the South Bay.

"I wanna have sex tonight," I sort of off-handedly said as we sped down Lincoln Boulevard in the wrong direction, until we were under tunnels and glaring lights. "I wanna have sex tonight" escaped a daydream sequence from my head through my mouth. I really just wanted to like someone who liked me back. To forge a connection in another city that would help me escape the smallness of the Westside. I knew that wasn't going to happen, at least not in the overly romanticized fashion for which I pinned on the daily. "I wanna have sex tonight" was more realistic, and I guess I just wanted to accomplish something. Anything. I'd always heard it said that women have it so easy when it came to sex. That we could have sex with anyone at any time. All we have to do is decide. So I was all, *What a grotesque notion! Let's give it a shot! I wanna have sex tonight. Hey, new girl that I'm not really sure I like or trust! I wanna have sex tonight!*

"Oh, yeaaaaaaaah?" she answered mischievously. "With who?"

"I don't know. Anyone, I guess."

God, how she smiled. "We can definitely make that happen."

If you ever find yourself in a car with a prospect driving into the unknown world of her male friends in a town you've never been to and she shows excitement when you say some self-destructive shit like, "I don't know. Anyone, I guess," beware, my dears, for a friend she is not. There are some women who have mostly male friends because their own male energy is intact. They are the ones who can be themselves around men and women alike, but just generally prefer breaking balls without it ending in tears and hurt feelings. Go meet a new group of boys with a girl like that and nine times out of ten you'll probably have a good time. On the other hand, there are those other girls whose connection to their own maleness is so flimsy that they have to feed off the masculine energy of the boys they surround themselves with. The ones who so despise being resigned to the scenery that they sweepingly reject all things feminine in some misguided attempt at camaraderie. The ones who seem to be in constant competition with themselves to prove that they're one of the "cool ones." To prove that they're not like other girls. Down with the homies, or whatever. I've been both kinds, and far fucking be it from me to judge. All I'm saying is, if you find yourself in a car with the latter kind of girl, just watch your tongue.

It took forever to get there, which is probably untrue. It probably took no more than twenty minutes, but I didn't know the streets and I didn't know the houses and time passes like molasses in the unknown. We drank Captain Morgan and Dr. Pepper in a house on a hill with a bunch of white boys in backward caps. I couldn't tell a single one apart from the other, and every time I tried to access the part of my brain that assesses the surrounding for feelings of *I could get used to this*, it just clicked and pulled like an engine that wouldn't turn over. *Fuck it, then,* I shrugged to no one in particular and focused on the only delight I could find. The thrill of discovery as my pallet awoke to the burning spice and pruney sweetness effervescing on my tongue. *Dr. Pepper and Captain Morgan. What is this holy grail buccaneer chalice of white-trash cocktails? Fuck it. I'll have several. Jack and Coke be damned!*

Yazmin and I went out to the street to smoke cigarettes. I stood on the brick ledge that surrounded a sloping lawn of ivy, holding dear to the red Solo cup in my palms. Practicing my balance. One foot in front of the other. "Did you really mean what you said in the car?" She exhaled with a puff of Parliament Light pretense. *Oh, fuck. I don't know? Did I?*

"Psssh. Girrrrrl, I always mean what I say." *Oh, goddamnit.*

"So it could be anyone?" *Fuck fuck fuck.*

I nodded.

And there was that goddamned smile again. Sharp-toothed and flashy like she'd just cashed in a whole stack of counterfeit chips. Yazmin pranced up the stairs and disappeared into the house on the hill I didn't know, to the white boys with backward caps that all looked alike, on the street I'd never remember.

A minute later he appeared. The faceless one. He took my hand and walked me half a block to a white Ford Explorer. "Oh, my mom has this car, but hers is the two-door Sport Edition," was all I said.

"Uh, this isn't mine," was all he said.

It was over before I even knew it started. "I'm Tyler," he offered as he zipped his jeans back up. *Remember that.*

"I'm Natascia."

The next morning I woke up in a sleeping bag on the carpeted floor of Yazmin's bedroom. Her miniature terrier puppy had gone into my purse in the middle of the night and chewed up the first edition *Phantom Tollbooth* I was borrowing from Dahlia. I gathered up all the pieces, cursing her adorable tiny teeth. A few weeks later Yaz pulled up to school in a brand-new black Nissan Sentra with a decal that read "Octopussy Posse" on the windshield, and that shit-eating dinosaur grin on her face.

"Hey, Tash! Wanna go for a ride?"

"Uh. Nah. I'm good."

# CHAPTER 10

D AHLIA DROPPED OUT OF SAMO or got kicked out or something. I don't exactly remember. Either way it turned out that her credits weren't the only thing nontransferable about her semester in Africa. You should have seen her though, the day she got back, right before Granny casually mention her father OD'd while she was gone. I'd never seen her skin sparkle so, like she had swallowed the Swahili sun and could hardly contain it. She'd gotten her nose pierced at the marketplace in Zimbabwe. A tiny, pale green jewel. Joan, the director of the newly formed Student Travel and Research High School, made her take it out immediately for fear of repercussions from Dahlia's mother. It was the kind of absurd injustice you only experience as a sixteen-year-old girl. Wanda was not that kind of mother, yet despite Dahlia's protests not only did Joan insist she remove the nose ring, but as punishment for having the audacity to make a decision about her own body, she was barred from going on the waterfall field trip in Zimbabwe with the rest of the class. But bless her soul, Dahlia feigned total disinterest in all things water and spent the rest of Africa with a piece of fishing line lodged in her nose until landing at LAX. As the captain announced their final descent Dali turned to make sure Joan was watching before she stuck the tiny green jewel back into her arrow-shaped nose.

God, I loved her for shit like that. She was the first person I ever saw defy adults with such ease. Like the time we went camping in Joshua Tree with the Church on Ocean Park and decided to spend the day just the two of us exploring the rock formations. We had a spectacular day, climbing, playing, talking about boys. By the time the pastor, and the park ranger found us, the sun was much lower than when we set out, and we were thoroughly chastised for our carelessness: "What if you would have fallen? What if you would have gotten lost in the desert? What if you were bitten

by a rattlesnake? You're not even teenagers yet! We are responsible for you!"
I hung my head low in shame like you're supposed to when grown-ups yell
at you. Not Dahlia. She stood headstrong at the top of the boulders, arms
crossed, eyes rolled. When they told us to come down I got on all fours to
descend, but behind me all I heard was a resounding no. I hesitated and
turned in disbelief. She was still cross-armed, chin raised, with the auburn
sun receding behind her.

"Come down right now!"

"No."

By the looks of it, Dahlia was prepared to give her life to those rocks.
I still couldn't believe it. *You can just say no to adults? Why had I never thought
of that? I mean, really, what could they do? Arrest us? We hadn't broken any laws.
Physically remove us? Maybe, but wouldn't that just end up bringing them shame?*
You could see them going through the same thought process, the pastor and
the park ranger. Once yelling and scolding failed, what were they prepared
to do? What was I prepared to give up? I appealed to Dali's leadership.

"Tash, you don't have to do what they say."

I knew she was right, and for the first time I realized how separate I was
from the folks around me. We are all just people, no matter the age, in total
control of the choices we make.

"Natascia, if you don't come down we are going to have to call your
parents to come get you. Is that what you want?"

*Shit. Fuck. The parental trump card.* No, that was not what I fucking
wanted. I could just hear my dad, the humiliation in his voice speaking to
the park ranger, apologizing for his daughter's lack of respect and his failure
as a parent. The two-and-a-half-hour lecture out of the desert. The promise
of never seeing Dahlia again. It wasn't worth it. I got back on all fours and
climbed down.

"Tash! Don't!"

"Come on, Dali. Just come down already. Let's go make s'mores."

The pastor and I still talk about that evening to this day. Still laugh about
it every time we see each other. And even now, as a full-blown adult, I still
apologize for my blatant disregard. He usually just raises his eyebrows and
shakes his head. "You two girls," he says. "You were something else."

The day she got back from Africa I waited at the apartment on Marine
for Granny to bring her home from the airport. I'd been accepted to that

private school too, to my absolute elation. But just as I was getting ready to start high school with my best friend in Africa, my folks broke it to me slowly that we just couldn't afford it. I was crushed. Dali was pissed. But if it weren't for her grandfather's trust fund, her family that subsisted on food stamps and welfare wouldn't be able to afford it either. Sitting on her stoop that afternoon, dreaming of all the things she'd seen without me, the people she'd met without me, I wondered if she had outgrown us. If she'd changed so much we'd just drift apart in a matter of months. She came rushing through the courtyard with her grandmother behind her, skirts swirling, skin glistening, bright-eyed, and grinning like a peach. She looked like a golden fertility goddess. We embraced. And not in the usual awkward Dahlia tap-on-the-shoulder-I-don't-know-how-to-show-affection way. We hugged like kindred spirits hug when they finally find each other. Like some *Anne of Green Gables* shit.

Sweet Lord Jesus, how she smiled! Really smiled, you know. Not drunken smiled, not "we're having fun, right?" smiled. Like, pure joy smiled. It was rare, and it took my breath away staring at her spinning into the kitchen, talking about new things and new friends. Girls named America and Mercedes, straight A's on math projects, sneaking out one night for a fishbowl full of neon blue alcohol, and something called *koeksisters*.

"No, not Cook Sisters," she corrected. "Koek—koek. Hahahhaha. No, not cock!" She pushed her lips forward and pulled her tongue back in her throat. "KOEK. No, it's not like a doughnut. It's like a magical sticky fried South African thing. It's like a koeksister!"

She asked us if we were hungry and Granny scolded.

"This food costs money, you know. We can't afford to feed all your friends all of the time. Gawd, don't they have homes?"

"Shut up, Granny!" Dali got up and looked in the fridge. "Look how much we have. You know, in Soweto they have nothing. Really nothing. They live in houses made from scraps of metal with dirt floors and they'll invite you in and give you whatever they have. They're poorer than we are, but they are happier than I've ever seen. Look at all this. We don't need all of this. And most of it will just go bad anyway."

She held a jar of Jif peanut butter. "God, I missed this shit, though. You guys want some of my dad's peanut butter?" she laughed. She never talked about him.

"Your dad's peanut butter?"

"Yeah, they call him Jiffy…some nickname they gave him in prison. Jiffy, Jerry," she shrugged. "I don't really get it." Granny scoffed and said something under her breath. I just rolled my eyes, but Dali looked right at her. "What did you just say?"

"Who, me? Didn't you know? Yeah, Jerry's dead. He finally OD'd. They found him under the freeway. Oh, for Pete's sake! Didn't your mom tell you? Oh, Gawd. You're crying now? Well, why on Earth wouldn't Wanda tell you?! You'd think your own mother would tell you! What? You didn't even like him."

"He was my dad."

"Well, maybe you should have thought about that and talked to him when he called once in a while."

Dahlia fled to the bathroom and wouldn't come out. Echoed whimpers escaped through the cracks of the door. Call him. Call him. I was going to call him. Granny pounded on the door and chuckled. She really did.

"Oh, come on, Dahlia! You have guests here!"

I'd never felt so compelled to deck someone in their dome. Elder or not. I looked Granny dead in her eyes. All the things I wanted to scream at her, but all I managed was, "Enough, Rosanna. Enough."

Granny clicked her tongue at me, rolled her eyes in baffled amusement, and walked home. I sat on the other side of that locked bathroom door willing my molecules to phase through the wood to hold her on the linoleum floor in the corner by the toilet. But she wouldn't let me in. When her mom came home and explained through the door how she didn't want to ruin Africa, Dali wouldn't let her in either. No one got in until Felix showed up. Felix was allowed. His parents were both long dead. Murdered over drugs or money or both while he was a toddler hiding in the closet. Or so he used to say. He went in without looking at me and they talked in whispers. And then he left and she still didn't come out. Not until everyone went home. Most of what was left of the Zulu Nation came pouring out of her cold coffee eyes that afternoon.

After that it was back to drunken "we're having fun, right?" smiles and I-don't-know-how-to-show-affection hugs. Back to driving around in Felix's primer gray Nova with bags of drugs in the trunk. A few months later, when Student Travel and Research went bankrupt, Dahlia landed at

Olympic High. The continuation school where futures go to die. It wasn't much, but she still had a spark of life left in her, and after she made the down payment for the house on Indiana Avenue there was still a spark of coin left in the trust too. Despite the Swahili sun receding from her skin, youth got the better of her, and she started dreaming again. She wanted to own a vineyard when she grew up. We'd laugh together at how she hated the taste of wine but wanted a vineyard. "Whatever," she'd say. "Maybe I'll use what's left in the trust to buy a piece of land in wine country, and you'll just run it for me, and you can taste all the wine and tell me if it's good or not." I was down. I'd walk the mile from SAMO high after school every day and meet her in the computer lab, and we'd look up property in Napa or Sonoma while we tried to wrap our teenage brains around the differences between steel and oak tanks.

"This shit's kinda complicated, Dali."

"Whatever, you're smart. Someone somewhere has figured out how to run a vineyard before. What do they got that you don't got?"

I hated when she was right, but I lived for compliments like these. We had been friends since we met at summer camp in '97, the year after she dated my brother. From the moment I sat my eleven-year-old tush on her lap by the ping-pong table, the sun rose and set for Dahlia. Her idiosyncrasies were the stars in my Big Bear night's sky, and if she wanted a vineyard, fuck it, I wanted a vineyard.

•••

THE FIRST TIME WE kissed we were outside of Will Rogers Park. In the middle of the road. She collapsed half crying, half laughing, 100 percent hysterically drunk.

"You don't understand," she blathered.

"Oh, God. What now? What don't I understand this time?"

"I like you! I really like you!"

"I know, babe. I like you too. Now get up."

"No! I won't get up! You don't understand…I have a crush on you…I like you and I don't like that I like you. You are beautiful and smart and honest. You know things and—" she couldn't go on.

My face must have exploded in light. *Oh, shit.* She was right, I didn't understand. But fuck it, I was down. I grabbed her stupid face and kissed her. Shut her right up. Then I pulled back, still holding her head. I must have looked like a idiot with a grin the size of Africa on my face. I AM FUCKING 100 PERCENT DOWN was all there was.

We went back to David Fox's that night and locked ourselves in the small bathroom. The one without the steam shower. Slumming it. We did whatever we could think to do to each other. Some combination of all the things the boys we had come to know came out all over our bodies. I couldn't believe how soft she was. Kissing a girl is nothing like kissing a boy. Nothing. It's like falling into a pit of marshmellows, tangled in pillows, covered in foam and flesh and all things that squish, and before your mind can catch up your body's already convinced you that you could actually live inside of her forever. You'll never want to come out. Never want to pull back. Never not want her lips on your lips. Never. I threw myself inside her. Fork and knife, spoon and hand. I wanted everything. Mine. Mine. Mine. I wanted her to be mine.

Somehow David Fox had unlocked the door and we caught him staring at us, naked. Fully erect. Revolting. She screamed, and I pushed him out with both forearms and locked the door again. We continued until well after the water ran ice cold. I spent the night beside her in her queen-sized bed as I had so many nights before. All those nights and all those naps when we were just kids. Why was this night different from all other nights? I wished for the miracle of the morning. I wished for everything I was still capable of wishing for. I dreamt of the little penguins on the bottle caps of Bud Ice that stacked at Will Rogers that night. Not all birds can fly. Maybe I'm a penguin. Sure, sure, sure. It all made sense. It could all be so simple.

When she awoke I held my morning breath, holding off the hangover with it, and squeezed out an impossible "hi."

*Her eyes, her breasts, her thighs.*

"Oh, God," she sighed and turned away. "I was really drunk last night."

Penguins. Damn. Neverfuckingmind. "Uh, yeah. Me too," and I got up to pee. Dehydrated. And then the hangover. Maybe it goes without saying, but breakfast was awkward.

We managed our friendship for another fifteen years after that. Always a rocky climb, always uphill. She'd get wasted and come on to me again. Like opening a pressure valve. She'd never want anyone to find out but somehow always managed to do it so someone would discover us. I think it just turned her on. I'd ravish her. Harder faster longer stronger. She'd always complain about the lack of dick between us. The cheap shot. I'd shove my fingers farther up, stick in another until she would pull back and scream, "I like it softer."

Fucking bitch. No, you don't. You like it like this. Rough. Drunk. In the shower pretending until the water runs Bud Ice cold.

After she got pregnant with Logan we never touched each other again. I guess three abortions were more than she could handle, and she was determined to keep this one. Our friendship disintegrated slowly into a series of breakups and makeups. She canceled her flight to Florence to have a baby and stay in Venice Beach forever. I moved to Italy without her. I remember screaming at her in the kitchen in the house on Indiana she half-owned with her mom the day she told me she wasn't coming.

"What the fuck, Dali?! How the fuck are you gonna raise this child? You're eighteen! Seamus' not coming back! You don't even have a diploma! And the trust is mostly gone since you bought this house! You've never even had a job! This is some Jerry Springer welfare shit. Come on, dog...don't you have any dreams left? You're better than this!"

"Fuck you, Tash! I was raised on welfare. If it was good enough for me, it'll be good enough for my baby, and if you don't want to get on board then fuck Italy and fuck YOU!"

But she'd call me at four in the morning, Firenze time, pregnant and bawling. "I can't believe you left me," she'd cry. "Your best friend is pregnant with her first child only once, and you just leave? You should be here with me! I can't do this! I'm going to give him up for adoption."

I should have never come back from Italy, but Venice Beach is magnetic. When she gave birth, I had to practically force myself into the hospital room. She behaved like I wasn't there. But then she'd call me when she needed to disappear. She knew I was the only one who would watch Logan without giving her shit for wanting to be eighteen. When she told me that she'd met with an adoption lawyer I fell over in the Trader Joe's on Pico and Thirty-Third. Skylar held me like that in the middle of the aisle. Seventeen still and on the floor telling my new boyfriend that I had to figure out how to adopt my best friend's baby. A month earlier I'd sworn before God and the pastor at the Church on Ocean Park that as godmother I'd protect him. I had no clue what that actually meant.

Dali changed her mind at the last minute, like she always did. Little Logan went to spend the weekend with his "new family." They were already calling him Vince, and in the afternoon of the first day he was with them, he conjured up a fever of 106. Dahlia rushed to meet him in the emergency room, turned her back on that prospective family, and for better or worse Logan came home with her the next night. Seven years and several abortions later came Lacey. All the joy that was left in Dahlia went into that baby girl. She kept planning the baptism and bailing at the last minute. She spent more of her time disappearing than ever before, and three more years and three more abortions later, no one knew Laura was on the way until the third trimester.

We had a good run, I supposed. We lasted twenty years, give or take. Mostly give. According to her, I'm a stuck-up, judgmental, snobby-ass bitch. According to the State of California, she is not fit to retain custody of her children.

# CHAPTER 11

Before Dahlia got pregnant with the first child she'd keep, when baby daddies were still just something they talked about between *The Andy Griffith Show* and commercials for Survival Insurance; before meth madness and family court hearings in Monterey Park, when leaving your baby with a friend for a few years was just something the mom in *White Oleander* did; before best friends became strangers on the streets they grew up on; before all of that, there was Seamus. The white boy from down the street. Venice local like a motherfucker. Not the new tote bag, $300 sweatpants, ayahuasca ceremony, seven-dollar coffee, loft behind Abbot Kinney, call yourself a local after five years type. No. The real Venice local. The conservative liberal, punk-rock skater, Camel cigarette smoking, doesn't think we have to do something about the homeless "problem," boardwalk tattoos, family in the same home for generations, God grant me the serenity type. Ginger, stout, already twenty-one with shamrocks on his elbows and three-dimensional rocker stars tattooed on his knees. Seamus used to hang out outside the Gourmet Coffee Warehouse (before it became Groundworks) and drink XTCs straight from the bottle. We'd always see him driving around in his green Toyota pickup with the Suicidal Tendencies sticker on the back and Dali's face would go stupid for a few minutes.

She liked everything about him until she discovered that he lived around the way. Then I think it was that closest she's ever been to absolute love. Dali still had real meet-me-outside-and-see-what-happens guts at this time. I can't remember exactly how they ended up meeting. She either walked up to him at the 76 on Rose and Lincoln, or she left him a note on that green Toyota pickup in the dead of night, or both. Probably both. Not long after, there was no Seamus without Dali. And there was no Dali without Tash.

The three of us were like that for a good while. Triangulated in triple to the hours and the days that moved so damn slowly in our youth. I think the only person who really dug the deal was Dali, though. She hit the best friend/boyfriend jackpot and the rest of us kinda hung on for scraps. Seamus was okay or whatever, but after having to regurgitate everything I'd just learned in history about the Civil Rights Act of 1964 in defense of affirmative action one morning at Café 50's, I quickly came to realize that there was only so much whiteboy I could stomach. I have no idea what his opinions of me were, but I do know my constant presence was the cause of both frustration and suspicion between the two of them. One too many Dali and I getting drunk and sneaking off to the shower while he was around kinda nights, I guess.

We kept it mad cool though, and mostly just enjoyed what we could of each other's company. I was pretty cavalier about popping pills at that point, and Seamus, bless his heart, always had some prescriptions on deck. Dahlia was my indisputable best friend, Seamus kept most of her craziness busy, and I had two people in my life that protected me from being alone all the damn time.

When Seamus moved out of his grandma's house around the corner from Indiana, everything started to go sour. He moved to the northern edge of Westchester behind Loyola. His roommate was some guy named Danny. The first time we went over Danny was holed up in his room with this blonde who couldn't wait to get the Sublime sun trampstamped, complete with Bradley Knowles's birth and expiration dates. I walked by on my way to the bathroom while they tumbled inside. *I wonder what it would be like to be in that room with him. To have a key to his place, and use this bathroom when I wake up in the middle of the night. I wonder if I could get used to this. Oh, well. Too bad he likes idiot blonde girls.* The Vicodin started to kick in on the way back from the bathroom, and this dark-haired goateed boy named Brandon showed up. Took about twenty minutes before we were making out hardcore down the block in his Hyundai. I did my best to forget all about Danny.

When he dropped me back off, Brandon gave me a ping-pong ball with his number pre-written on it in silver sharpie, and I was like, damn! Does this smooth-ass motherfucker have a box of these in the center console for girls he makes out with? I laughed and told him I'd call him or whatever and walked back to the house feeling strangely like I'd cheated on someone but didn't know who. I picked some flowers, left them on the kitchen table where someone could find them, and went home dreaming of a whiteboy to call my own.

Nothing ever came of Brandon. He told Seamus I was a bad kisser, which I call bullshit on to this day. I happen to know for a motherfucking fact that I'm a good kisser, Vicodin or not, so fuck that lying-ass fool for life. Whatever. The next time we were over, Danny told me he had broken up with the blonde girl, and in the same breath mentioned that he took care of the flowers I left. Sure enough, they were sitting in a beer bottle, watered and fresh as the night I picked them.

In all my years of romantic psychosis someone had finally taken the bait. Finally some random boy I'd attached a series of starry-eyed ideas to had done so to me at the very same time. Seamus and Dali were pumped, and they both went to work straight away. Danny really likes you, and you should come over, he's a really great guy, you guys'd be perfect together, and then we could all hang out, blah, blah blah. Danny opened up, told me all about the kids who made fun of him when he was young, told me about his father and how their relationship was strained. Then he told me how it made him crazy that first night I disappeared with Brandon. "I barely knew you and I had a girlfriend, I know," he remarked, all doe-eyed. "But when I heard you were off with Brandon, I don't know, I just couldn't stand it. I felt like you were mine somehow. Is that weird?"

No, no, no! It was all too easy! I kept trying to find something wrong with him, but the first time we kissed it was like the Niagara fucking Falls. I was mortified. I had no cover. He was proud as he held my underwear in his hands, like it was his accomplishment. But he had no follow-through. Something about being intimidated by me. *Why do all these boys go soft? I'm just a little fucking girl. What is so goddamned intimidating?* "Well," he said. "We could get up and go to that party or we could just lie here holding each other like this." I rolled my eyes and jumped up. "I'm going to the party. You can do whatever you want." He laid in bed holding the soaked zebra-striped electric blue thong I'd borrowed from Yazmin that one morning and looked at me like I'd just broken his heart.

I was a cunt. There's no other way to describe it. I don't think I wanted to be, but it was this unstoppable force that surged out of me like some villainous mutant superpower I'd yet to learn to control. He was so sweet too. Pure sugar. Holding my hand walking down his neighborhood he'd say something saccharine as fuck about the moon and my lips while he picked jasmine for me. I'd tell him his breath smelled like something had rotted inside his mouth, and he should see someone about that. He'd go to the dentist and get his broken tooth pulled, and I'd check my pager like I had somewhere else to be. I didn't know how to sit across from such a resounding yes, so I disappeared for a while. On to other boys and other houses, but mostly back to the yellow walls of my bedroom.

Maybe a month passed, maybe two. Dali and Seamus bought a beagle puppy on a whim one afternoon and named it Laura. They were always buying animals they couldn't take care of. Dali's mom, Wanda, wouldn't let us in the house with her: "Come on, man! No more animals!" It was coming on summer and neither of them would let up about Danny, and because I really didn't have a good reason not to, I agreed to go with them to take the puppy to the Westchester house on the one condition that they'd promise not to leave me alone with him.

We stopped by Pavilions in the Marina and I gave Seamus money for a bottle of wine. The four of us sat in the living room and watched *Evil Dead* for the first time, and to my absolute entertainment and delight I managed to have a good time. Dahlia and Seamus disappeared into Seamus's bedroom, and Danny and I couldn't keep our hands off of each other. It was the first and last time we had sex.

A few weeks later Dali snorted glass for the first time in the bathroom of the Westchester house. We had to give the puppy away. Then all of the animals started dying. First the two chinchillas Dali and Seamus had gotten for each other. Months apart. After the second one died, Dali just put a blanket over the cage and left it until Wanda discovered it days later rotting in her room.

Next to go were the dwarf bunnies from Alan's Aquarium. Dali's two mutts had torn through the makeshift chicken-wire bunny run we put up in the side yard until we could build something more permanent. It was pure carnage. The ferocious game of predator and prey. I was at a callback for *Our Town* after school when I got the 911 page. Dali was in hysterics, but I decided to stay at the audition in the stupid dress Granny made me wear. "Who auditions for a role in *Our Town* in bell-bottoms, for Pete's sake!?"

Dr. Frank gave me the whole, "Uh, nice dress, Natascia," before I blew the audition trying to pronounce Antietam. Dali spent the afternoon alone sobbing in the green Toyota pickup at the Albertson's on Ocean Park while Seamus bagged groceries inside. They picked me up outside of the theater room after dark. We got burritos and drank beer. Nobody said much.

I ended up getting cast in *Our Town* as the lead role of ticket-taker, and not long after opening night Dali confessed that she couldn't go through with another abortion. She wouldn't be moving to Italy with me when the semester ended and our dreams of owning a vineyard died before they even had a heartbeat.

Before leaving this godforsaken town, Danny pried open my bedroom window and threw a gift onto my bed. My neighbors saw, and my mom and brother thoroughly chastised me for having some psycho boy break into our house. By the time the public humiliation was over and I got to my bedroom, I was ready to throw the whole fucking thing away and never look back. But curiosity got the best of me. It was a mango. A mango and a Ziplock bag filled with various trinkets. A plastic number two, dried flowers, orange construction paper with two hearts drawn on it, some crayons, a picture of two ducks, a single die, a photograph of a boy in a tree, and a letter copied on fax paper that tied it all together.

*Natascia—*

*Even though I don't believe in luck, you and I must be some lucky ducks to have met in this big pond called life. I am willing to roll the dice and take the chance of getting hurt to be with you. What do you say? You're fresh as a flower, so I picked this picture to give to you. 2 hearts smelling jasmine, smiling talking about love. These gifts were chosen for you. My heart is hers to love…*

I was inexplicably repulsed and called him with a fury I am still ashamed of. Pretended I'd never strategically hinted that my bedroom window faced the street and was always unlocked. Pretended I'd never left any goddamned flowers on his goddamned dining room table. "Don't ever break into my house again!" I raged 100 percent cunt all over him, hung up the phone, and crashed onto my bed humiliated and fuming. I tore through the whole damn mango. Didn't even bother getting a knife from the kitchen. It was ripe as hell, and the juice got everywhere. Down my arms, my chin, and the sheets too, but I just kept eating it. Even when the only thing left was the giant seed, I sucked and gnashed at it until mango threads were stuck in every tooth.

I saw him once after that. Logan had just been born, and I shouldn't have been back from Italy, but there I was. Venice Beach again. Skylar and I had started dating, like in a serious fashion, and for some stupid reason Dahlia and I decided that October 17 was a great day to do something crazy. Seamus still hadn't met his son, and after ignoring several belligerent voicemails that summer from Danny threatening suicide unless I called him back, I guess I sorta felt responsible. On a whim we stole a giant hollow Styrofoam snowman from the neighbor's porch on Lake Avenue and filled the inside with impossible idiocies. Seashells, feathers, candles, pictures of Logan, and a couple of letters for a couple of boys who lived in Westchester. One all about fruit and the other about a baby. We sealed it up with packing tape, shoved a violet rose in the poor snowman's hand, left it on their front porch, and drove away.

It was another couple years before Seamus ever met Logan. But Danny? He took to that shit like a fly to honey. Hit me up that very same night. The minute I saw his number on my pager I knew it was all a lie. I didn't mean a word of it. I called him back though, and agreed to go bowling because what else could I do? We went down to the lanes by the airport with a bunch of his friends I didn't know. He'd been working out that summer and weighed about one hundred pounds more than the last time I'd seen him. After an awkward dinner at the diner attached to the alley, with folks I had no interest in, I told him I wasn't really feeling up to bowling, so we sat in the car mostly, and he told me more about his father and what it meant to get my letter. He tried to kiss me. I pulled back, said something about wanting to take it slow. I told him I'd call and we could see about starting over. I called Clay instead and disappeared that night. From Skylar, from Danny, from Dahlia and Seamus and Logan, from my yellow bedroom on the street I grew up on, from Los Angeles, from the United States, from the continent of North America, from the Western Hemisphere, from the Earth, from the Solar System, from the Universe, from the Mind of God. For just one night. Skylar stuck around for seven years after that, and I never saw Danny again.

# CHAPTER 12

IN HIGH SCHOOL I WAS all of the emotions, all of the time. There was no elation without deep sorrow, no discovery without the pepper of guilt, no confusion without apathy, and certainly no triumph without dread. I had no idea how to contain any of it, how to quiet any of it, how to simplify any of it, and I was sure that if I didn't figure it out soon, I would die. Not melodramatic teenager, like, *Oh my God, I'm dying*, die. Not like that. Like, not make it to eighteen die. Like, front page of the high school paper die. Like, segment on the six o'clock news die. Like, memorial service in the Greek die. Like what a tragedy, taken before her time, she had such a bright future, how did we miss the signs die. I didn't know how to make it through the never-ending ticktock of the cuckoo clock, so I fucked my way through most of it to stay alive. It didn't matter if I hated the other person, if I even knew them enough to hate in the first place. I was (nearly) always at peace in the act itself. Before I could be a ball of anxiety, and after, fuhgeddaboudit. After was the fucking Russian roulette of emotions. But in it, I was alone. I was calm. I was totally at peace in the suspended moment before the unknown. The silent stillness of external madness. The supreme focus in the bustling coffee shop. The rhythm, the breath, the belonging to a moment. This is where I am. This is where I'm supposed to be. The thundering hearth, the unstoppable heart, the mixed martial art of firing synapses. The reverence and awe of total devotion.

Even if it's sex that gets me into whatever predicament I'm in, it's almost always sex that gets me out again. My greatest ally. The resounding yes. Loneliness is unbearable. Shame is unimaginable. Rejection is heartbreaking. But sex? You can touch sex. It's real. Undeniable. Indisputable. The linear and the nonlinear. The one and the zero. Sex is the great turning ground where anything can happen.

I had sex with Kyle Newman one of those nights in the dojo. I remember practically nothing about the surrounding circumstances. Only that it happened. We weren't even friends, he and I. Not really, anyway. He was just in the same circle of friends as Johnny Pine and them, and one night I ended up in his bedroom with a bunch of people where we smoked copious amounts of ganja until everyone was either gone or asleep. Then he and I kissed for the world record of worst cottonmouth. The next morning we woke up before everyone else and he drove me home in secret. We made each other swear not to tell a living soul. I never did, either. Not at least until now. Here's hoping there's a statute of limitations on secrets made in teenage depravity.

# CHAPTER 13

SPEAKING OF TEENAGE DEPRAVITY, the night with Kaspar transpired in much of the same fashion. The only real difference at that point was I didn't give a shit who found out. My brother had been sent away to live with our uncle in Italy after the broken jaw and the gun in his bedroom, so there was no chance he'd hear for at least a year. I only mention that because along with being another of Johnny Pine's friends, Kaspar was also in the same grade as my brother, and of all the people in all the world I could give a shit about, I couldn't stand the thought of my brother knowing these parts of me. But, like I said, he was gone, and aside from him I couldn't give a flying fuck who found out. In fact, I was kinda hoping the rumor would spread right back to Johnny's ears, and for once he'd give a shit.

I didn't like Kaspar any. I was just bored and saw an opportunity. We were hanging in Ashley's backhouse in Mar Vista. The fridge was always brimming with Coors Light and a bottle or two of Malibu Rum. There was a pool table, a flat screen, and an Xbox. A real boy trap. I won't call Ashley's mom an alcoholic because far fucking be it from me to judge. However, I will say that when they moved into the mansion on Mountainview a few years later she had a wine cooler custom built into the laundry room. It was one of four wine coolers in that huge house.

Back on Marco Avenue in Mar Vista, where Ashley's stepfather owned the three lots on the corner, her "backhouse" was a single-family home about the same size as the house I grew up in. It was connected to the big house through the yard by a well-manicured lawn, a sweeping deck, and a lap pool. NBD. When it was still under construction Barb brought us over to show off the palm frond wallpaper she'd just installed. "Look, Ashley! A tropical pool house! Isn't it great?" But Ashley was sad. She didn't want to have to leave her childhood home on Chelsea, in Santa Monica.

"Yeah, Mom. It's great, I guess."

Barb hit the fucking roof. "You are so ungrateful, Ashley! Snap out of it! Natascia loves it. You love it, right? Wanna be my daughter? Hahahahahah!"

We used that backhouse/pool house as much as we could, and Barb was pretty good about leaving us to it. Unless, of course, she was in the cups herself, and then she'd develop a morbid obsession with being a mom, and making sure she knew exactly what we were up to. Chardonnay is a hell of a drug.

Ashley was hooking up with Oliver Blunt on the down low, and one night he came over and brought Kaspar with him. After tapping the everloving shit out of the Rockies, it was me and Kaspar, and the loft above the living room. It was over just as soon as it started, and I was left staring at the black bottoms of his filthy feet as he lay snoring. He probably hadn't showered in days. Fucking surfers.

# CHAPTER 14

HONESTLY, THERE ISN'T MUCH to say about Ethan except that I hated his guts from the first time we met. I really have no concrete explanation for my hatred other than I found his disposition absolutely despicable and he more or less felt the same about me. We used to really dig into each other all the time. I'd tell him that everything that came out of his mouth was tainted stupid, and he'd tell me to kiss his white ass. Never a kind word between us.

He spent the night in my room beside me one night. The first boy who ever did that. We didn't have sex. I thought about it plenty and nearly said fuck it more than a couple times but found myself so intensely self-conscious. He kept saying, "Just pieces of cloth. The only thing between us is thin pieces of cloth." Couldn't even form a proper sentence. My mom walked into my room the next morning. Sixteen years of privacy, and the one night I have a boy in secret she opens my door to say good morning. I threw the giant white down comforter over Ethan's head, and miraculously she was none the wiser.

"My love, I'm going to be on set all day, but there's food in the fridge, and please, for the love of God, try to keep things clean. Call me if you need me. But also don't. I'll be busy."

"Okaaaaay, Mom! Bye! Wait! Can you leave me some money?... pleeeeeease! Come on, don't look at me like that! It's the summer!"

When she left I made him leave too. Just pieces of cloth. In the shower I wondered what it would be like to have him beside me. White, naked, wet. What would he think of my body? What would I think of my body in his eyes? In a shower, sober and nude. *Isn't that what couples do? How do you have sex in a shower anyway?* No, no. It was too much. I made the right decision sending him away.

We all went out later that night. Some party in the Palisades. We managed to stay out until the morning, mostly driving around. Ethan and Paul Kennedy dropped me off at home around four thirty and the line rang in my bedroom.

"Hey! You wanna hang out some more?"

"What? You guys just dropped me off!"

"Yeah, I know, but the doughnut shops are just opening and Paul and I were just thinking how much you'd like one. Come on. Doughnuts? Coffee? Fresh. Piping hot. We're still in Venice. Come with us."

It's the only nice memory I have of Ethan. Him and PK in the front seats, me in the back, the quiet early morning streets of Santa Monica, the sun rising, and a dozen doughnuts between us. After that we were back at it. The insults, the competition, the hatred and repulsion that magnetized us to each other.

The day I got my first tattoo on the boardwalk, Genevieve took me to some lame get-together with Pali people. It was her bullshit idea of celebrating my new ink.

"Really, dude? Pali people?"

"Yeah, Giovanni is going to be there."

"So what?"

"So he's Italian. You guys can speak Italian or whatever."

"Oh, great! Now I have an assignment."

I hated speaking in Italian to strangers. I hated Pali people. And Ethan was going to be there. But I went, because in those days "no" was a unicorn. We laid into each other immediately.

"You're a fucking idiot, Ethan, and you'll never amount to anything."

"You're a fucking bitch, Natascia, and you're gonna die alone and sad.

We fucked in the front seat of his SUV that night.

# CHAPTER 15

I HAD A FAIRLY typical Los Angeles childhood. My parents divorced early; I watched too much TV; and, like everyone else in this godforsaken city, I wanted to be an actor. Growing up amongst the throngs of waiters and baristas, you learn quickly that even speaking such things aloud shaves years off your life. Worse still, in a town obsessed with the notion of talent with a capital T, telling someone you want to be an actor instantly transforms you into a caricature of yourself. In LA, one of the first things you learn as a kid is to be hyper-vigilant of your image, lest you disappear into total irrelevance like the rest of the toons in this town. Still, breaking into monologue and song anytime just enough people were watching, spending recess writing plays and choreographing music videos, sneaking into R-rated movies on the weekends with my brother for "research," I couldn't very well tell people I wanted to be an engineer when I grew up.

I once asked my father who his favorite actress was, hoping to learn something I could use.

"Meryl Streep," he told me.

"Meryl Streep? That blonde lady in *Death Becomes Her*?"

"Ha. Yeah, that one. And that's not her only movie, Tatti."

"Wait, she's not that pretty. What about Michelle Pfeiffer, or Pamela Anderson, or something?"

"Ach! They can't act worth a dime. You asked me who my favorite actress is, not who the prettiest is. Anyway, I think she's beautiful."

And like that I was going to be Meryl Streep when I grew up—except maybe prettier. I spent hours daydreaming of becoming a star, wondering what it would take to make it. I remember walking down the promenade among the street performers and wondering, "What is it that the Chili Peppers got that this dude playing his guitar doesn't?" All you had to do was turn on the TV or radio to know it wasn't talent. LA is a surplus of talent, an overstuffed suitcase busting at the zipper with talent. Talent is the lie that leaves you doubled over the producer's couch, tits out, signing your soul away in company contracts for that cherry sweet promise of fame—and fame is just a promiscuous green fuck fairy at the end of the talent rainbow. I didn't know what it took to make it, but growing up in LA I sure as shit knew it wasn't talent. But I figured you have to start somewhere, and my somewhere was the Adderley School for Performing Arts and the Lincoln Middle School Madrigal Choir.

Somewhere between rehearsals in the Palisades and choir competitions, my girlfriends and I became obsessed with a particular television show from the seventies that featured three women which, for reasons of not getting sued by some rich assholes, I'm not going to name. It was the mid-nineties, the Spice Girls were at the top of the charts, and girl power was in. Lunchtimes were split between memorizing lines from *Ruthless*, harmonizing "Lo, How A Rose E'er Blooming," and breaking into the iconic pose from this TV show any chance we got. This was before they did the horrible remake of the show, before YouTube, before Google, and before Netflix in a time when finding out more about a show in the seventies meant asking your parents, catching the occasional TV Land rerun, or looking at slow-loading studio stills through a general Yahoo! search. In the seventh grade, bell-bottoms, oversized collars, halter tops, and feathered hair completely captured our twelve-year-old imaginations.

I wanted to be the blonde one. I even tried to get her haircut one day. I sat in the barber's chair at Supercuts in the Marina, trying to ask for that seventies feathered hair look without wanting to give too much away, and ended up with straight bangs, tears, and a vow to never cut my hair again. I was a brunette and no amount of Sun-In was going to turn brown to blonde. With nearly orange hair and straight flat bangs, I eventually acquiesced. Fine, fine. I'll play the brunette, but I get to be the pretty one!

I'd spend hours online looking her up, wishing for a flat stomach and small boobs. Back when you could still buy vintage clothes in downtown Santa Monica and everything was a bargain, I practically slept in the bell-bottoms and awkwardly fitted halter tops I'd dig up on weekend trips to Muskrat or Aardvarks.

The brunette. Good looking, for sure, but somehow less memorable. She wasn't like the blonde one. I'd never be like the blonde one either, so I resigned myself to being one of the brunettes—the pretty one—and continued my research for the part. Naturally, when the chance came to sleep with her first-born son years later I couldn't pass it up.

I met Grant when his best friend Austin was dating Kimberly Anderson. Austin was always dangerously unstable, and their fights were brutal. He'd get violent and scream, she'd run away, he'd buy her something made of white gold, she'd come back, and on it went. Grant was always there, always in the middle of the abuse, until Kimberly eventually carried on right into his arms. Austin wasn't very long for this world in general, but regardless of any infidelity, Kimberly Anderson didn't help. She wasn't the last girl I'd meet who would break something that was already broken, just the first.

The night I slept with Grant was one of those sticky Hollywood nights. We didn't often venture out of the Westside, but this particular night, carried by the Santa Anas, we found ourselves on Sunset Boulevard laying waste to raw fish at Tenmasa. One fake ID between the lot of us, the bottles of Saporro and sake stacked faster than the Japanese women who didn't care we were underage could clear them. We snuck off in pairs to snort lines in the bathroom, each pretending the others didn't know. At this point the bangs and Sun-In had all but grown out, but staying true to my vow, my hair was now down past my hips.

I was on the verge of getting out of high school, taking eight classes that semester to graduate early. That afternoon as part of my acting final, I performed act one of *The Bell of Amherst*. I didn't play Emily Dickinson. I was Emily Dickinson. Afterward Dr. Frank apologized for having never cast me in a single play. He made it up to me by giving me an A in Acting and Film and told me not to bother turning in any more assignments. There was at least a month left till the end of the semester. That night we celebrated.

Crammed in the bathroom with Genevieve at Tenmasa between white lines, pondering the razzle-dazzle of my hometown for the millionth time, I looked at her as she handed me back the dollar bill.

"How does this all work, V?"

"How does what all work, Tash?"

"This. This place we live in. How come some people make it and some die alone with their dreams?"

"What?"

"You know, like how do some girls break into Hollywood, or end up with rich guys who pay for everything? I mean, it can't just be talent or who you know, right?"

"What are you talking about?"

"I mean, I get it. Like, you have to be pretty, but is that it? There's plenty of pretty girls in this town, but that can't be it. I'm pretty, I think. I mean, not pretty like that, but I could be if I wanted to, maybe."

"Tash. Oh, my God. You are pretty. Seriously? You are, like, so pretty."

"Stop that. You know what I mean. Kimberly Anderson is pretty, but she's nothing special. And somehow she dated Austin, who always bought her shit, and now she's with Grant, and I'm sure she'll marry some rich dude who will buy her a BMW, and she'll never have to do shit for what she's got. There's gotta be something else. Something I'm missing. Maybe I just don't have it in me. Whatever IT is."

"Dude, what's this about anyway? You don't want some rich dude husband. That's not you."

"I know, fool! But that's what I'm saying! Why is it not me? And how do we both know that? All I'm saying is that even if I did want one I couldn't get one because I don't have whatever IT is that they go for. I don't know. Maybe I'm too smart, or maybe if I had a flatter stomach or was nice or something like that. I just feel stupid and cheap if a guy even tries to pay for something. It's just so obvious. You're the guy, you wanna fuck me, so you buy things. I'm the girl, I want things, so I let you fuck me. I mean, do they both just pretend they don't care how unoriginal they are, or do they not even realize how fucking phony it is? Oh, my God, do they not even care? Is that it? Do you just have to resign yourself to being cheap? Wanna split this last line?"

"Yeah. But, wait, why would you feel cheap if a man pays for you?"

"It's just gross. I have to, like, sit there and pretend that he's not doing it to fuck me. I mean, I know I want to be an actor, or whatever, but is this real life?!"

"Dude. It's really no big deal. These guys have grips of dough, and sometimes that's all they have. I mean, this fool Grant's mom was an actor in that seventies TV show we can't name. You think it matters to him if he pays for some random girl's sushi?"

"Wait. Back the fuck up. Grant's mom what?! Which one was she?"

"Yeah, dude. How do you not know that?"

"Which one?'

"The brunette."

"WHICH ONE!?"

"The pretty one."

The check had already been paid when we got back to the table, and V just winked at me. I wiped my nose, pretending I had allergies, and thanked Grant awkwardly. Then I remember waiting for the valet. I don't remember much after that. Piling into his car with everyone else…the steep hill pulling out onto Sunset…dead man's curve…and then the hallway. The hallway to his room was covered in photographs of his mother. Ad campaigns, editorials, movie posters, pictures with other famous people. There were awards. I remember running my hand across the glass that covered them, trailing behind him. I remember the darkness. And then I remember waking up.

The room was agog with question marks, spinning and swirling in my stomach. And it was brown. I rolled over and saw him lying naked beside me, snoring. I'm dead, I thought, sitting on the toilet. I've died and been sent to a living hell where rich people fuck whomever they want and paint their bedrooms brown.

I wasn't different or unique or lucky or talented. I was just like everyone else in this bullshit town, fluttering toward the flickering candle of glitz and blaming my burnt wings on blacking out. I sulked back into that rotten bed with the sheets that matched the walls and lay there unmoving, stiff as a corpse, hating my guts for what I could not remember having done. I touched his back with as much niceness as I could scrape together. He groaned. Then he peed. Then he put his clothes back on and led me back down that hallway. This time I didn't even look. I didn't want the pretty one staring down at me. I didn't want to know what it would be like to have that life. Fuck the fame, the credit cards, the white gold. I didn't care anymore. We got into his car. Drove down the long driveway. He pushed some buttons, and then suddenly we were back on Sunset and in traffic. *Ugh*.

"So, where do you live?"

"By Venice High."

"Ugh."

The last time I saw Grant was at a party in the Palisades. Genevieve and I huddled around Brendan Rossi's new nitrous tank, huffing the extra-large birthday balloons and selling the smaller blank ones for a dollar. This big linebacker-looking bro with empty eyes came up with Grant on his right, Austin on his left. His name was Donald, and he was peripherally connected to the Pali douchebags who broke my brother's jaw the year before. V and I said hello. No one said hello back. Donald reached out and decked Brendan hard in the face and Grant grabbed the duffel bag with the nitrous tank. They all ran. Hand to God, I don't know what came over me, but I ran too, as fast as I could. When they jumped into Donald's SUV, I jumped into Donald's SUV, right into the backseat with Grant, tangling my arm around the nylon strap that held the tank. Nothing but Grant and the strap existed in that moment. I raised my eyes to meet his with a sudden sober fury.

"Grant. Let. Go."

"Get the fuck out of my car, you crazy bitch!" Donald screamed.

"Grant, Brendan is my friend. Don't do this."

"Fuck you, bitch! Get the fuck out of my car!" Donald tried again.

"Grant. Please."

He didn't say a word. His eyes locked with mine, the tension in his arm giving ever so slightly.

"Fuck this!" Donald peeled off, and the strap tightened again.

I didn't give a shit about Brendan Rossi or his stupid nitrous tank, but for the life of me I wasn't going to give in. Either the nitrous made me dumb enough to be brave, or maybe I was just tired of these fucking rich private school boys taking whatever they wanted. Tired of all the fights at parties. Tired of witnessing the humiliation of all the males around me. Tired of being a helpless little girl. I don't know. But there I was in a stranger's SUV, speeding into the hostility of white male privilege with nothing but stubbornness at my side, and there was Grant, who still hadn't said a word.

"Grant," my eyes stung. "Just let go. You don't have to do this."

"He's not letting go, you dumb bitch. And now you're fucked!" Donald cackled.

Grant finally spoke. "Natascia. Listen to me. You have to get out of here. You have to let go."

My stomach dropped. His cell phone rang. It was Genevieve.

"Grant! What the fuck! You let him drive off with her?! Put her on the phone now!"

"V?"

"Tash! What the fuck are you doing?!"

"It's wrong, V."

"Do you even know who you are in the car with?! Where are you?"

"I…"

"Put Grant on the phone!"

"Hello? I know…I know. I know! Okay! We'll take her back."

"Fuck that!" Donald just kept on laughing.

"Turn around and take her back."

"Fuck that! She jumped into my car. She's stuck with me now."

"TAKE HER THE FUCK BACK!" But Donald just pulled over and stared at me, grinning. My arms were still locked in a death grip around the duffle bag. Grant looked deep into my eyes.

"Natascia, listen to me. You aren't going to get this back."

"Grant…"

"Natascia, please. You've got to get out of here. Now."

"GO!" he shouted. I did. They drove away fast and hard. I eventually found the party again. A few years later I heard that Donald met with a violent death. Austin OD'd, and Grant? Well, I never saw Grant again.

# CHAPTER 16

MY BROTHER GAVE ME a heart-shaped amber pendant for my fifteenth birthday before he was sent away to Italy. It weighed about four ounces and was the most beautiful piece of jewelry I had ever owned.

There's this photograph of me from that summer. We were at the first post-camp reunion at Bart Novak's house. My hair is still in braids. I'm wearing a navy blue button-up collared shirt from Express, with a white spaghetti strap undershirt from The Gap, and my favorite faded bellbottoms from Contempo, which are just out of the frame. I borrowed the cheetah print sunglasses my mother bought on Melrose and the amber pendant is resting between my naturally perky fifteen-year-old breasts. Big Ray is behind me in the shot, pretending to lick my ear and I'm staring off into nothing, oblivious of the photographer.

I hadn't seen Diego since they asked him to leave camp that summer and he went ghost. I knew he'd be at Bart's party, but I didn't know that he'd pull a condom on me in the middle of asking why he'd disappeared: "I knew I'd see you today, and I brought it. You know, just in case." I should have slapped him but I didn't. I just shook my head and walked away.

He showed up after homeroom a month later, on the first day of school. Pancho, the security guard who held post on Seventh and Michigan, let him on campus despite having graduated two years earlier. They were old friends, I guess. They had that camaraderie you get when Spanish is your mother tonque. I was a Junior who didn't give a shit about school enough to wear more than sweatpants and a tank top on the first day. Diego stood outside of the language building holding the strap of his messenger bag across his chest, cheesing it big-time. I was flattered, blushing even. Until I remembered the sweatpants.

"What are you doing here?!"

"Came to see you."

"How did you know where I'd be?"

"Whitey told me you had Spanish for homeroom."

"How did you get on campus?"

"I told Pancho I wanted to surprise a girl."

"What do you want from me?"

"I wanted to apologize about the party. I wanted to see you."

"Well, here I am."

"Yeah, you look beautiful."

"I'm in fucking pajamas!"

"Can I see you again?"

"God, Diego! Can I stop you?"

He smiled and we walked back to the gate on Seventh and Michigan together. I teased Pancho about breaking the law. He teased me about making boys want to break laws. We all had a good Spanish laugh. After Diego left I went to find Shannon. She was one of the reasons Diego was asked to leave that summer. One of the many girls who "made him" want to break laws. She'd understand. She just rolled her eyes. "After all that he came to see *you*? What an asshole. Stay away from him, Tash."

*Stay away from him, Tash.* She might as well have shucked three dozen oysters, poured champagne on my pussy, and fucked me with a chocolate dildo while giving me a strawberry-shaped hickey. Yeah, Shannon. Out of all the girls who caught his fancy this summer I was the one he came to see. You're right. What an asshole. I'll just stay away from him.

We made a date a week later and he never showed up. I hadn't been stood up before, and I remember thinking I hope this motherfucker got hit by a car, or something. He called me later that night.

"I'm so sorry, I got hit by a car on my way to drop off a résumé."

Well then.

"Oh, Diego! I'm so sorry! Are you all right?"

"Yeah, just banged up and my bike's fucked. Now if I do get a job I won't have any way to get there. I really need a job. I don't know what I'll do if I can't get one."

"You'll get one, you're so great. You'll get one."

"It's not that simple, Natascia."

"What do you mean?"

"Sure, I'm great, and usually if I meet people they can see that right away. But, just dropping off a résumé? The minute they see Martinez it goes to the bottom of the fucking pile."

"What? That can't be true. Even now? Even in California?"

He laughed. "Yeah, Natascia. Yeah."

We started talking on the phone every night, reading the same books, going on long drives, hiking the Santa Monica Mountains at midnight, talking about personal legends and destiny and what it would be like to choose the life of a warrior.

The next summer Diego wasn't allowed to work at camp, but he drove up to Big Bear one night, and they mercifully let him on the property for me, for an hour. The Y is forgiving like that. Martinez or not, everyone gets a second chance, a third chance, a fourth. We walked Ragger's Trail in the beaming moonlight, holding hands under the mountain stars. He told me he just had to see me. He loved me. He'd already enlisted with the Air Force.

We only ever had sex once. We had just come back from Top of the World on Mandeville Canyon. Chronologically speaking I have no idea at which point in my sexual trajectory this was—I just remember deciding to do it. Lying in the trunk of his mother's Ford Explorer. Him on top of me.

"Tash, are you okay?"

"Yeah, Diego. I just…I don't know. I just don't feel anything."

"What do you mean?"

"Are you inside me?"

"Yeah."

"I don't know. I just don't…feel anything."

Except for the nights in the mountains, Diego and I existed mostly on the telephone, and in the written word. It was only a handful of months after he started basic training that the towers came down in New York. I moved to Italy before the war and he was stationed in Charlotte. We wrote multiple times each week about me coming to visit when I got back from Europe. He'd tell me how much he loved me. How much he missed me. We made plans.

Diego was like me in so many ways. Full of passion, full of spontaneity, full of dreams, full of shit. I remember the internet café I was in when I got my "Dear John" letter. It was the one near Santo Spirito with the sign on the window in English that read "We have ice-cold Dr. Pepper. You're welcome." A euro and a half later, and it was, "You should follow your heart and not someone else, and in me you'll always have a good friend."

That's it. No explanation, no excuse. One week it was, "Don't ever tell me again not to miss you so much," and the next it was, "Dear Tash, the country's on the brink of war..."

The only real reason I came back from Italy was for summer camp. Half a week into the first session, Caleb broke down and told me that while I was in Italy Diego had married a stripper named Penny. Blonde.

I wrote to congratulate him.

He wrote back:

"Try this on for laughs. Penny is from Irvine. Her dad was in the Air Force, so she's like an Air Force brat. She was born in North Carolina. Anyway, we met, blah blah blah and so on and so on. Well, peace out, I've got work to do, and there's a war going on."

The war was inevitable. Unavoidable. Manifest Destiny on a spherical world where the West inescapably becomes the Middle East, and round and round we go. Diego may or may not have deployed. Four years later the war silently raged on, and I got an "anonymous" email with a link to a missed connections ad on Craigslist. The listing described the first time we met: I had just gotten off the bus to camp. He'd been there all summer. He walked straight up to me and looked me in the eyes. Hello, I'm Diego. Hello, I'm Natascia. I went up to the director's dorms to drop off my luggage. He caught me in the hallway. Leaned in so hard I fell back and hit my head on the wall. He looked like he wanted to take a bite out of me. *I didn't want you to move across the country just for me. I wonder where we'd be by now if I asked you to move...*

We wrote back and forth for a month after that. He was about four kids deep and having problems with his wife. Then ghost. Old habits. Blah blah and so on. I expect I'll hear from him again someday. Maybe when his kids have grown or his wife finally leaves him. Sometimes I think I'm only ever good for these men in their absolute despair. *You're just so easy to talk to. I feel like I could tell you anything. You just get me, Natascia. Goddamnit. You just get me.*

# CHAPTER 17

I MOVED TO ITALY when I was seventeen, and sometimes I wonder what it would have been like to go alone. To be able to live in the full reinvention of myself without a constant reminder of who I used to be. I didn't do that, and every time something new presented itself, begged me to try it on, Sabrina was there reminding me of who I was supposed to be. Sabrina had been my friend since middle school choir. After Dahlia bailed on Italy, I somehow convinced Sabrina that she should shove all of her remaining credits into one semester so she could leave high school, her friends, and her family behind and take off across the world with me. I still can't help but wonder why in God's name I felt like I needed a witness.

I was dead set on growing up, getting my own apartment, and taking care of everything myself. I had some money Nonna set up in an account for me after the second time she'd won the lottery, right before she died. It wasn't much. A few thousand dollars. It was all I had left of her, and I thought she'd approve of my using it to move home. My mom was more or less behind me, making jokes about moving all the way to America just to have a daughter who would grow up and move to Italy. And my pop realized pretty quickly that there was no way to stop me. All he could do was remind me to be careful with every breath he took. They were courageously supportive.

Sabrina's folks? Not so much. They took a whole lot of convincing and twice as much planning. Everything had to be calculated. Train schedules were researched, lodgings secured, food budgeted, phone numbers written down. Two seventeen-year-old girls living on their own in Italy? After the first two months, when school is finished, what then? Where are you going to go? How are you going to get there? Where will you sleep? How much is that going to cost? They called a joint family meeting to discuss. I rolled my eyes through most of it as my mom calmly answered their questions about the motherland with grace. Every time I mention the word "adventure," Mom would kick me under the table. *Play it cool, Tatti.* "We'd just feel so much better if we knew you two were living with a family. It's a really great way to get the whole immersion experience, especially since Bri isn't fluent like you." I couldn't believe what I was being asked to agree to. Move from one family into another. Have an old-school Italian mother watching my every move? I looked over at my mom and summoned all the telepathy we'd been building between us since my womb days.

She squeezed my hand under the table and said, "She's is right, Tatti, and it won't be so bad. Think of all the good food you'll eat, and the other students you'll meet. And at least this way I know I can send you off to Italy by yourself and Nonna won't turn in her grave."

Ugh. "Fiiine! But only for the first month. Then I'm getting my own apartment!"

After spending a few weeks in Torino with my uncle, Sabrina and I hopped a train to Firenze, moved into Ninni's house, and it wasn't all that bad. Except for the week I was sick as a dog and Ninni asked me if I was walking around in bare feet because I wanted to die. Or the time she called me a thief because Sabrina and I used the hot water in the bathtub to wash our underwear so we didn't have to pay her five euros to use the washing machine. Except for that, we did eat incredible food, our Italian got better, and damn near everyone we came to know could somehow be traced back there.

Including Martin, the chiropractor.

•••

NINNI'S WAS REALLY TWO flats in one joined by the kitchen. Family on one side, students on the other, dining room table at the center. Gavin, Nigel, and Martin had been living in the big room with the bunk beds. There was a single on the same side of the hall that was about as big as Harry Potter's first room in the Dursley house, where the nice old American man lived who brought me syrup like a normal person when my cough kept him up all night. Then there was the girl's room with two twin beds, and enough flowered duvets and closet space to feel at home *ish.* Every two weeks the students and the rooms would shuffle. We moved in, Nigel moved out. The old man left, Rhonda moved in. Gavin found a flat, Martin went traveling, and Sabrina and I moved to the room with bunk beds. By the end of our stay we wondered aloud to Ninni what it would be like if we stayed another month. *"Impossibile,"* she said. The rooms were already booked.

And thank fucking God at that.

Sabrina and I enrolled at the Istituto Europeo. Her parents researched it, and it was cheaper, but mostly everyone we knew went to Lorenzo di Medici and studied anything from art restoration to photography to wine tasting. Valentina and Mariana were from Colombia, Lupe and Pilar from Mexico, and Axel was from Sweden. Victoria, Gemma, Gavin, and Nigel were all Brits, and Martin was American like us, but from Oregon or Colorado or some such place where Tevas and waterproof pants are deemed appropriate outerwear. I had approximately zero interest in him as a sexual creature. He was just someone to play cards with, meet for cappuccinos after class, drink booze, and run through piazzas with. You know, like the rest of them.

Until Sienna. It was supposed to be just a day trip. Get out, see some culture. Something to email the moms about. *Look! I'm productive! I have friends! We are adjusting well! Everything is going great! Send more money!* We took the bus down from Santa Maria Novella and spent the early part of the day just walking around. Martin and Nigel kept pointing out different places of historical significance. Where this saint was buried, where that relic lay. I was all, "Yeah, these churches are great or whatever, but when are we going to eat?"

We landed in Piazza del Campo at some such café with the rest of the tourists and proceeded to get cut off around the seventh carafe. *"Non c'e ne pui rosso,"* or so the matron who very well could have been my Nonna insisted. We took communion until nightfall, laughing through pasta and cigarettes, the glory of time historically stretched before us.

Then it was dark, and there was no more red wine to be had, and somehow we'd become aware that the busses had stopped running. Firenze was suddenly so far away. Sabrina and Nigel calculated our check to the last cent, threw down an annoyingly precise amount of euros, and ran to the bus station half worried, half sobered by the prospect of being stuck. I just kept laughing. *I'm not running to catch shit! You'll never make it! This is the stuff adventures are made of!* I ran the opposite direction just to be contrary. Martin ran after me. We hid for a while somewhere with steps and bright light.

"Aren't you going to call them, Tash?"

"Haha! Can't! No minutes left on my SIM card." I kissed him. "Let's get gelato!"

Martin and I sat on the streets of Sienna, tongues slathered in frozen cream, lost from everyone we knew with nowhere to be and filled with the afternoon's unholy sacrament. We made out between licks.

"Natascia, this is great. You're great. But you're drunk, and all the old women are staring at you."

"Of course they are! Let 'em look! Nonna's always watching!"

"Natascia, we don't have a place to stay tonight!"

"I know! Isn't it great?"

Martin smiled and shook his head. "I'm going to find our friends. You'll thank me in the morning."

He found us our friends, and a hotel room. Sabrina kept complaining about having to spend money.

"Lighten the fuck up! Now you'll have a story for your grandchildren."

"Well, can you at least ask her if she'll give us a discount since we are checking in so late?"

"Oh, sweet Mary and Joseph!" I tried to haggle terms at the front desk with the matron on her behalf in my best-slurred Italiano. This woman looked at me like I'd lost my damn mind and sneered, *"Passaporti! Tutti!"* I turned to Sabrina with my hand up, gesturing to the old woman. "You heard her."

Friends found, beds procured, identities secured, everyone safe, boys and girls, two by two. Nigel and Sabrina down the hall. Marty and Tash and an antique key to an ancient room. We murdered each other, Marty and I. Blood on the bed, blood splattered on the walls, blood soaking the floors. Hundred-year-old dresser drawers, frescos from the time of Michelangelo, glass lamps with dim bulbs, and heavy velvet drapes in royal indigos down to the floor, sacrificed in the blood of the lamb. I went to the bathroom to use the bidet; Marty followed. Blood all over the bathroom.

Hours later when the slaughter tapered like the candles in that ancient room, the sun and the birds found our bodies in a pile of sheets. I peeled my eyes open to find not a trace of blood left anywhere. *Was that just a dream?* I showered slowly and delicately as one must in a bathtub in Europe, careful to minimize the inevitable flooding of tiles, and I wondered how the night fared for Nigel and Sabrina. I dressed in yesterday's clothes and left Martin to a soaked WC to knock on Sabrina's door. Nigel answered, and we both broke into stupid smiles.

"Morning, Nat. Bri's in the loo. I'd better check in on Marty, then, eh?"

I blushed and pushed past him to find her. She was standing over the sink in her underwear washing her face with cold water, and the feather's touch of a washcloth. I sat on the toilet watching, jealous of her elegance, wondering how someone could look so fucking angelic after a night of drinking. *I bet this bitch drank three glasses of water before bed for good measure.*

"So, Bri?"

"So what, Tash?"

"So you and Nigel? Did you bone?"

"Ugh! No!" She giggled and slapped my arm. "He wanted to. But we just kissed a little and I took a bath."

"Of course you did. *Sempre la principessa!*"

"What's that supposed to mean?"

"Nothing, Bri. Nothing. I fucked Marty."

"Yeah, Tash. We heard." She turned to face me. "How was it?"

"It was wild, Bri. My vagina is fucking killing me, and I feel like I have an anvil on my head, but I feel free or something. I don't know. I guess that's what it's like to sleep with a twenty-five-year-old man."

"Yeah, I guess." But she didn't know. "So do you like him?"

"Meh," I shrugged.

"How do you do it, Tash? Like, just sleep with people whether you like them or not? Aren't you worried about being a slut?"

"Oh, please, Sabrina. Don't give me that. I do this shit so people like you can live vicariously through me. So you're welcome or whatever."

The bathroom got real quiet. Bri looked back into the mirror. "We have to be out of here before eleven or they'll charge us for another day."

I rolled my eyes and got off of the toilet. "Dude, chill."

In the hallway, Nigel's eyes met mine like a high five. Back in our room Marty was kind, warm, and as gentle as our hangovers begged us to be. I was curt. Princess Blizzard, Queen of Sleet and Snowdrift, Master of Ice, Wizard of Flurry, Slush Puppy, Frozen Bitch. I grabbed my jacket without a word and triple-checked under the bed and in the drawers for anything left behind. We met Nigel and Sabrina in the hallway under dark sunglasses.

"Let's go get our passports back," I said.

As the only one fluent, that business fell on me—as did the curses of disapproving elders. The matron awaited us behind the front desk. When she saw me her face scrunched into the shape of disgust I knew so well. The look of every Italian grandmother that has ever lived. A look so Catholic, so Roman, so eternally biblical. Her abhorrence: medieval. My shame: written in stone. *Vergogna. Maleducata. Rovinata.* She handed back our passports with a sharp tongue. I took them with burning ears, and Sabrina muttered something about the free continental breakfast. I shot her a look and made for the nearest bar to pay for espresso in peace. We spent the morning waiting for the bus back to Firenze in the quiet piazza, watching *bambini* in their Sunday best. Bri took pictures.

On the ride home, and the walk back to the flat from Santa Maria Novella, I gave the avoidance game my best shot. *Better establish the end of the adventure before this one gets any ideas.* If you'd seen the way Marty looked at me on that bus ride you would have done the same.

•••

THERE ARE ONLY TWO other encounters with the chiropractor worthy of note. The first being the night he cracked my neck. Marty had just completed his licensing and Europe was some sort of final hurrah as a young man before getting down to it. He'd been adjusting the gang for months, but any time he did all I could hear was my pop's voice telling me to be careful. I'd usually just decline his offer and watch.

Until the night at Ninni's when he walked into our bedroom and straight -up asked Sabrina to leave. I laughed so hard I had no time to be offended. He was a skinny, gangling, eyeglasses- and REI-wearing motherfucker—but he had balls, I'll give him that. I nodded to Sabrina, locked the door, and pulled on the thigh-high, red-and-white-striped stiletto boots I'd just blown a hundred euros on, and took everything else off. Then it was the massacre of the innocent all over again. A sinful delight. As we lay on my twin-sized bed covered in flowered duvets, watching the blood drip off the walls, he held me too close and asked, "Do you want me to adjust you?"

"I'm pretty sure you just did."

He laughed and kissed my forehead just sweetly enough to make my stomach turn.

"I don't know, Marty. I'm scared. Will it hurt?"

"It shouldn't. I'll be careful. Trust me."

Famous last words. The next thirty minutes were spent weeping. He gave me the worst tension headache that side of the Mediterranean, like a crown of thorns in an arbor knot around the dome.

He left Florence soon after. Took off to who knows where with his North Face backpack and Patagonia fleece. It was nearly another two months before the gang got CC'd on an email announcing his return and requesting a place to crash. Sabrina and I had long moved from Ninni's into our own flat. Aegir had just asked me to be his girlfriend, and Francesco was texting me every day, but, "Sure, Marty, you can crash with me."

And crash he did.

Gavin met him at Santa Maria Novella while I cooked dinner for the lot of us. Mozzarella pomodoro, orecchiette with fresh peas and panna, and a *semifreddo al amaretto e ciocolato*. Nigel crossed the river to join us. The OG gang back together. When the bell rang I ran to the balcony in my apron and blew open the shutters. There was Marty on the cobblestone streets of S. S. Borgo Apostoli, hands wrapped around the straps of his North Face backpack, and Gavin in full broadcast Welsh smile, bottles in hand: "Rapunzel, Rapunzel! Let down your key!"

We drank Splügen beers, smoked hashish, and not a bite remained. Marty stayed with me that night on my twin bed in that closet of a room. We giggled for most of it, and sex was more gentle and tender than I'd become accustomed to with him. He told me about his ex-girlfriend and how he missed spending the nights nude with her eating Chinese takeout, about his tattoo and how he used the elements of water and fire to represent the yin-yang, and about his plans for setting up his own practice upon his return to the States. When he got up to cross the kitchen to go to the bathroom he didn't bother with his clothes. Bri caught him in the hallway, they both screamed and laughed and woke up Mimi in the third room. The chutzpah on that dude. The night was sweet and kind. When morning broke, and the boy in my bed looked at me with wide eyes and open palm, my asshole clenched and I decided, *Fuck it, maybe I'll actually go to class today.*

The last two months in Firenze we were at Loch Ness every night. It was a little member's only bar by Santa Croce that catered mostly to international students. A short shot from the secret bakery that opened at two in the morning, and next door to the all-night kebob shop. Loch Ness was the great turning ground in that little city. One night you could end up in a shouting match with a couple of Algerian boys a breath away from physical violence over the politics of gender and the pending war, and the next night you could share a spliff at the foosball table with two Fiorentini who wanted to know all about growing up in LA and if we knew George Clooney. The music was good, the booze was free, and the culture was rich. We knew everyone, everyone knew us, and then there was Francesco.

All the bartenders I ever hooked up with, fell in love with, or tipped too much owe it all to Francesco. It took maybe a night and my name and I never paid for another drink again. He never really had a chance with me, but I liked the way he flirted and kissed, and we had an understanding. At the bar I was his. Outside of the bar, nothing mattered. We only ever went on one date. He took me to some swanky hotel in *Piazza del la Republica*, and when I tried to order a Negroni he shook his head no, said I needed something more feminine, and ordered me a Bellini, murdering his chance before we were even five minutes in. Fucking Italian men.

On Marty's last night we went to Loch Ness with Gavin and Sabrina in tow. They busied themselves showing their membership cards and waiting for each other. I just nodded to OJ, the security guard at the door, and disappeared into the crowd, high-fiving, hugging, and double kissing all the people whose names I no longer remember. When Francesco saw me he swooped out from under the bar in that dramatic, romantic, *siamo solo noi* Italian kind of way, picked me up, swung me around, and stuck his tongue into my stomach. I just laughed staring into his eyes, hands wrapped around his bald head. "Well, *buona* fucking *sera*, Lupo Cativo!" I exclaimed when he set me down.

"I'm standing right here, Natascia." I'll never forget the look on Marty's face after he said that.

"So what, Marty?"

"What do you mean? So I can see you kissing him, and I'm standing right here!"

"SO WHAT, MARTIN? You left. I still live here. I have a life here that has nothing to do with you! These are my people. This is Francesco. This is what we do together. I have a boyfriend named Aegir on the other side of the river too. I'll probably see him later tonight. I'm not just going to pretend like none of that is true because you decided to hang your hat in Florence for a couple of days!"

He walked straight out of Loch Ness. Gavin shot me an "oh, Nat" look, patted me on the back, and followed Marty out the front door. Sabrina's jaw was on the floor.

"Jesus Christ, Tash!"

"Not tonight, Bri. Not tonight."

Francesco smiled, *"Amore mio,"* and went back behind the bar. He poured us a couple of shots of whiskey, looked me dead in my irises, and said, *"Adesso ho capito, Cappuccetto Rosso! Adesso, ho propio capito."*

# CHAPTER 18

O NE NIGHT AT LOCH Ness we played foosball with two Italian Americans, first generation like me. They came back to our apartment that night. I fucked the shorter, less attractive one. His name was Nico. Probably still is. Bri took two Advil and just fell asleep beside the nice-looking one. I think his name was Beto.

She ended up on a date with him about a week later. Went to his house on the other side of the river. He made pasta with fresh apples. I guess that was all it took. She came home the next morning swooning and never heard from him again. Except for the time we got on the bus to go to cooking class. He looked over at her, got up, and got off at the next stop.

As for Nico, well, I would have forgotten his name by now if he didn't share it with one of the DC boys back home. And so as not to ever, ever have anyone confuse the two, on every list I made henceforth he was known as Nico Italy.

# CHAPTER 19

PIAZZA SANTO SPIRITO SITS like a desert in the city. A sanctuary for drifters, artists, and mutts on rope leashes. Crowned by an unadorned basilica whose perpetually locked doors whisper memories of the catechism. The dust of the Holy Ghost like a sacred filth, swept from storefront thresholds in daily prayer. At its center stands a beer bottle fountain cascading in pattered cadence like a blessing over mandolin and concertina. Piazza Santo Spirito. *Le carrezze del straniero. Dominum nostrum. Porcha miseria al li mortacci suoi. In nomine patris et filii et Spiritu Sancti.* Nigel would talk about his new flat often. About the people of House Santo Spirito. About all the Icelanders he was meeting. And about Aegir, who played guitar.

We met on the Arno, midway between our two flats, divided by the constant river. Just west of Ponte Santa Trinita, if you give the wall a jump on the south side, and balance your way down a steep grass hill, you'll find yourself on a perfectly lovely patch of pavement that is mostly devoid of river rats during the day. Gemma and Victoria took the train up from Rome, the Latinas of House Pitti came out in full force, and Nigel promised Santo Spirito would be in attendance. We would finally meet the illustrious Icelander. We descended on that river a parade of nations. The regal Mexicans in blue jeans and beauty mark, the sumptuous Colombians in millefiolle of scarved fabric, the fearless Welsh in trainers and rugby shirt, the uncanny English with their good cheer and quip in hand, an Italian ambassador for quality control, a couple of slapdash American girls for a little grit and character, and the Stranger personified by all things *Ísland*. An early springtime sun and the brisk rush of the Arno river. A merry little picnic. Sabrina, Gavin, and I trekked the hour on foot to the Penny Market, and loaded our backpacks up with cheap meats, cheeses, and the sort of wines that would turn Nonna in her mausoleum grave.

The squatter's luncheon was in full swing. Sabrina was nearly as rouge as the wine when over the wall the breath of Santo Spirito poured in. Down the hill came a tower of a man in corduroy, wool, and velvet. Six foot seven, shoulder-length strawberry blonde unbrushed hair, full beard to match. With a guitar in one hand, and a bottled Belgian beer in the other, this bespectacled prince of nine realms, born of sunlight, moonlight, and spotlight, of fish and fowl and meat, man of salt and sea and tundra, man of black-and-white film and Gauloises, of bread and butter, coffee and spliff. Aegir who never changed his socks. Aegir who sang Dylan and Cohen and Prima. Aegir who had me before song, before hello, before language.

I knew the words to every song he sang. He'd blast through harmonies and I'd hold with all my might to the melody, trying to catch resonance and pitch like snatching a blizzard of dollars with one hand. When he sang *Buona Sera, Signorina*, my heart fluttered like the Ta Ra Ta Ta Ta of a sixties Italian pop song. I gave him my best Keely Smith, diaphragm, deep throat, dry sass, and skinny charisma. His eyes and mine like the spinning fields of Tuscan sunflowers, ever turning toward the light. Just us and the music we knew better than anyone else there. Giorgio, the only full-blooded Italian, complained because we sang the English version of "Buona Sera," and because that is what Italians do. Quality control and complain. "Pssssshhhhhttt!" we both dismissed him. "Prima is King!"

When sunset was upon us, Penny Market wine proved to be too much for our dear Sabrina, and before twilight had fully peaked she went from rouge in the cheeks with laughter to bathing in a pool of lavender vomit against the violet sky. Some gals just can't hold their box wine. Gavin, blessed Welshman that he was, took it upon himself to personally piggyback her the six kilometers to Ninni's. He was something else, our Gavin. Even after her burgundy pants leaked all over his Rugby shirt, and he gagged on the Ponte Vecchio, our man took a breath and powered through. They don't make 'em like that anymore.

I was obliged to return with them and explain in my most impeccable slurred Italiano how Sabrina had gotten "sick," just needed to sleep, and *"grazie mile* for dinner, Ninni." Ugh, to explain. Is there a verb more vile in all human existence? With Bri nestled in a spinning bunk bed cuddling water and a rubbish bin, shouts of *"mi raccomando!"* faded into the night as Gavin and I ran back across the river to House Pitti to fall in love with

Firenze over a gallon of Fontana di Papa. Him with a fresh shirt. Me with a fresh crush.

Aegir and I kissed the next evening at MayDay bar. Over White Russians garnished with strawberries. Over politics garnished with art history. Over music garnished with tobacco. Over cobblestone garnished with streetlight. Prickling beard and tickled cheek. Tippy toes and tower. The unsalted Florentine bread of war. The fiery passion of a thousand Tuscan suns. A man of gigantic confidence in my callow mouth. Afterward I floated to Ninni's for our last night there on motherfucking Lisa Frank rainbows and unicorns. I packed suitcase and backpack with swollen magenta vulva and technicolor butterfly heart. One final night for giggles, and gossip, and girlishness. One final night for bunk beds, and curfews, and family dinners. One final night as maiden faire. Tomorrow we move. Tomorrow we live. Tomorrow I become a woman and cease these childish things.

•••

WE WOULD SPEND THE mornings making love. The man had a full beard and tremendous stamina. I'd pull him back up to me. "Is everything okay?" he'd ask. "*Amore*. It's like sandpaper down there," I'd reply. We'd been dating for about a month and a half. I'd moved in and we were sitting at the dining room table finishing a meal I had just prepared, which, if memory serves, consisted mostly of fried potatoes. He must have been in a good mood that morning because he hadn't stood over me in the kitchen criticizing my every move. He wiped his mouth, lit a Gauloises, rubbed his belly, and with nonchalance worthy of a king, said, "You know, I think I like you. Before, I wasn't really sure if I did. But, I think I like you." My jaw dropped, and as I cried silently washing the dishes, he got up from the table and disappeared in the bathroom until most of his beard was gone. He emerged petting the massive blond muttonchops he'd left with a shit-eating grin. "For you," he said. Then he grabbed his guitar and walked out the front door.

There were at least five different nationalities coming in and out of Santo Spirito on any given day, and I never ate better in my whole damn life. The flatmates mostly gave each other a wide berth in the kitchen, unless one of us insisted on learning. Not Aegi and I, though. We were always standing over each other, cursing the ruination of gastronomy. I don't want to give you the wrong impression here. Aegir was an incredible cook, and now that I'm older and have grown into my own craft I can see the nature of his instincts were always spot on. He had a thing for onions and gorgonzola. Lots of panna and speck. And he was a mean baker. I write that quite literally. If I even dreamed of opening the oven while one of his cakes was baking he'd chastise me at length for my ignorance. I learned a lot from him, as much as my arrogant seventeen-year-old self would hate to admit. Still, one time I caught him taking a blade to basil and I just about blew a gasket.

We were unbearable in the kitchen. Downright incorrigible. And we got our share of raised eyebrows and long sighs from the rest of the flat. It never bothered me much, though. I mean, it bothered me to my very core, you understand, but it didn't faze me. At the end of the battle, one of us would usually relent with an "I'm sure it'll taste fine," and Aegir would open his legs in a gangly wide stance so I wouldn't have to crane my neck to kiss him. I was always happy. Even when he was mean, and I fucking hated his guts, I was happy to do so. And man, could he be mean! Like the time I came home with sandwiches from the bakery by Santa Croce without beer.

"There's no beer? That's just plain rude."

"Well, how was I supposed to know you wanted any, Aegi?"

"From now on just assume I always want beer and don't ever come home without it again."

Or the one night I came home late to find him on the landline in the hallway, sitting hunched over on one of the dining room chairs. I opened the front door and he kept his back to me. Didn't even look up in acknowledgment. He stayed whispering on the phone by candlelight for what felt like hours. When he finally crawled into bed he wouldn't touch me, which on a twin cot with a six-foot-seven man is no small feat. But he didn't sleep. He just fumed. I'd never seen him like that before, and I was afraid he'd gone back to being unsure if he even liked me. Trembling, I laid the palm of my hand on his bare back and asked if he wanted to talk about it.

"No, I don't!"

The next morning he pulled a picture of her from his wallet. Ophelia. His girlfriend right before me. She looked like Enid from *Ghost World*. So much cooler than I'd ever be. "That was her last night on the phone. Long distance. She was angry with me. God, I just miss her so much sometimes."

But it didn't even hurt me to hear it. His pain was so reasonable, so human, and I adored him so profoundly, that I would have done anything for him if only he would have asked.

I could publish a whole zine about him and fill it with the little drawings he used to make of himself. Aegi's vanity was so pure, so gentle, and I was in a perpetual state of awe and jealousy every moment we shared together. Being with him made me wish I were good at something. Like really good. Like quiet the room with my operatic voice good. Even when he was mean all I wanted was to impress him like he impressed me. To gather public accolades and admiration. To be the undisputable best at something great. And maybe then I'd manage to keep his attention.

It was the first time I fell in love with a musician, guys, so cut me some slack.

In the bedroom we were equals. Giving and taking in that I'd-like-to-try-your-charity-until-you-cry-now-you-must-try-my-greed kind of way. It was a fumbled synchronization of pleasure and discovery. And in case you are still keeping count, he was my fourth first boyfriend. He was the first man I truly enjoyed having sex with, the first blowjob that didn't feel like a job, the first man whose body I craved, and the first man who brought me to heaving sobs during the act. We were fully in it one afternoon. The antique windows of our room blown open, the shouts of the piazza below, the frescos on the walls swirling in amber and gold. I was practicing getting out of my mind and into my body, determined to master the art of orgasm but still sort of flashing in and out of the moment. He turned me over, pulled my hips up to him, and something just snapped. My body shook with terrifying sorrow. I began sobbing uncontrollably and he stopped and asked me what was happening. But I couldn't speak. It scared the shit out of the both of us, but there was nothing to be done save to move through it. And bless his heart, my Aegi. He didn't freak out, didn't make me feel weird. He just held me, petting my hair until it passed.

Nothing about him was familiar to me, nothing about him was like home, yet tangled with him on what became our tiny twin bed, I had never known that kind of belonging. And I knew when it was over I'd never know it again. Still seventeen in the land of my ancestors, with this Viking of a man, my body was indisputably mine, and I was giving it because I wanted him, because he wanted me, because it was the right thing to do. When it did finally end, without fail the three things that would inevitably bring me to tears were the memory of the shape of his belly, the taste of his toothpaste, and the afternoon he drew a bath in that tiny bathroom and called out to me.

"Take a bath with me!"

"What?"

"Take a bath with me."

"You're a Nordic giant. How's that going to work?"

"Take a bath with me."

"*Amore*, you barely fit in there yourself."

"Take a bath with me."

"You're crazy! I'll never fit!"

"Take a bath with me."

"Seriously?"

"Take a bath with me!"

Most of the water ended up on the floor. He laughed and held me to him as we sorted out limbs. "You Americans. You worry too much."

He gave me a ring before I left Florence. Our flatmate Julia, who was studying to be a gemologist, identified the stone as labradorite right before she proclaimed it the most beautiful stone in the world. She and I held it up to the light and watched it change colors. Brilliant blues and grays, hints of brown and green, and gold like a fog above it all dictating the light. "I love it! It's so beautiful!"

He shrugged. "I gave the guy some hashish and he gave me a good deal on it. It reminded me of you."

The Colombians were going to Greece after their semester ended and Sabrina convinced me to go. Except for the night I nearly got raped on the beach in Mykonos, or the day Sabrina told me I was a horrible friend before leaving me alone at the taverna by the sea, I managed to have an okay time in Greece. Still, all I could think about was getting back to Firenze and to Aegi. When we did get back I left most of my shit at Valentina's new apartment, packed a backpack for Santo Spirito, and vowed to never leave him. A week later, Bri was down my throat about traveling again. We were at Santa Maria Novella, arguing in front of the ticket kiosk.

"This was the plan, Tash!"

"Bri, I've never had a boyfriend before. Everything I want is in Florence. I could give a shit about Sorentto, or Naples, or wherever the fuck. Please try to understand!"

"Tash, you said we'd travel. I came on this trip with you not just to stay stuck in Florence while you explore your relationship with Aegir."

"I know, I know, Bri. But things have changed. I didn't know this was going to happen. I love him, Sabrina. Please don't make me do this. Can't you just go alone?"

"Tash, I'm not going to travel in Italy alone. My mom would freak out! Come on. This is fucked up."

I bought my fucking ticket to fucking Sorrento to leave the next morning.

"Well, I hope you're happy."

"I am, Tash. Thank you."

We sat on the steps of Santa Maria Novella smoking cigarettes and watching the Romani mothers beg for money.

"Are you okay, Tash?"

"I'm fine, Bri. I've gotta go. I've gotta go find Aegir."

"Well, are you sleeping at Valentina's with me tonight?"

"No. We are going to some party tonight, or something."

"Tash, our train leaves at six a.m."

"I know, Sabrina! I know our fucking train leaves at six a.m.! I just paid thirty euros for the ticket."

"Well, do you really think you'll make it on time if you go out tonight?"

"Yeah, dude. I'll meet you tomorrow morning at the train station."

"You promise?"

"Yeah, Bri. Sure."

The party was about a forty-minute walk from Santo Spirito to a part of the city I didn't even know existed. Some massive villa. There were fire dancers, and musicians, and artists of the post post-modern sort. It couldn't have been more my scene if it tried. Beers were a euro, and Aegi kept asking me for money. I kept giving it.

We made it back to Santo Spirito at dawn. The dogs that stood guard as their owners slept on the steps of the basilica growled as we came up Via dei Michelozzi. I had just passed the best night of my life and I'd be damned if I'd let some dogs tell me where I could and could not walk. This was my Piazza now. But Giorgio called out, Dirk and Leti veered, and right before I got to the base of the steps so they could smell my moxie, Aegir grabbed my hand and pulled me back down the street. "No!" I shouted at him, and tried to break free.

"No! You can't let dogs dominate you like that, Aegi! They wouldn't have attacked me!"

"Goddamnit, Natascia! You don't have to be so crazy all the time!"

"They wouldn't have attacked me!"

"Okay, Natascia! Okay! That very well may be true. But I have no interest in finding out!"

We took the long way around the Piazza, everyone's shock subsiding into nervous laughter, and me kicking and cursing. Aegir wouldn't let go of my hand. When we got upstairs to the bedroom we shared with Etienne, I sat on the windowsill looking down at the dogs that had curled back up with their humans in the once-again peaceful Piazza. "Don't you have to go soon?" he asked from our bed.

"Um, yeah. I guess. I have a few minutes, maybe I'll just rest awhile." He smirked at me and shook his head as he opened the covers. I crawled into his arms. When my cell phone rang I convinced myself that I didn't hear it. That I was sleeping. She came back from Sorrento four days later. Things were never the same between us.

Months later, with our flight back to LA a mere ten days away, Sabrina said, "*Venezia,*" and, "You owe me."

It was a tearful, rushed, early morning goodbye in the hallway beside the landline. "Don't worry too much," he said with a squeeze. "We'll see each other again. I just know it."

I was playing with my labradorite ring as we pulled out of Santa Maria Novella on our way to a rain-soaked Venice. The taste of his toothpaste was still fresh in my mouth when I realized I'd left my favorite silk scarf tied to his bed, back in Florence. "I'll keep it for you until I see you again," he texted back.

I lost his ring somewhere in that flooded city the very next day.

•••

It was fifteen years before we saw each other again. Five thousand, four hundred and seventy-five days. At least. Really, it's a miracle we even managed it. I was flying back from Amsterdam and had a layover in Keflavík. With customs and connecting flights we knew we'd only have about an hour to see each other, excluding drive times to and from his home, but fuck it. It was better than nothing. After getting my passport stamped in Iceland I was pulled into a little room to be more thoroughly searched. I had been flagged at random. Despite having all of my personal belongings ruffled through, and the pat down, I was all smiles and couldn't help myself from flirting with the customs agents. These Icelandic men couldn't help themselves but to smile and flirt back at me. When they asked what I was so happy about I told them, "I'm going to see my first boyfriend! We haven't seen each other in fifteen years!" The men kept smiling, and cheering me on. "Good luck," they told me as they handed me back my things.

Aegir stood on the other side of the interrogation room near baggage claim with his two-year-old son. He looked exactly the same. A little older, maybe a little rounder, but it was my Aegi, in the flesh, and no doubt about it. He was real. Like really real. He wasn't just someone I'd made up fifteen years ago, and Italy wasn't just this story that never really happened. He happened. I happened. It was real. I was real. My Aegi, covered in wool and corduroy and velvet. Full hat and scarf and boot, and his son…a tiny blond, snot-crusted version of him. Oh! All the times I imagined a child between the two of us! All the ways I fantasized this moment! Five thousand, four hundred and seventy-five days to remember, to forget, to long for, to let go of, to hold dear, and to try to drown out. Five thousand, four hundred and seventy-five days of all the things I'd ever wanted to say, and here he was waiting in an airport for something, anything. "Remember me?" was all I could manage. He held me so close, the Icelandic wool sweater scratching my face like his beard used to when we were younger.

"Of course I do," he answered in unironic disbelief. "How could I ever forget?"

It was freezing outside. Not like the Netherlands in November freezing, either. Like sideways rain and wind from the Arctic sea. The smell of salt and sulfur and chance. It was a weather that was altogether so foreign and frightening. A weather so grandiose and powerful that even a drizzle can provoke a cellular level of urgency. Aegir, with his two-year-old son in tow, as calm and sober as Odin walking through Asgard, turned to me and said, "We should really get moving."

On the passenger seat of his car were half a dozen new CDs and a gorgeous book of photography about his Icelandic band. "Those are for you," he told me as I moved them aside.

It took maybe half an hour to get from the airport to the seaside town of Keflavík. We got out of the car to the smell of the crashing tides and fish. "Does it always smell like this?" I asked.

"Like what?" he replied.

"Like seven tons of fish laid out at your door?"

He shrugged his tall, lanky shoulders and laughed. "I don't know. I suppose so," he said, walking me up the carpeted mildew steps that led to the apartment in which he lived his life as a family man.

Anna was a picture of loveliness. She came in from the cold minutes after us, wrapped in wool and scarves and blue jeans. Her cheeks flushed from the wind, her hair long and beautiful. She did what I imagine all mothers and wives do and apologized for her appearance and the appearance of the house. I hugged her and told her she was lovely, and I was so glad to be welcomed. "I'm so sorry you can't meet Sigridur," she told me. "She'll be getting out of school right when you'll probably have to head back to the airport." Sigridur. Their firstborn. Aegir and I almost met years back in San Francisco. He canceled the trip last-minute when he found out Anna was pregnant with Sigridur.

"Oh, that's all right," I responded. "I'll meet her next time."

We sat at their kitchen table while their son, who spoke no English whatsoever, did his best to slather Skyr yogurt everywhere but his mouth. They just let him have at it, didn't fuss over the mess like so many American do. Aegir made me coffee from the espresso machine he'd bought when we lived together in Florence. "I still have it! Can you believe it?" Truth be told, I couldn't believe any of it.

"You have to excuse me, Anna," I laughed through the tears that had a mind of their own. "It's just…I never thought this moment would ever really happen. I'm just so happy to be here, with the both of you…" I looked over at their son. "This is just…so…lovely."

She kept telling me things about Aegir as we ate chocolate covered licorice, and I did my very best to hold back saying "I know" at the end of every sentence. "It's a shame you are only here for an hour," she sighed. "If only you could stay longer. We could have a nice dinner. He really loves to cook, and he's actually quite good at it."

"I know" slipped out of me like a smile.

She just smiled back and started telling me about the bakery he'd opened up in town and how it had been such a success because of Aegir's star power. "Oh, yeah?" I asked.

"Oh, yes. He's quite famous around here," she beamed. Aegir and I stepped out on the balcony to share a cigarette alone together while Njord put his might on display for us in the sea below. Just like that an hour had gone by. They made arrangements for the kids in Icelandic with each other. Anna and I embraced with their son in her arms right before Aegir and I got in the second car together to drive back to the airport. My tears on a never-ending stream outward.

"It's just...so amazing, Aegi!"

"What is?"

"To see you like that. To see you as a father. I mean, I pictured it so many times, but I never really thought you would be one. You just never struck me as the family type."

"I never really saw myself that way either. And it's strange, you know. It really doesn't feel like me. But, I don't know. It's really quite beautiful. Having children. I wouldn't change it for anything."

I laughed and cried as he told me more about his life, his music, and the things in his heart. He never married Anna. He said he just couldn't bring himself to do it. That he loves her, and he loves their family, but that he just couldn't bring himself to do it.

"You know me, Natascia. I love my children, but there is so much more to me than that."

"I know."

"I really wish you could stay."

"Me too."

We spent the rest of the drive talking about the old days in the apartment. "I really loved you back then," he confessed. "I just didn't know it at the time."

I kept crying. "I just...I'll just...I just...I love you, Aegi. I'll never not love you."

He held my hand across the gearshift. "So what about you?" he asked me. "What are you doing now?"

"I don't know," I replied. "I mean, I wrote a book. It's not published or anything, yet. But I'm giving it all I've got."

He smiled. "Finally!"

"I think you'd like it too. You're in it."

"I know I'd like it. You were always such a good writer."

"Maybe next time we see each other I'll be the one giving you copies of my work!"

"I'd really like that," We pulled into the airport.

We took a selfie at the top of the escalator outside of customs. With tears in both of our eyes he kissed me as we embraced, and I didn't know how I'd ever let go again. *He's really real. It was really real. It all really happened.*

My passport was still flagged from arrival so I had to go back into that tiny room with all of the same customs officers. Only this time instead of smiles and flirtations, I was all tears and nods. "What happened?" the same customs agent from before asked. "Did he not show up?"

"No, I saw him, and I met his family. And it was just...really lovely," I replied, clutching the photography book he'd given me.

The agent smiled back tenderly and motioned to my book. "Did you get that here in the airport? Do you know this band?"

"No," I shook my head. "He gave this to me. This is his band."

The agent's eyebrows went up, and he spoke in Icelandic to a few of the other male officers. I flipped open the book to a picture of him. "This is your first boyfriend?" he asked in disbelief.

"Yeah. I haven't seen him in fifteen years and we only got an hour together."

"He's really quite famous," the agent replied.

"Apparently," I laughed.

"You're all set to go," he told me, handing my things back. "And don't worry so much. You'll see him again. I just know it."

A few days later Aegir sent a photograph of himself wearing my silk scarf around his neck. The one I'd left in Firenze fifteen years ago. The message read, "It's very good when you have a cold #stillhaveit.

# CHAPTER 20

"I LIKE CAMEL TOE."

The room exploded. Josh Klein turned the strip of paper over in his hand, looking for some clue. He nearly choked on the words as he read them again. "I like camel toe? Dear Lord! Who wrote this?"

The short boy in the back with the long blue hair wearing a Harlequin and Poison Ivy T-shirt sheepishly raised his hand. The entire staff lounge turned to face him. His cheeks were like a couple of extra-large cherries.

"What's your name, man?"

"Skylar."

"Well, Skylar. That's the best damn icebreaker I've ever read! Welcome to camp, dude!"

•••

NESTLED ON THE NORTH side of Boulder Bay, the Santa Monica YMCA boasts having the only summer camp on the lake of nearly two-dozen others on Big Bear Mountain. Sailing, canoeing, kayaking, swimming. The typical American summer camp, except maybe a little more run-down. The doors and windows of the cabins came down some time in the late seventies and didn't start going back up until the new millennium. But you could get away with shit like that in the eighties and nineties. Raccoons would run in and out of the cabins digging through care packages while you slept, and if you snuck out at night you could bet the next day would be spent picking up rocks. Nobody's parents sued, and insurance companies weren't so hard-lined. Shit was more natural back then, and we loved it. Arts and crafts, archery, BB guns, formal dances, campfires, ghost stories, and lanyards. Days of hiking, jumping off the dock, and learning how to sail. Nights making lifelong companions, coming-of-age breakthroughs, friendship bracelets—

all that wholesome shit. My parents may have raised me, but camp taught me everything else.

Nearly the whole summer passed before anything happened between me and Skylar. We were down at waterfront, sitting on the dock as our campers created memories of their own on the lake. I had already decided that he was mine, and in that moment I decided I'd let him know. I stood up, walked behind him, sat down on the dock, wrapped my arms and legs around his body, and held him tight like someone's girlfriend would do. He leaned back against me and we just sat there like that until the canoes came in.

A few days later we took our breaks at the same time and had dinner at El Jacalito in town when it was still over by the Bowling Barn and Alley Oops. I sat across from this blue-haired boy and slowly realized I was on a date. *Fuck.* It felt strange to order meat when I knew he wouldn't. I think I just had what he was having and asked him questions about being raised as a vegetarian. He did his best to answer as he shoveled bowl after bowl of pico de gallo down his throat. Skylar wasn't a big talker, but he never had any problems eating. He must have been more nervous than I could imagine on that date, but we were becoming fast friends and I knew he wanted to be there for the right reasons. After I came back one day from the library in tears, having just read emails from all my friends who were still in Italy, he sat down on the steps of Dorm C and told me he understood. He had lived in Amsterdam and knew what it was like to come home and have no one really interested in hearing your stories. "You can just tell them to me," he said. "I wanna hear about Florence."

We made out in the trunk of the Jeep as Barry drove us back to camp that night. Skylar smelled of raw onions and garlic something foul. He said I had a cat tongue and wondered how in God's name it could be so rough. *I don't know. Maybe I burned it on melted cheese?* I didn't mind anyway, about his breath. I was there when he ate all that pico de gallo. I felt like we were in it together.

On the last night of camp everyone cleared out of the boathouse and it was me and Skylar between row after row of bright orange and red life jackets. We stayed up until sunrise, never quite making it past second base, just sort of stuck in a pickle between shortstop and third.

The next day we waited for the buses together. My girls and his boys on the lawn chairs by the pool. I sat sharing a seat with Skylar, my arms and legs enveloping his body. We loaded up the buses, and the kids in his cabin sat right next to mine, the eldest girls and the eldest boys. It was tradition. I saved him a seat next to me, but Skylar decided to get on the other bus, last-minute. I just didn't get it. When we got back to the Y, he found me, asked if he could take me home in his mustard yellow '73 Charger. "Nah. I'm set."

I asked him about that day throughout the next years we spent together. Why he didn't just ride the bus with me. He'd always just shake his head, without explanation. "I don't know, Tash," he'd say. "I don't know what I was thinking."

A few weeks later when August was tightening its noose, I started at Santa Monica College. Day one on a new campus and who the fuck do I run into? Blue hair, knit sweater and all, standing over the school map. He hadn't seen me yet, and I nearly turned around to walk the other way. No, I thought. You'll always regret it if you do.

"Hi, Skylar."

"Oh! Hi!"

"You never called."

"I know. I'm crap at the phone. Give me your number again."

"Whatever."

"I'll call, I swear. I need someone to cut my hair for me."

"You're cutting your hair?"

"Yeah. It's time for a change. You cut hair, right?"

"You'll have to call to find out." He called a week later.

We made a date for September 20th, Dahlia's nineteenth birthday. She wasn't talking to me anyway. After she gave birth to Logan, I was relegated to the shit list of post-partum doldrums. Only people who were 100 percent supportive of her pregnancy were allowed to see her and the baby after the birth, which left them pretty isolated. Anyway, after Italy I was less inclined to drop everything and play Duck Duck Goose with Dahlia's emotions. There was a whole wide world to contend with. Stonewall away, bitch.

When Skylar and I finally did sleep with one another, his hair was still blue. The sun was setting through his west-facing window on Third Street, and the white and yellow walls of his room blushed vermillion. Vermillion. A red so bold, so regal, you'd swear it was governed by gold. Vermillion. To say the room was crimson would be a straight lie, and carmine would be blaspheme. Scarlet too rich, and ruby positively infantile. Red is inaccurate. It wasn't just red. It was Santa Monica sunset brilliant and glowing. It was smog and bay breeze and chemistry. Mercury, sulfur, and monoxide. Pathetic fallacy like a motherfucker. It soaked everything, stained my corneas, and with every breath of passion we sucked in the dust and flushed vermillion. *Don't ever leave me.*

For the nearly four years we were together we were inseparable. We lived together, ate together, slept together, worked together, took the same classes together, and traveled the world together. We listened to the same music and had the same friends. Skylar and Tash. You could hardly tell us apart. Thanksgivings, Christmases, Hanukahs, New Year's Eves, Passovers, and birthdays. Christmases were always the best. Skylar would build me something out of wood, or start one of the big projects in the house we were always talking about. It was always still unfinished by Christmas. He'd stress out about it like mad. In fact, this toy chest he built me out of pine and walnut still sits in his old room in his father's house. Unhinged, unfinished, unclaimed. My name and the symbol of Firenze pounded in copper on the front.

But Skylar had a way of making up for his unfinished work. I've never known anyone who elevated wrapping to such an art form. For my nineteenth birthday, he bought me this perfume I wandered into a shop in Florence looking for. We traveled there in '03 to live with his best friend, Corey, for a month or so before moving on to Munich and Vienna. He bought the perfume in secret later that same day. When he gave it to me four months later in December it was completely sealed shut in a box of perfectly sanded, unfinished pine. I had to break it open in order to find out what was inside. God, I miss shit like that.

Once, for my twenty-sixth birthday, the last one we celebrated together, the one he had to lie to his new girlfriend about going to, he bought me a cheap bottle of Trader Joe's wine and built a box to hold it in. Scrapwood from one of the rotting piles stacked around his pop's woodshop. Weather-worn, clunky hinges that hardly fit, and an imposing silver handle. At first glance you'd never be able to identify it as Skylar's work. The man was fastidious as fuck, to the point of comedy. When he worked for Saul's pop in construction he would spend hours sanding drywall before painting it. Major used to tease him, "It's not art, Skylar." But it was. Everything Skylar did had to be done right or he couldn't do it at all. The curse would leave him spinning his wheels in paralysis for weeks at a time. Just sitting there, staring at the walls, thinking of all the things he NEEDED to do and all the ways he NEEDED to get them done, and what he NEEDED in order to be able to get them done in the way they NEEDED to be done that he'd get so overwhelmed by the process he couldn't actually do anything.

When he handed me this clunky, beaten-up box, with edges that hardly matched, I looked at him with furrowed brow. He looked back with delight, and flipped it over. It fucking hinged on two ends so not only could you get the bottle out, but you could open the entire box to reveal its insides. And get this, the inside of the box had been sanded and finished to absolute flawless perfection. What a fucking psychopath. Pure whimsy. Pure genius. Pure Skylar.

•••

A COUPLE OF MONTHS into the us we became, we were having sex like crazy, like new couples do. Before we moved in, before we traveled, before I love you, we were lying in my bed at my mom's house and he said, "I can't wait until the time when we see each other and don't have to have sex."

"What the fuck is that supposed to mean?"

"No, nothing. Just that I don't want to have sex all of the time. And it will be nice to see you and to not have to do it."

After the first six or seven months, Skylar got his wish. We did a lot of seeing each other and not having to do it. He and I gradually developed into best friends, and then we were just roommates. Bank accounts, grocery stores, paying rent in our parents' houses, learning how to drive in the Charger, then the Chevy, then the Buick, then the Toyota. Running errands, cooking vegetarian meals, feeding our dog, going to camp, saving money for the next big trip. Lather, rinse, repeat. We had come to rely so intensely on each other that there were times when I thought I could just live with the sexual rejection. That I'd never find someone who knew me like Skylar did. So what if we never had sex?

It was rough, but I worked my ass off to remain faithful. I really did. Slipped up a couple times though. Kissed Marcus Allen in his dark green Chevy Malibu one night. Nearly died from guilt and anxiety until I confessed. Skylar sat there trying to console me. I was shaking so bad as I told him. But he instantly forgave me. Said he understood. Said he'd pushed me to it. Said it wasn't anything we couldn't work through. Fucking killed me that he blamed himself for it. I didn't deserve him.

I tried to break up with him so many times. He'd be sleeping, or on his way to it. I'd be there gasping for breath. I'd put my hand on his back, or try to kiss his neck, wondering what the excuse would be tonight. "I can't do this anymore, baby," I'd tearfully sigh. "I love you, and I don't know how I'll live without you, but I can't keep living like this."

We'd stay up all night crying in each other's arms. "Maybe we don't have to decide tonight," he'd eventually say. Exhausted and relieved, we'd fall asleep together and in the morning we'd look at each other through puffy eyes, so delicately, so gently, and with so much kindness. We'd spend the next day ditching school, or work, or both, and go have fun somewhere and just smile. Ride roller coasters and drink chocolate malts, soda fountains and ice creams, all the throwback fifties nostalgia we both loved, and for that day it would seem like there were never two people who loved each other more, and maybe, just maybe, that would be enough for now.

It never was. I remember the day I came back from human sexuality class confused and in tears.

"Skylar, I think I'm gay."

"Okay. Why are you crying?"

"Because if I'm gay, then is being with you just keeping me from being my true self? And if I'm gay, does that mean I have to come out? Is that how everyone is going to see me from now on? Gay Natascia?"

"I don't know, baby."

I had no idea that queerness was a spectrum.

That morning, wailing in Skylar's arms, I didn't understand any of it. How could I be in love with Skylar and still love Aegir and still want to sleep with other people? And how could all of this be true if I was also secretly attracted to women?

A few weeks later I came home from Human Sexuality again. This time in absolute elation. I'd learned a new word that changed everything.

"Skylar! Did you know that there are some people who don't believe in monogamy? Like, they just don't fucking do it, and their partners don't do it either? Like, they have actual agreements about having sex with multiple partners, male and female, and they talk about shit when it comes up. But if their partner loves someone else and wants to have sex with someone else it isn't cheating and it isn't the end of the relationship!"

"Yeah, I've heard of that before."

"Polyamory! Isn't it wonderful! Doesn't the word just drip with honey! I mean, this whole time I thought I was fucking crazy! I thought something was actually wrong with me. Like I was broken or something. But I think I'm just different! Maybe I'm just polyamorous! Maybe I'm just QUEER!!!!!!!!"

"That's really great, Tash. I'm really happy for you."

"Well…"

"Well, what?"

"Well, do you think that is something you could do with me? We could still be together, we could just sleep with other people if we wanted, but it would still be us, forever."

"No, Tash." He laughed nervously. "I can't do that."

"Oh, come on! You can't possibly believe in monogamy. You don't even believe in marriage! Monogamy is just something we are raised to believe we want. That we have to have this unattainable golden standard to be happy and successful. That one person has to give us everything we need. But that's impossible! We're never even told there's an alternative to this kind of lifestyle that doesn't include loneliness and a broken heart. One person can never be everything because life doesn't work that way, and what we need and want is constantly in flux. Real life is messy, and polyamory is open communication about the ever-changing realties of being alive! Monogamy is the opposite of that. It's just about holding each other to an unrealistic standard that excludes everyone else who tries to come into your life. Don't you see, Sky? Two people can love each other to no end and also fall in love with other people because that's just life, you know? And it doesn't always mean that their love for each other falters or that they're cheating on the other person. It never has for me. I've always loved multiple people at the same time, and I used to think there was something seriously wrong with me. But maybe that's just how love goes and our thinking about it is so wrapped in convention we can't see love for what it really is!"

"Look, Tash. I get it. I know that I'm conditioned to believe in this shit, and I am conditioned to become jealous if you love someone else. But even if intellectually I know that, I still feel the jealousy. I still want monogamy.

I can't help that. But I'm happy for you. I really am. You should live your life and explore polyamory. You just can't be with me if you do."

"But if it is just a belief, surely you can change it!"

"I don't know, Tash. Maybe if you just slept with women I'd be okay with that. I could at least try it. But not if you slept with men. I'm sorry."

"Jesus! Don't you see the double standard in that!? I could love and fuck a woman just like a man, but because she's a woman you wouldn't feel threatened?"

"Yes, of course I see the double standard in that! I know I've just been conditioned by a patriarchal heteronormative society to behave this way, but knowing it doesn't change the fact that it's there."

"How is that possible!? Isn't identification the first step to changing a problem?"

"I don't know, Tash. I just know what I want. And I want one woman who wants one man. I love you, Tash. I really do. But I don't think I can give you what you want."

"But I don't want to lose you!"

"I don't want to lose you either!"

"No one's going to love me like you do, Sky."

"Come here, baby. Someone will love you better than I can. You'll see."

"But we don't have to decide today?"

"No, we don't have to decide today."

•••

If I HAD TO PINPOINT when all the trouble started it would have to be when we went to Florence together. Corey, Skylar's best friend, was living there and invited us and a couple other camp friends to stay for a month in his huge flat in Piazza Della Signoria. It had only been a year since I'd lived across the river with Aegir, and reminiscing one day at the internet café I emailed him to tell him I was back. He was back in Iceland by then but got all excited and said he'd try to come down to visit me. I foolishly thought he actually might, so I panicked and told Skylar, which is the precise moment he realized I'd never told Aegir I was dating someone else. To be fair, I'd never really had a reason to—Aegir and I hardly ever corresponded anymore—but Skylar didn't see it that way. He picked up his shit and left to go to Rome without me. I spent the night taking our friend Barry through my old city.

We started at Loch Ness with OJ and the Swedish bartender whose name I don't remember. I must've downed a whole bottle of Jäger by the time I'd made my way to MayDay. All the old folks were there...wondering how Aegir was. By the time Skylar came back from Rome I was locked in the bathroom half-naked and puking up licorice-flavored White Russians. We never really talked about it after that, but that's right around the time he started claiming he "just wasn't a sexual person."

I wish I could report that was where it ended with Skylar. Every year or so I'd slip up and kiss someone else or confess that I wanted to. Every year or so he'd blame himself for my actions. Every year or so I'd try to break up with him, but we'd never make it last through the night. We both knew it had to be done, but we just kept on not deciding.

I suppose if this were a different sort of story I would've gotten pregnant, guilted Skylar into some version of marriage, and lived unhappily ever after—at least until the shame and relief of divorce and custody set us free. I guess if this were a different kind of story Skylar and I would have played out the legacy of our parents with each other, me getting fatter, him getting quieter in his anger. But this is not that kind of story. This story is written with an unlikely hero. In the birthplace of the Third Reich, this Jewish Italian girl found some small salvation. His name was Wolfgang.

Wolfgang was one of the Germans Skylar and Saul met on their whirlwind Indonesian surf tour. Kinda smallish in stature, blond, blue-eyed, devilishly handsome, and aloof in that German way. Sixty years ago our friendship would have been impossible. I wonder what our ancestors thought of us. Me, Skylar, and Wolfgang. Two half Jews and a Bavarian.

We should have never taken that trip together. If we were being really honest, it had been over for at least two years, but the flights were booked, plans were made, and fuck it. Maybe we could enjoy Europe one last time as a couple.

Wolfgang met us at the train station in Munich by way of Torino. It was past midnight but we'd have no problem checking into the Easy Palace Hostel, where he worked. The subways and busses had stopped running promptly at midnight, as they always do across Germany. "Let's just walk there," Wolfgang said. Despite the Austrian wool coat that Skylar bought me the year before in Vienna down the street from Wolfgang's flat, this LA girl was near frozen in the Bavarian winter.

"How do you people live like this?"

"What are you talking about, Natascia?"

"It's never like this in California. So fucking cold. This is unlivable."

"Ach! Open your eyes, woman!" Wolfgang scolded. "Where else in the world can you walk miles through the park? Look at the trees covered in white, look at the midnight sky, listen to the perfect sheet of virgin snow crunching under your boots. Don't you see how romantic it is?"

Skylar stayed pretty apathetic to my presence for all of Germany, even after we moved from the communal hostel rooms of the Easy Palace to the privacy of Amos' loft room in his family's house. Even after we had countless reunions with the Germans, Skylar stayed quietly indifferent. But Wolfgang was all aglow. He talked to me, made me laugh, bought me beers, and made fun of me every chance he got. When Skylar wanted to go to bed, Wolfgang would insist we have another beer, even if that meant having one at the gay bar.

When the German gays got hostile about the presence of a female in their sanctuary, Wolfgang flirted with them until they bought us all a round of beer. We left the gay bar that night and Wolfgang's taunting went too far. I shot him a giant snowball in the face, and then I got one back. We ended up on the pavement wrestling each other in the ice and snow. Skylar just stood there watching everything, saying nothing.

Wolfgang laughed when we got up soaked. "Let's go get another beer!"

"No," Skylar said. "We are going home."

Wolfgang and I said goodbye.

Skylar and I spent another night in bed with his back toward me.

Then it was New Year's Eve and Willem was having everyone over to his parents' house for fondue. Skylar and I ate approximately nothing. The fondue looked amazing, and for the first time in years I wanted meat. How much longer am I going to do this? I wondered. Travel to these wonderful places and not experience the food. If Skylar weren't there I would have had some for sure. I would have been someone else for the night, someone I didn't know. Someone who was full of adventure and romance and joy. But I couldn't stand the thought of Skylar looking at me with any more disgust than I had grown accustomed to. All the German women had dressed up for the new year and were so beautiful. I envied every one of them.

It was loud around the table, an intangible boisterousness that I neither understood nor could be a part of. It looked fun to be Bavarian, to dip meat in sizzling pots of broth, to glitter and flirt across the table, to wonder if you'd get some tonight. Skylar spoke German enough to laugh, drink, and play along. I watched everything. Everyone was so busy texting, gossiping, barking at one another. Hands reaching across the table. Another prost. A flurry of excited energy. Then abruptly everyone pushed back, started to leave. Wolfgang looked over at my confusion to explain, "We have to leave or we'll miss the last train into town," and, "No, leave it, we'll clean it in the morning."

And then we were all running in the snow, and then we were all skipping the fare on the streetcar, and then we were all on a bridge, fireworks exploding around us. Skylar turned to me. "Happy New Year, Tash." Another fucking New Year. We kissed, all the passion long gone. Pretty soon I was hugging about a dozen Bavarians whose names I mostly don't remember or never really knew. Then Wolfgang appeared and my face was rosy like a fourth grader.

"Happy New Year, Wolfgang."

"Happy New Year, Natascia."

Skylar found us like that, smiling, staring into each other's eyes. "C'mon, Tash," he laughed nervously. "Let's take a walk."

"What? A walk? We'll lose everyone!"

"Nah, we'll be right back. C'mon, Tash! It'll be fun!"

He was almost never drunk. That was usually my department. But he seemed cheerful and insisted. I didn't want to leave that bridge. I don't know why I went with him. I don't know why I did about eighty percent of the shit I did in my early twenties. Habit, I suppose. He held my hand and we wandered.

"What are we doing, Sky?"

"I just wanted to get away from everyone. Just to be with you alone." He was drunk and we were lost.

I can't remember how we eventually got to the club. I just remember Amos having to come down to the door to make sure we got in. Everyone was there, wondering where we'd been. I fucking wondered myself. We put our coats down in some backroom filled with fold-up tables and chairs stacked on their sides. Skylar kept drinking and the night promised to push awkwardly onward. Until the look.

"I have to go," Skylar blurted.

"What? Go where?"

"I have to lie down."

"You can't be serious. You're just going to leave me?"

I watched him push through the makeshift coatroom and close the door behind him.

Klaus found me first. He was the kind of dude who always looked high. Demure, almost. We never spoke all that much. Every once in a while he'd stop to translate something to me. Handsome, I guess, if you like that sort of grown boy thing. "Where's Skylar?" he asked.

I shrugged. "He's passed out back there somewhere."

That was all it took. Klaus grabbed me a little too close to the breast and pushed his mouth onto mine.

"What the fuck, Klaus?!" I pushed him back. "Don't fucking do that!" He just laughed.

Klaus grabbed me again. Harder. And a shot of lighting fear went right through the root of me. I pushed him again. "Stay the fuck away from me!" And this cocksucker just kept on laughing and grabbing. I tore through the crowd to the coatroom. Skylar'd made himself a bed there. Industrious motherfucker. But he was dead to this world. Totally unmovable. *Fucking Skylar. I'll never forgive you for this.* I closed the door to the coatroom. Klaus was staring at me from across the bar. *Creepy motherfucker. Amos. I have to find Amos.* Amos was Skylar's closest German friend. We were staying with his family for the second time in a couple years. He'd help, right? But Amos was at the bar talking to some girl, and when I told him about Skylar and Klaus, all he said was, "Ach! Klaus is fucking strange. Don't worry about it. Just stay away from him." He slurred, then he turned back to the girl, carrying on, beer in hand. Klaus kept staring straight at me. *Fuck.*

"Well, hello," volunteered the voice of an angel.

"Oh, Jesus! Wolfgang!" I grabbed his whole body and held him like a life vest.

"Where have you been? I haven't seen you since the bridge. Where's Skylar?" I told him about Skylar and the coatroom, and crazy fucking Klaus.

"Klaus? Klaus is fucking crazy!"

"I know! He's freaking me the fuck out and I don't know anyone here!"

"You know me. Come on." He grabbed my hand and didn't let go. Walked right up to Klaus. They barked Bavarian at each other for a while. Wolfgang was about half his size. Klaus looked at me and said something to Wolfgang, who waved him off drunkenly. Shouted something behind his back, and pulled me away.

"What happened? What did he say to you?"

"Ach! Klaus is fucking crazy. Just stay with me. I won't let him ruin your night, I promise. Come on. Let's have another drink."

"Okay. Don't leave me."

He didn't, either. Not for a second. Klaus kept looking over, but he stayed away. Wolfgang kept his word. Hours of holding my hand. Introducing me to everyone. Translating everything they said. We drank together, and danced together, and when I had to go to the bathroom, "I'll take you there," is what he said. Still holding my hand.

We waited in line, and then he waited until I came out. "Thank you, Wolfgang." And I hugged him. "Thank you, truly." I pulled back and looked at him. *This is it, Natascia. You'll never be able to talk your way out of this one. You'll never be able to come back from this. Skylar will never, ever forgive you. Never. You don't have to wait till the morning. You can decide right now. Right now, forever. Do it, Tash. And never look back.*

I took his gorgeous German face in my hands and kissed him. And he took my Jewish face in his hands and kissed me back.

"What are we doing?" he asked. I pulled him closer. "You're the devil," he said, holding me tight. "You're the fucking devil."

We stayed like that in the little corner by the bathroom. Kissing for God knows how long. The red walls we pushed up against pushed back. The golden light from the bathrooms flickering in and out as the doors swung open and shut. Red engulfing everything around us. It was deep. And dark. And foreboding. A red you could almost hide in. Bloody. Dirty. People kept passing us to relieve themselves. Amos found us like that. He left us like that, too.

Then it was dawn and all of the lights came on and the color drained from every dusty corner of that beer-soaked basement room. We stood there, arms wrapped around each other in florescent glow.

I didn't know what to say. "I have to find Skylar."

"Come on," he declared, and took my hand. We pushed our way through all of the sudden whiteness. Skylar found us. Wolfgang let my hand go, and the rest of who was left of the boys appeared. Klaus too.

"Hi." Skylar was well-rested, sober now.

"Hi." I could barely look at him.

"Have fun?"

"Sure," I shrugged. "Feel better?"

"Sure."

Outside it was morning but still dark. Snow covered everything like a fog. The last time I saw Wolfgang he was getting out of a taxicab we shared with Amos and Klaus. Our goodbye was obligatory and abrupt. The taxi pulled away and I looked back at him through the rear window.

Skylar and I awoke in the late afternoon of the new year. He rolled over in Amos' loft and came on strong, tried to make love to me.

"I can't." I'd never turned him down. "I just can't."

He hugged me and we lay there quietly.

That evening we caught the train back to Willem's parents' house to clean up the fondue. Everyone was there. Well, nearly everyone. Not a one of the glittering German girls had returned to do chores and their absence was just that. No one expected them. No one felt the loss of their glamour. But Wolfgang? His absence was everywhere. The broth had grown a fine sheen of mold overnight. It had been about four years since I had touched meat, but I didn't give a good goddamn.

"Where's Wolfgang?" Skylar asked.

I pulled out chunks of half-cooked, coagulated rotten meat with my bare hands.

"He went back to Vienna early this morning," Amos replied.

"What?" Skylar seemed offended. "He didn't even say goodbye?"

Amos looked at me. "Nope." I kept my mouth shut and my head down. My heart in my throat. I emptied all the ashtrays into the garbage brimming with crumbs and mold.

"That's fucking weird," Skylar scoffed. "Did he say anything?"

"Nope, he just left."

The next day on the train to the airport, surrounded by our luggage, I looked at Skylar. "I can't do this anymore."

"Tash."

"Sky."

We didn't say much more. At least not anything that mattered. I didn't tell the truth. Maybe I convinced myself I could manage without it. Maybe I convinced myself it would only hurt him more and it was unnecessary. A couple days back in LA, Skylar had already mostly moved out. I showed up at his pop's house.

"I have to tell you something."

He laughed. "Who is he?"

"Wolfgang."

"Well, I hope you two are happy together." He laughed again. "I knew, Tash. I knew when I saw your face in the club that morning. I knew when he got out of the cab. And I knew when he left for Vienna. It was obvious. I'm not stupid." Then he took me in his arms and held me as we both cried. He told me it was his fault again. That he drove me to it.

Sometime later—maybe a year, maybe two—when we were still the best of friends, Skylar and I drove the Toyota to the Bay so I could interview at Mills College. Wolfgang and Germany came up.

"Oh, whatever. Look, I'm not saying that I did the right thing, but I saved us."

"No, Tash. You didn't."

"Yes, I did. We were never going to break up so I did the one thing I knew would make it final. And I'm not going to apologize for it. I was brave."

He laughed and shook his head. "No, Tash. That wasn't brave. That wasn't brave at all."

119

# CHAPTER 21

THE ONLY ME IN LA without Skylar was the "high school, black hole, booze and boys" me. So when Skylar exited stage left, good old Isabella entered stage right. She'd had a baby the year before with that asshole she started dating as soon as she left SAMO. He always kept a tight leash on her in that machismo sort of way and I hated him for it. Isabella was a dandelion, fragile and free. Luis only loved her for whom he thought he could make her, and Isabella, bless her heart, had just enough total self-loathing to think she deserved that kind of love. After they had a daughter, I tried to be there for her, but it wasn't until Luis left her and the baby and that I was single again that our friendship truly sparkled. Without missing a beat, we did everything together. Went to class at SMC, studied in the library, got a job at the Brickhouse, stormed the streets of Venice, traveled to Mexico, and even moved in together at one point. But it was all the boys that really braided us together, and Santiago was at the start of it all.

It was inevitable. Anyone after Skylar was going to be an absolute disaster.

Santiago and I first met in an ROTC class our senior year of high school. It was the only class offered during eighth period and I needed the credits to get the fuck out a semester early. I'm not sure why he was taking it, but Santiago was there every day with some stupid dad joke, always talked about the sun, and always laughed at everything I said as if I were the most amusing person in the whole world. And his smile—I'm talking hall of fame.

We were from different worlds, Santi and I. I belonged to the world of reputation. Of drugs and booze and status. The kids who pushed the limits and fueled the flames of gossip. Judd Apatow's freaks. I hadn't been a virgin for God knows how long, and I would have eaten high school Santiago alive. He had no place among us. He belonged to the domain of studying and taking SATs, of growing up at an age-appropriate pace, of having good relationships with your family, of real friends who truly cared for each other's well-being, and shit. Even though I was making a mad dash for the exit door, I was still in high school, and all that still mattered enough to stop me from taking any attraction to him seriously. Just the same every day as eighth period approached and the school emptied, I would wonder, *Is today going to be the day I smash that hall of fame smile up against the wall?*

•••

Now LET ME GET one thing straight with you. It was never cool to go to Brennans. There was nothing happening about that spot, and as far as I was concerned it was borderline shameful to even step foot in that shithole. Anyway, for some reason I'll never quite understand, on Thursday nights in 2005, everyone started to think it was a really great idea to go to Brennans. No one ever even watched the turtle races out back. We just all started going there, drinking cheaply, and complaining that there wasn't a doper place to be.

The first time I stepped into that shitbox, all I wanted to do was leave. Isabella wouldn't let me. "C'mon, Tash! Just let yourself have a good time!" I didn't want to spend another night in my own darkness, so fuck it. Six shots of Jäger and a couple of New Castles later, very little continued to matter. It was worth it, too, like bringing a mitt to the stadium to catch a foul ball; sticking around in that disgusting diviest of bars paid off when Mr. Sunshine appeared with his hall-of-fame smile.

He had that look, you know? The one where you can tell someone's not a virgin anymore.

"Why do you keep looking at me like that, Tash?"

"Like what, Santi?"

"Like you wanna say something."

"Well, that's because I do wanna say something."

"Well, out with it, *mujer*." I buried my blushing in my hands, hid behind my long wavy hair, and giggled like I was in high school. "No! I can't!"

He laughed, pushed my hair back, and told me another stupid joke.

"Okay! Okay! I'll tell you! Just no more corny jokes, please."

I told him about ROTC, about wanting to push him up against the staircase in the history building, about being sixteen and nervous, about his smile, about…and then he kissed me. His lips were soft and full, and he smelled clean like soap and February air. The lights came up in that greasy-ass bar. He asked for my number and called a few days later, and then he picked me up in his mom's car. He gave me a mix CD, and we parked on Ocean and Bay and listened to it and probably had sex in the backseat.

It's not that I was intoxicated and can't remember doing it. I just remember other things from that night. Like when Frank Sinatra closed out the CD with "Save the Last Dance" and Santiago proudly proclaimed he had to get his corny side in there at some point, and I thought to myself, *what a fucking dork*. I remember the car radio running through the whole CD with the engine turned off and thinking that I should probably tell him the battery would drain but then deciding against it and just letting him make the mistake. I remember waiting for AAA with flushed cheeks. I remember thinking how glad I was to be with someone who wasn't Skylar. I remember thinking about the imminent doom of the rebound and then thinking, no, this is Santiago. He's one of the sweet ones. I'll be fine.

I didn't want to be his girlfriend. I didn't want to be anyone's girlfriend ever again. I just wanted to hang out sometimes with someone who wasn't Isabella, listen to music, and have sex. I wasn't shy about that last part either. No, sir. I had no patience with being coy anymore. Anyway, it was Santiago, and he was such a nice boy. What did I really have to lose?

I remember the moment everything changed. He picked me up in his brother's car and we drove by the camera store he worked at in Westwood. We'd just finished devouring ice cream sandwiches from Diddy Reese and he was telling me about his latest photography project. I pushed him up against the wall of outside the Bel-Air Camera, kissed him hard like I'd always wanted to. He pushed me back and said, *"Cálmate*, mujer," as he laughed nervously. Then, for what always felt like no reason at all, he faded away.

A month would pass. I wouldn't hear from him and then he'd send me some idiotic message about enjoying the sun and smiling. He ignored any attempt I made at seeing him.

I had never experienced anything like that, and to this day, male or female, friend or lover, this is the one thing that just about anyone can do and I completely unravel. Fuck neutrality. My very sanity comes apart at the seams the moment I am ignored. When I first read *1984*, like everyone reading through the climaxing scenes of torture, I had to seriously consider what Big Brother might do to me that would break my spirit so wholly and irreparably. Imagine my total disbelief when I realized through Santiago how little it would take. Some kind of systematic vanishing in plain sight. Ghosted in reverse. Like, I'm the ghost but I have to continue to exist without a trace of acknowledgment. All it would take is some version of that and I'd be delighting in things that were double-plus good for the rest of my life. I feel like a right fool admitting it, but since he's always watching anyway, Big Brother already knows, and now you assholes know too.

I had a helluva time sleeping at night and got to be so goddamned fidgety in the day that I annoyed myself. I was in a constant state of anxious rage and every cigarette, every cup of coffee, every vibration from my cell phone that wasn't from him threatened to snub me out.

I didn't talk about him all the time, or anything like that. Or maybe I did. You'd have to ask Isabella. In my recollection I was pretty contained and private in my nervous obsession. Still, Iz could always tell when it got to be bad. She'd never push me to talk about it and would always listen if I had something to say. Never judged me for giving so much of a shit. Never reminded me that he was just a rebound. Never snapped at me to just get over it. She'd just look at me and say "Paradise Cove" and I'd let out a melodramatic sigh of relief and nod back. We'd pull into the nearest liquor store to buy the most expensive bottle of champagne we could afford with our tips from the Brickhouse and drive up PCH in the Toyota blasting the mix CD I'd made for that asshole but never had the chance to give him until we pulled into the long driveway that still charged a reasonable amount for parking back then. We'd grab two champagne flutes from the bar and sit by the shore until long after the bubbles ran out.

Paradise Cove is a bougie little private beach in Malibu open to the public for a price, which kept most people we knew away from it at the time. Paradise Cove was neutral territory. Not Venice. Not Santa Monica. No one to run into. No Natascia I had to be. If I ever did want to talk about it, about anything, which was hardly ever, Paradise Cove was the safe zone, for us both. Mostly we just sat quietly, sipping champagne. Sometimes we'd dream big lives together. Wondering how life would look through thirty-year-old eyes, forty-year-old eyes. Owning our own restaurant, publishing my first book. Holding my first Academy Award. The two of us and her grown-up daughter. Non-romantic life partners in a non-conventional family. But mostly I remember the quiet. Paradise Cove was just as much about what wasn't said as what was. We never gossiped there, and we never complained. Never bitched about the gentrification of Venice, the places we used to know white-washed to oblivion in yoga pants and kale. Never lamented being slowly edged out of our neighborhood through surging real estate prices. Never uttered the words "douchebag" or "yuppie." Paradise Cove was sacred ground. Sometimes we'd talk about Mexico, about former lovers, childhood memories. Sometimes we'd just weep. But mostly we drank champagne in silence, and for those few hours there was stillness and it didn't matter if I existed or not.

It'd been nearly a year since we'd last spoken when I learned Santiago's father had died suddenly. I called him. It seemed like the right thing to do. I figured I'd just leave my condolences on voicemail and that would be that, until he answered on the first ring.

"Hello?"

"Hi... How are you?"

"My dad died."

"I know. I'm so sorry."

"He's gone."

"I can't even imagine how much pain you're in right now."

What else could I say? I listened to his grief and told him I was there if he ever needed someone. I told him that and all the other things you say to someone, which never truly comfort them as you'd intended, but which you say anyway. And it should have ended there for me and Santiago, the boy with the dynamite smile. We should have just dropped it and never picked it back up again. But apparently one's twenties are reserved for the kind of idiocy and self-loathing one can only master through repetitively beating the metaphorical dead horse of romantic naivete.

Three years after his pop died, in 2009, we picked up right where we'd left off. I had just moved back to Los Angeles after graduating Mills College. Everything inside me was different, but LA was just like she'd always been: constantly reinventing herself as a new version of the same old girl—promiscuous and enchanting, nurturing and cold-hearted all in the same breath.

We were at Trader Joe's on Thirty-Third and Pico buying snacks for her now six-year-old daughter, and there was Santiago, bagging groceries. Iz did most of the talking, like she always did, and I just stood there matching his idiot grin, simultaneously wishing I could run and being grateful for her gift of gab. Then it was, "This weekend is my birthday. I'm having a BBQ, and you girls should come."

We spent about an hour at that BBQ. That was all I had in me. Santiago was all smiles, and sunshine, but the memory of the nice guy turned Casper years earlier had etched itself into my skin.

A week or so later we met at the Alibi Room. Before we were even halfway through the first drink we were knee deep in the full recapitulation of what happened between us in 2005, and by the end of the second drink we had come to some sort of semi-formalized agreement about taking it slow and being explicit in our communication. By the third drink we danced between flirtations and stories of the years that had gone by. And by the fourth, his father rose from the dead and we found ourselves lighting candles at the *ofrenda* in memorium. I went home alone that night, relieved and confident in my ability to get drunk *and* take it slow. I was different, despite LA, and maybe he was too, but I was absolutely determined to pussyfoot my way through discovery.

The next time I saw him I shouldn't have. It was late. Not crazy-no-good-booty-call late, but late enough for a Tuesday. He told me to come over, said a bunch of people from work were at his house and he wanted them to meet me. He'd been drinking, but I couldn't quite tell how much until I arrived. He was way too happy to see me.

"This is Natascia," he kept announcing to his coworkers. He sat on the kitchen counter of the house he grew up in, that his family had long since abandoned after the death of the patriarch, and cracked open can after can of Tecate in declaration. "Tecate! My father drank Tecate!"

I should have left while I could still see the door. I should have politely smiled and excused myself, let him walk me back to my car, hold my hand and kiss me, and watch me drive away. But I didn't do that. I sat on his kitchen counter with him, drinking Tecate, until I was on my way up the stairs to his bedroom. He kissed me, and I grabbed his face.

"I don't want to have sex with you tonight."

"Okay." He kissed me more, pushed me down onto the bed.

"Wait. I mean it. Slow down."

"Okay." We kept kissing. He took my shirt off.

"Wait, goddamn it. I don't want to have sex with you. We can keep kissing, and we can even touch each other a little bit, but I fucking mean it. I don't want to have sex with you tonight."

"Okay." He took off his pants and then mine. We were in our underwear kissing on his bed. I know, I know. I walked right into it. It wasn't long after he started rubbing his fingers through me that he pulled it out and stuck it in as if I wouldn't notice the difference. I pushed him off.

"What the fuck, Santiago?!" His face went white.

"What part of I don't want to fucking have sex with you tonight did you not hear?" I grabbed my clothes without ceremony.

"No," he pleaded as he reached for me. "No, I'm so sorry. Please don't go."

"No, fuck that. I can't stay here."

"Wait then! Let me at least walk you down," he scrambled for his pants. I pushed out of the bedroom he'd grown up in and down the stairs, not caring if he was behind me.

"Can I at least walk you to your car, Natascia?"

"No. No, I've got it."

"Can I at least call you tomorrow?"

"No. I don't know. No. I have to get out of here."

"Please? I'm sorry. I'm not myself. Please don't just leave like this!"

"I have to go. I need to think. I need some time. I have to go."

"Take time. Take whatever you need. I'm so sorry. Just don't shut me out. Just, please. Call me, okay? Just call me. Let's talk about this."

It wasn't that the outcome of the evening was totally unpredictable, but rather that I'd let the very obvious transpire. I felt the fool. Subject to the violations of my own stupidity, my own unwillingness to do something different, to not be coaxed and led. Isabella was completely checked out at the time in what many years later I'd learn was a meth-induced downward spiral of her own. When I told her what happened on the phone she offered nothing but "I'm not really good at holding this stuff, Tash. I don't know what to say." So I called Mary Jane in the Bay, the friend I'd made at college as an adult. She bought me a plane ticket to Oakland and I flew out the next day.

Despite being in the middle of finals, Mary Jane came through and offered sanctuary, and kindness unparalleled. She did her best to convince me that I wasn't an actual piece of shit who deserved this treatment. That the violation was on his end, but I was sure I knew better. Santiago did nothing to me that I hadn't signed up for in some way, and nothing she could say would convince me of anything else. I wasn't fourteen anymore. I wasn't drunk. He wasn't several years my senior. I had no excuses.

At some point during my time in the Bay he and I found each other on Facebook Messenger. "This is new for me," he wrote. "I'm just not used to being the asshole. I'm always the nice guy, and with you I always end up being the asshole."

When I finally got the courage to hit him back and hold him accountable, Santiago took a good long time to respond. When he finally did it was to say that he was over it and he didn't want to talk about it anymore. A couple years later I got a text about the sun and smiling. I told him to do us both a favor and lose my number.

I kept seeing him around town because this place is fucking Mayberry. He started working at the Wurstküche on Lincoln Boulevard, and there was always one reason or another that I had to be there for something. It was awkward at first but eventually we became friendly again, and when he invited me to his house for another BBQ celebrating his thirtieth birthday I brought a tall can of Tecate and shook his hand. "For your pop," I said.

I ended up dating one of his coworkers whose story didn't make the cut for this book, and when shit fell apart with us and I needed to move out of our apartment fast, Santiago offered me the extra room at his place for way below Venice prices with no deposit. I took it because life is weird and messy, and it was the least he could do.

# CHAPTER 22

THE KID'S NAME WAS Zero. That's not a nickname, not circumlocution, not some sort of literary cleverness intended to provoke the reader's capacity to wax poetic on metaphors à la AP English. The kid's name was Zero, and I fucked him on the cliffs of Big Sur with the deep Pacific crashing below.

I went to Esalen with my mom in the Spring of 2005. She could tell that I was losing it and decided that getting out of LA would do me hard good. We enrolled in an African drumming class because it seemed like the least New Agey thing they had on the menu, but it turned out to be pretty lame all the same. I banged on the djembe for four days with a bunch of white people, drank shit loads of herbal tea, and still my thoughts were of being ghosted by Santiago. Despite Big Sur's majesty, the sulfuric baths that poured freely from the rocks, and all the vegan food I could ever want, I was bored.

Zero was the son of one of the drummers leading the class. I don't remember his father's name. He was the long-haired, ultra-cool, pot-smoking Boomer with an ear for complex rhythms and time signatures. The quiet white man assisting the Nigerian instructor. Zero was the restless one. The sort of assistant to the assistant. Always fidgeting, always walking around the room, speeding up the rhythms, and being scolded to slow down. He stared at me a lot. He was somewhere between seventeen and nineteen. I was probably twenty-two. It was probably illegal or whatever. He was probably a virgin. He certainly had the look.

We hung out one night in the lounge, smoked some pot his dad had given him, found a pathway along the cliffs, and sat down on a stone bench. Then I may have raped him or whatever, but only in the legal sense. He seemed to be enjoying himself plenty. Afterward he held my hand and

I let him. We walked down to the baths like that, holding each other in the steaming sulfuric waters. He forgot to take off his silver necklace and it tarnished immediately, and we shared the most luxurious shower I've had to date. The showers at Esalen lay nestled in the cliffs above the ocean. It was late and the baths had all but emptied. Zero and I pushed open the sliding glass walls that divide you from the abyss of night and sea below. The boy turned on all ten showerheads, full steam. The bracing ocean breeze, the sharp sting of hot shower rain, the faint stench of sulfur, and our two young naked bodies, giggling and caressing. I let him kiss me, let him touch me, let him do whatever he wanted. Gave him the night.

The next morning as I was packing to leave, he brought me wildflowers he'd picked along the way. I gave him my number because it seemed like the sensible thing to do and said yes when he asked to take me to Royce Hall a week later. We met at Real Food Daily in Santa Monica. He ordered hibiscus tea and seitan and was an insufferable shit to our server. He wouldn't even look up at her, just barked his order and rolled his eyes until she left. Something was fucking wrong with that kid. I insisted on paying the check and left a huge tip with a hand-written apology. After dinner, we met his dad at UCLA and saw Zakir Hussain slaughter the tabla. Zero and his pop counted beats on both hands, and I kept my eyes closed and teary for most of the show. It was a fine night for an ending.

# CHAPTER 23

Marcus and I have been friends since we were kids. My pop moved to Santa Monica a year or so after the divorce, around the time I was nine. Marcus Allen was a story at nine I would have never predicted. Don't get me wrong, he was a good-looking kid—but, meh. My list of crushes was always pretty full, and I thought that, like everyone else, he was into Genevieve, the bombshell who looked twenty at thirteen.

All of that changed the moment he pulled up to a party twelve years later in a 1965 Chevy Malibu. It was deep, dark green like midnight in the forest, and he was so beautiful sitting in the driver's seat that I kissed him despite being Skylar's girlfriend at the time.

Marcus had grown up, started wearing his hair back with just enough product to suggest that he might be into Elvis, but not so much that he lacked any originality like the rockabilly throwback crowd. He wasn't rocking a pompadour, or anything. He just looked like he glanced in the mirror before he left the house.

"Wanna go for a ride?"

"I really shouldn't," I demurred as he closed the door behind me.

Anyway, that was it for Marcus and I for a few years. It wasn't until after Skylar, after Santiago, after Esalen that we really began our affair. Marcus had started a band with his friends. They were a sort of punkish, metalish thing. He'd grown his hair out and would perform with no shirt and black jeans at 14 Below on a semiweekly basis, doing his best Jim Morrison/Iggy Pop impression. I had approximately zero appreciation for what they considered music and what he called performance. Still, Isabella and I went to all their shows because that is what you do when your friends make something that is important to them. You show up and support, whether you have an opinion of it or not.

We'd always end up in a whiskey haze on top of each other. Sometimes we couldn't even have sex on account of the whiskey and all, though we'd give it the old Santa Monica College try. We carried on like that for a while, caring only enough to maintain late-night affections. Marcus and I never really wanted all that much from each other, save friendship and the occasional comfort. Though I did almost meet his mom once.

This was way back when he was still sleeping on a mattress in the kitchen of the apartment he grew up in on Fifth and California. He kept raving about his new Egyptian cotton sheets after one show and why didn't I come over to feel how soft they were. I scoffed at his total brazen shamelessness before eventually relenting. He was about a fifth deep and I wasn't too far behind when we pulled up to his mom's. We crashed in through the front door and it was all of ten seconds of uncomfortable disbelief before I put together that the mattress on the ground, five feet from his mom's bedroom door, was to be our Egyptian cotton love tomb for the night.

"But it's Egyptian cotton!"

"Your fucking mom is right there!"

"Whatever. She's gonna love you!"

Be that as it may have been, I never gave her the chance. I snuck out of there just as soon as he fell asleep, which wasn't too long after he hit the pillow. No amount of Egyptian cotton would ever cover that *sin vergüenza*.

Speaking of which, there's no telling how long we would have kept that shit up if I hadn't gotten pregnant. I guess theoretically speaking that baby could have belonged to one of three men, but hand to God I was absolutely sure it was Marcus's. Skylar and I had more sex after we broke up then we did in all the years we were together combined, but we'd always had unprotected sex and had never had any problems. It couldn't have been his. And as far as I knew it couldn't have been Sebastian's because I still wasn't sure if what he and I had done even counted as sex. Maybe I just wanted it to be Marcus's because I needed someone to be mad at for my own carelessness.

That sweet little baby would have been a teenager in middle school herself making her own lifelong friends now if I'd had the courage to face how I'd disgraced myself. I was a shit person then, but the only good thing I had going for me was that I had enough sense to recognize I was not fit for motherhood.

In the end, it wasn't Marcus's baby, and by the time I told him I'd been pregnant I'd already had the abortion.

We saw each other every once in a while after because Mayberry. The fucking Westside. A place where eventually everyone in your past becomes your present and becomes your past again. Just this last year he hit me up and asked me if he could take me out for a drink. I spent the first part of the night listening to him shower me with praise. After about twenty minutes of that shit I just couldn't take it anymore, and I finally told him I'd found out it wasn't his baby about a year after yelling at him outside his apartment. I never had the courage to tell him before. "That's okay, Tash," he sympathized. "I'm glad you're telling me now. Shows what an amazing person you are."

I didn't feel very amazing, but I didn't feel like protesting. Then he looked at me and declared, "We could have loved each other, you know. If you'd decided to have that baby and it was mine, we could have raised her together and fallen in love and made a beautiful life as a family. It wouldn't have been perfect, but we could have made it work. I just know it."

# CHAPTER 24

THE BABY WAS SEBASTIAN'S, and there isn't much to that story either. Sebastian and I were never meant to have sex. Never meant to mean anything to each other.

I had just come back from Mexico with Isabella. We took her daughter out there to meet her family as the non-romantic life partners we were. I remember being really broken up about Skylar on that trip. Missing him, missing us, feeling like I had ruined my life. Between that and having to take care of her daughter while Isabella fucked off with one of the neighbors by her tía's house in Coacalco, between the constant pressure of her conservative family not understanding our relationship, between being scolded like we were twelve for wanting to explore the country and all the ghosts that kept visiting her in the midnight panic of her dreams, between being a vegetarian in one of the gourmet hubs of the world and being forced to consume mostly lechuga and *queso con tortilla y salsa* until her family got frustrated and took us to McDonald's because, quote, *"hay papas fritas, y son vegetarianas,"* between all the probably delicious but horribly parasitic *barbacoa y raspados y coca pinche cola* the million *tíos* and *tías* kept shoveling down her daughter's two-year-old mouth while waving off our protests that she was VERY lactose intolerant and not used to that kind of food, between the emergency trips to public bathrooms for diaper and full wardrobe changes, or midnight wake-up calls of a possessed toddler screaming *sangre sagrada* clutching her stomach in anguish for three weeks straight, between all of that figurative and literal shit, it wasn't exactly the kind of vacation I'd imagined.

I was happy as fuck to get back to LA and to go up to camp for the last week of summer. Skylar and I were still friends, and lovers like never before. "Not a sexual person" my ass. Corey held the annual camp reunion at his father's beach house on the Venice Boardwalk. There was never anything between Sebastian and I. Truly. Sebastian was Corey's college roommate when they went to UC Berkeley together. Skyar and I used to drive up to the Bay to visit them often when we were still a couple. It's not that Sebastian wasn't good-looking or interesting. I just knew he wasn't for me.

After a few bottles of Jägermeister and the usual sing-a-long camp shenanigans, Barry led the bold down to the shore at Breakwater for a midnight posse. Stripping my clothes off and jumping through the waves with the rest of them, it seemed innocent enough. A typical night with camp friends. Except on the way down, Sebastian and I took the stairs in tandem, and at the sand we held hands running and laughing, and by the time we were out of the water and all our clothes stuck to our sandy wet skin, everyone else seemed to be way ahead of us. Somewhere between the sand, the boardwalk, and the stairwell, all the laughter turned into kissing.

We stole away into one of the empty bedrooms while no one was looking, tearing at each other's damp clothes and laughing so much. *What was so goddamned funny?* We tumbled some and ended up in the walk-in closet with the sliding mirrored door nearly shut and shit got kinda real. Fast. I stopped it quick. Or at least I thought I did and got up to check and see if the door was locked. *Am I really doing this?* I went back to him in the closet to finish what we had started. "Um...I'm finished," he declared gently as I got on top of him again.

By the end of September 2005 I kept looking for traces of blood. When I wiped, staining my underwear, the bed sheets. Anywhere. But blood never came. It had to be Marcus'. Or Skylar's. It just had to be. Not Sebastian's. Never.

The abortion took two and a half months. Every complication God could throw at me without killing me, He did. I think I can still have children if I wanted to. I hope I can, anyway. It took maybe a year before I finally came to terms with it. *Maybe it was Sebastian's baby?* I still didn't know for certain until the day he came into the restaurant for a smoothie. He didn't even know I worked there. We hadn't seen each other since the closet and had never spoken about that night. I brought the smoothie out to the table he was writing at and sat right down.

"I have to tell you something."

"Okay."

"I don't think it was yours because I don't even think we really had sex, but I got pregnant and had an abortion, and whether it was yours or not, you were the only person's it could have been that I never told."

"I...it...what do you mean we never really had sex?"

"Well, I don't know, I don't really remember. I just remember you saying you were finished after I got up, like you didn't want to anymore, and we had just started."

"I said that because I was finished. Like in the literal sense."

"Oh. Well, that explains it." I sighed.

"What are you writing about?"

"You'll never believe me if I tell you, Tash."

"Oh, yeah? Try me."

"It's a short story about a boy who always suspected he'd gotten this girl pregnant. But he never knew for sure." We were both in tears.

He came over to the garage that night in secret. I read him the letter I had written our baby. Told him about the abortion and all the complications in bloody detail. We held each other on the couch Corey's parents had given Skylar and I when we moved in together. Me just sobbing the rest of it out, him just holding me and stroking my hair. We woke up in the middle of the night like that, still on the couch. He got up and took his shoes off and climbed into the loft bed Skylar'd built for us when we lived in that garage together years back. "You're not leaving?" I asked him.

"No," he said. We just slept side by side with all of our clothes on, holding each other in grief and silence until the morning came.

# CHAPTER 25

A FEW YEARS AGO I was scrolling through Instagram and came across a term I didn't know. Thirty seconds later on Urban Dictionary I realized that I'd known what a fuckboy was years before the term had been coined. His name was Rafa, and he taught me just how dull casual sex could be.

I met him at one of Isabella's father's unnecessarily extravagant parties. This particular party was held somewhere between the Valley and Hollywood in a huge house that was built to look like a castle. You know, one of those permanently vacant production houses across the city that has no soul because it was never meant to be a home to anyone. I don't understand the mentality there. Renting out a castle one night for a party. Filling it with folding chairs and tables and Sternos and the shameful scratches of someone posing as a DJ. Shuttling guests from a parking lot in limos, probably paying at the door if you're not the boss's daughter's non-romantic life partner. And for what? Just to say you went to a party in a castle in Hollywood, or the Valley, or whatever? Spare me.

Isabella had to be there, which meant I did too. Rafa was Isabella's "cousin," which is to say that their fathers crossed the border together, bonding them for life. Before getting to the party they all talked about him, the prodigy soccer star just retuning from Brazil. *Soccer, huh? Brazil, huh?* Sounded interesting enough for the night. When he got there he was just a bitty thing, not even twenty yet. Skinny with a goofy-ass grin, wearing the same haircut he'd probably had his whole life. *Neverfuckingmind.*

The night wasn't a total bust, though. The Mariachi Divas preformed in full fifteen-piece feminine majesty, blowing away the dust bunnies of the night with diaphragm and trumpet. Not long after, they were nominated for a Grammy, and not long after their set ended at the party it was kind of a wrap for me. I found myself languid on a beanbag chair in one of the turrets with Isabella and her cousin, lamenting that I couldn't get high.

"This spot's blown, Iz. I'ma roll a joint."

"Dude, don't you dare light that in from of my dad."

"Ugh. Let's catch one of those limos back to the Corolla and blaze then, 'cause I'm tryna be out."

I don't know how many years later, Isabella's pop opened another restaurant and was having another party. Again I was expected to be in attendance. Fully prepared for another dull night, I wore an unnecessarily short skirt hoping for some fun, but ten minutes in, the party was more or less the same deal sans castle. Same Sternos, same dried-out food, same lame-ass conversations. "*Mija*, your *primo*'s coming. He's been in Brazil again." Blah blah blah. Iz pretended to be listening, and I just stood there wondering how much whiskey I could manage without her dad reminding me that men don't like women who drink. A few minutes later she had to run some errand in the kitchen and I was left alone, drinking bourbon from a plastic cup when this handsome little devil walks right up like he knows me.

"What are you drinking there?"

"Do I know you?"

"Why don't you go pour me one and find out?"

"Why don't you go fuck yourself? What are you, like nineteen? Twenty?"

"What's it to you?"

"Primo!" Isabella screamed.

"Isabella!" He screamed back.

Some kind of late-blooming puberty had hit him like a parasite, consuming all the boyishness before spitting out this confident, dark, stacked little man. You could tell he played soccer in South America now. You could tell from his long wavy locks and that ass. I couldn't believe it, I really couldn't. The thing that made it so much more incredulous was the cockiness. "Hey," he said. "Pick your jaw up off the floor." He took all my hits and dished them right back until after fifteen minutes I wasn't sure if I wanted to smack him or fuck him or both, but I knew for certain I wasn't going to let him decide which came first.

"Izzy," I said. "This spot's blown. I'm outta here."

"C'mon, Tash. Don't do that."

"Yeah, Tash." He smirked. "Don't. Let's all go back to my boy's house."

"Nah," I shrugged. "I'm good."

"Tash, goddamnit!" Isabella pleaded. "Don't do this. You always leave. Just stay with us. We'll have fun. Please."

"Yeah," he joined in. "Just come," but he said it like he spelled it C-U-M in his head.

"Uh, nah. You guys go ahead. I'll see you tomorrow, Izzy. See you around, Primo."

That's when Izzy really laid into me about always bailing on her at her dad's parties and how I'd said I'd be there, and how I always complain about being alone and this is how I end up that way and some other guilt-trip shit blowing up my motherfucking spot in front of this fine-ass cocky boy who had no business knowing any of it.

We all walked outside together and stopped in front of her burgundy '79 Jaguar with matching cracked leather interior. "Get in," she says to me. "Oh, no, Izzy. I'm going with him."

We never made it to his boy's house. I made him pull over somewhere on the south side of Santa Monica and climbed on top of him while he was still in the driver's seat. Had myself one of those full-body-shaking, fifteen-piece mariachi set orgasms in about thirty-five seconds flat. Made him drop me off at home after that.

Our encounters got less and less interesting over the next couple of years. By the fourth or fifth I remember longing to go out on a date or something, just to spice things up. Anytime he led, the amount of porn he watched was embarrassingly evident. It just got boring. There's nothing more dull than having sex with someone who is absolutely indifferent to your existence.

Fucking Rafa was just like going to a party in a castle somewhere between Hollywood and the Valley. It's supposed to be exciting, supposed to be glamorous, and you go just to say you did. But amid the folding chairs and chafing dishes, the Sternos burning low, you get bored and hate yourself for believing the hype.

# CHAPTERS 26 AND 27

I N MY FOURTH YEAR at community college I took a Latino/as in Contemporary Society class through the sociology department because Magdalena Morales was teaching it and I would have taken fucking advanced applied calculus if that woman taught it. She was a force, both formalized and colloquial in style, and she believed in me. She once told me that she considered me a future colleague, and any assistance she could offer was just assistance she was eventually offering the department and the field in general. I don't know if she meant any of it, but that kind of compliment from that kind of professor is the kind of thing you think about right before you jump off the cliff that makes you turn around, drink some water, and go home.

Magdalena talked me through the shame of my abortion when I could barely make it through class, told me about a magical place just for women in the Bay called Mills College, and ultimately taught me that sexuality, gender, and damn near everything else exist on a spectrum. For a young girl discovering her queerness in the confusion of a monogamist-driven hetero world, she taught me that all of my expressions of sexual and romantic love were a-okay.

"But I don't know if I'm gay, Profé," I'd lamented in melodramatic anguish. "Ach," she waved off. "Sexuality is a spectrum, mija. Always changing in society and the individual. It might be complex, but it ain't that complicated. You don't have to worry about defining yourself by it—or by anything else, for that matter. And don't tell my colleagues I'm saying this because we fought so hard to get people to understand that homosexuality isn't a choice, but what if it could be? And what if we lived in a world where we didn't have to excuse ourselves for being gay by convincing straight people that's it's not a choice? You wanna talk about gay pride? Real pride?

What about the pride in choosing an alternative lifestyle because it suits you better than the heteronormative stamp you're born into?"

Like I said, folks. A force.

Every time she spoke it was like church bells ringing out on Christmas Day. I was all ears and third eye. Open as fuck. I probably would have never slept with Jamie, and ultimately that girl Stacey by default, if she hadn't responded the way she did when she found out the three of us paired for a project.

"Huh. You and Jamie?"

"Well, and Stacey too."

She waved the sound of her name off. "You and Jaime. I can see that."

"See what?"

"The two strong, outspoken, educated young people in my class."

"Psssht. No way. It's not like that, Profé."

"Oh, no? He's a nice-looking Bolivian boy. And you're both so passionate and intelligent. I could just see you staying up all night drinking cafecitos and debating the finer points of *la revolución*."

Where previously no thoughts grew, the seed exploded in ripe soil and I couldn't get Jaime off my mind. I went over to his Mid City apartment a week or so later. That girl Stacey from class that always struck me as too bubbly met us there too. Jaime brought out snacks and the three of us, but mostly just he and I, discussed Article X of the Treaty of Guadalupe Hidalgo, Octavio Paz, and the psychosocial notions of borderlands. A couple hours into our passionate play, his girlfriend came home. When she saw Jaime with two other white girls deep in study she must've hit some kind of massive internal wall. She stormed around the apartment broadcasting discontent in that no-everything's-fine WASPy way. I kept looking up at every huff to catch Jaime's eye. Don't worry about it, he kept dismissing through ESP. But more than worry, I just wanted to remove myself from the passive-aggressive, static-filled room. I gathered up my notes and books, said a very rushed "see you in class," and high-tailed it back to the Westside. That girl Stacey stayed another hour or so.

The next day before class began Jaime dropped off a letter on my desk. In great intimate detail it described the personal study of a Master's in Psychology with the intent of becoming a therapist. It apologized for unnecessary unwelcoming behavior, for projecting romantic jealousies, confessed personal and professional shame for her behavior, and declared desire for a future friendship. It was signed by Jaime's girlfriend.

"Hey, Jaime! What is this about?" He rolled his eyes. "I don't know, dude. She insisted I give it to you."

"Just me? Did Stacey get one?"

"Nah. Just you. Stacey stayed for too long and when the house was finally empty we got into a huge fight about how you left."

"What the fuck? I barely spoke three words to that woman."

"I know, I know. She's fucking nuts."

It was so easy for him to say that. That whole "my girlfriend is crazy" thing. I saw something else. I saw a woman who was very in tune with the movements of energy around her. I saw a woman who could see into the future, and a man whose very survival depended on convincing her that she was crazy. For all I knew he could have put her up to writing that letter himself.

"I don't know, Jaime. If she's so crazy, what are you doing with her?"

"I don't know. It's complicated. I've been trying to leave her for months now, but I haven't been working and this city is expensive, and we've been together for so long. It's not easy to just pull the plug. I don't know. I'm waiting till the semester's over."

Despite the color guard of red flags in synchronized routine swirling around us, Jaime and I kept studying together. I'm kind of a sucker for dark-skinned skinny boys. He wore Thrasher shirts and Vans with pulled-up socks, and had that young Latino, punk-rock, socialist revolutionary thing going on. Profé was right. We could talk for hours emotionally and intelligently about politics under the Bush regime, about the failures of the Cuban revolution, about the economic collapse in Argentina. And then we'd talk about his girlfriend and how he wished he could just leave.

At the end of the semester, Profé assigned us a final project. "What are the masks you use to present yourself to the worlds around you?" I baked Torta di Mele, made risotto al funghi, and brought in espresso with a fresh jug of hazelnut milk for my classmates to enjoy. Jaime put up a framed picture of his lady and read a letter describing his undying love and devotion.

A few weeks into the summer Isabella and I were down at the El Rey to see Jurassic 5. Jaime and his friend Lalo met us there. We were standing at the bar taking down double bourbons when that bubbly girl, Stacey, walked straight up, like, "Hey, guys!" I looked at Jaime like "what the fuck?"

"I invited her. My bad," he whispered in my ear.

When the show was over we were all outside under the marquee. I stood on Jaime's skateboard and he held my hands, doing his best through bourbon shots to teach me how to skate. Isabella and Lalo were already making out, and Stacey was just fizzy bubbly around the lot of us, getting progressively more forward and slutty with every giggle. When Chali 2na came out into the crowd on Wilshire Boulevard, I jumped off the skateboard and ran right up to him.

"Hey! I'm so sorry, you must be getting a lot of this tonight, and I usually don't do this, but if I don't I'll always regret it. I just want to shake your hand and tell you how much I appreciate your lyrical skills."

"Oh, well, then get over here, girl," and he pulled me in for a deep embrace. He smelled magical, like sandalwood and Play-Doh and earth. I almost forgot to speak when he asked me my name.

Someone called out to him that it was time to bounce and he could bring his new girl too, if he wanted. "So how about it, then? You wanna come and meet everyone?" I looked back at Isabella with Lalo, and Jaime who was now teaching Stacey to skate, and I might have said yes but opted for something much more coquettish like, "Maybe next time." Chali 2na smiled, shook his head, and said, "Be good, Natascia. I'll catch you next time."

"Not if I catch you first, Chali 2na fish!" We both laughed and walked back into our respective lives.

"What are you doing, Tash?" Isabella goaded. "Why didn't you go with him?"

"Nah, Iz. It would have ruined it. But damn, he smelled magical. Not like a fish at all!"

We all piled into the Corolla, crammed into Lalo's Mid City studio apartment, and commenced to edge out our own not-so-glamorous after party. There was a mattress on the floor and a daybed and some of Jaime's shit was stacked against the wall. Izzy and Lalo went at it on the floor. Jaime, Stacey, and I sat on the bed together in aroused disbelief of the show at our feet. He grabbed Stacey and kissed her, and when he went for me, my "what about your girlfriend?" came out coy as fuck.

He nodded in the direction of his things on the floor. "I moved out."

I didn't care if it was true or not. Me, Jaime, and the hypersexual bubbly one went at it. So above as below, until dawn, exhaustion, and the spins caught up with us.

Jaime and I kept seeing each other through the summer. Mostly because Isabella and Lalo kept in touch. The four of us usually ended up in some version of that first night, minus Stacey. I eventually lost interest. Jaime disappeared into the ether, and Isabella launched herself further into a cloud of meth and Jameson-induced debauchery. It was a few years before she came out of that and by that time Jaime was just a memory, Isabella couldn't even remember Lalo's name, and God only knows what became of Stacey.

# CHAPTER 28

R ONNIE GAVE ME MY first two cars. The Chevy and the Buick. Ronnie, Tommy, Eddie, and John all lived on the same street they grew up on, in their parents' old houses in Venice. Born, raised, and eventually died on Indiana Avenue. Little did Dahlia know when she bought the house in between Eddie and Tommy with most of the money in her trust that she had also inherited a middle-aged, blue-collar legacy. The first week her family officially moved in we were putzing around in the backyard and Eddie hollered out through the fence about the Lakers' game. "You girls should come over," he boomed. "We're making chili!"

We were fifteen-ish. He was well past forty-five.

Ah, Eddie's house. A reliquary to the sixties and seventies. A waterbed, a koi pond, a hot tub bursting through the asphalt, a dormant, bright orange '68 Challenger with black racing stripes in the two-car garage surrounded by salvaged electric Budweiser signs and hidden under the eternal duster of Someday. Eddie's house. Rooms filled with television memorabilia, velvet concert posters, and wind-up tin robots. Record players with glass tube amplifiers, avocado-green diner bar stools, floor lamps with shades of gargantuan circumference, and a succulent garden lit to cascading LED state-of-the-art perfection. Eddie's house. Where file cabinets overflowed with invoices for electrical work, and coil stoves perpetually bubbled with stewed meats and homemade BBQ sauces. Where the refrigerator had its own special door for a lifetime supply of Bud Lights. Where conversations almost always included the words "corner store" and "Havasu." And Eddie...stout and rosy from too much red meat and beer, with a neck that looked like a chin that looked like a neck. Never able to sit in one place for more than thirty seconds, constantly moving in the middle of his vintage castle like a bombastic toad lord, heralding us with stories of Dogtown.

That's how it went in Venice back then. The moment Dogtown Z-Boys hit the theaters Venice pride spread like the goddamned pox. If you were over the age of forty in the year 2001, every other word out of your mouth spelled P-O-P. The year 2000? Fucking crickets. But in 2001 it was *Hecho en* Venice this, and Locals Only that. All of a sudden if you knew one of the original Z boys, like even if he was a grade below you and you thought he was a dork, you were somehow relevant because you saw them skating at a party once or broke into one of the backyard pools with them this one time. In 2001 growing up in Venice was a lifestyle choice, a point of pride, a fucking brand. That one time you saw Jay Adams hop over a fence to bail a party the cops broke up was like sweet nectar from the tree of life, and if you could only find some local teenage girls to breathe the story to, your middle-aged existence would be revived in all the golden, washed-out glory of your seventies high school days.

Eddie loved telling those stories as much as he loved telling us how shitty Led Zeppelin sounded live. He'd sit on the edge of his black sectional leather sofa, over the zebra area rug surrounded by pink walls, and tell us about his wild days, before he got "sober." About how if you mix cocaine with just the right amount of water you could take down a gram in one snort. Then he'd act it out on the great glass coffee table, guffaw until his rosy skin turned stewed tomato, and get up again for another beer. Eddie's house was the hub of all things unsavory on Indiana Avenue, but Dali's mom never seemed to have a problem with her teenage daughter hanging there. So that's precisely what we did after school every day.

I'd walk from SAMO High to the continuation school down the street to pick Dali up, and we'd hightail it over to the fridge with endless Bud Lights. Eddie would put the *Dave Mathews Listener Supported* concert DVD on the big screen for us because "you girls love that shit," and his blue-collar cronies would file in one after another from three thirty to sundown. Plumbers and pool men, contractors and mechanics, all of them born and raised on or near Indiana Avenue. It was an odd bunch of men. I never understood their conventionality, nor did I ever really appreciate the total unconventionality of our developing friendships. I suppose it would have made more sense if all these men hit on us or something, tried to make it with the young teenage girls that would be at Eddie's when they got off work, but it wasn't like that. We were like the furniture. All of us. And when they weren't feeding us, or fixing our cars, or complaining about their wives and girlfriends, they'd mostly just tell us stories of the old days.

Eddie gave me my first job organizing and filing the invoices from his electrician business. He even took Skylar on a few years later as an apprentice. And when Logan was born he became his de facto godfather. Not that it was all wholesome and normal. There was that one time Eddie lost his mind about something or other and took all the pictures of Dali and I in oversized shirts and basketball shorts in his hot tub, and tore them to bits before throwing them on Dali's doorstep. Or the time he got in a screaming match with Granny and shoved her. And after Ronnie gave me the Chevy for nothing but the promise to get it out of his name by sundown Eddie hit the roof because I was a girl and didn't know shit about classic cars. But he eventually accepted it and taught me how to adjust the carburetor, and check the oil, and would always cheer when I rumbled down the block past his house.

A year later Ronnie sold Skylar and I his pristine baby blue '83 Buick Regal with matching interior for a hundred bucks so we could have a car that didn't have holes in the floorboard. Skylar and I split the cost and drove away that afternoon covered in blue velvet. We had her for all of four months before I got into my very first car accident. I'd only had my license for half a year and this yuppie in an SUV made a left turn from Oxford onto Howard when she clearly didn't have the right of way. I kept driving because I clearly didn't have the instinct to stop. It was her fault, but I was uninsured, young, and shook up as fuck.

We didn't have the money or the will to get it fixed, so we sold it for fifty bucks to some pals of ours who needed a car pretty badly and stuck to the Chevy for a while despite the holes. My license got suspended, but we ended up with a two-grand cash settlement, so it wasn't all that bad. Skylar and I opened a joint account and invested most of it into hydroponic grow equipment, because my Sky was one smart cookie. Even after we broke up, Skylar and I maintained the joint account and our investment, and for the next few years money quite literally grew on trees. I started pushing dubs and eighths with relative ease. When I'd sell out of the homegrown shit and the door'd be knocking, I'd head over to the first dispensary on the Westside to pick up a few things for a few clients. And that, dear hearts, after all this, is how I met Damian.

No matter what I came to the dispensary for, Damian always made sure I left with a little something extra. Whether it was a couple of loose joints, one or two lollipops, a new triple-fudge quad-dose brownie, or a little nug of something that just came in from Humboldt that I had to try, Damian always had treats and a full, bushy-eyebrow smile to match. A year of this passed and I took my spoils without thinking much of it other than it's fun to be young and cute. Don't get me wrong. I could tell there was something there, and he was the kind of handsome that made you hope someday someone would eventually say something, but I don't know. I didn't know how to start something with a perfect stranger, and what's more, I wasn't really sure I wanted to. The whole idea of dating is repulsive. Meeting a total stranger and systematically attempting to get to know them as the two of you dance between the projections of each other's minds, all while swapping spit and hormones and shoving genitals. I don't know. I can count on one hand the amount of actual dates I've been on, and I still think even that's too many. I'd rather just slowly get to know you, you know, in your natural habitat and shit. Even if it takes a few years before I decide to share a drink with you. That way when we're sharing a drink we're just catching up, as opposed to the awkward alternative I watch people struggle with all around me.

So it'd been a year already. He was the hot guy at the ganja shop, and I didn't even know his name. I'd just go up the back stairs hoping he was on shift and I'd get a lollipop or something. I'd blush through whatever words were exchanged, swoon behind bulletproof glass, and take my spoils down to the car where Izzy was waiting to see what he gave me this time and to ask again if I had finally said something. The answer was always no. That was sort of enough for me. I could have done that for another few years and been perfectly happy fantasying the rest. Until one fateful evening after Isabella had finally gotten her own fake medical license to buy and I brought her up the back stairs by my side. It took all of three seconds after being admitted before this bitch opens her big fat mouth, and the next thing I know his name is Damian and he's us meeting us at the Otheroom in an hour for beers.

She made me let him buy our drinks and I had to listen to him thank Isabella and tell her how much money he'd spent on ganja just to get my attention. They had a real good laugh at my expense.

"Oh, isn't Natascia just the most naive girl you've ever met?" and "if she were left on her own she'd probably have gone in for another year without saying anything," and "yeah, she really needs help, but that's what makes her so cute."

I ordered another Chimay Blue on his tab with steam coming out of my ears, and when Damian excused himself to go to the bathroom I turned to Iz and said, "Don't ever do that again."

"Do what?"

"Don't make things happen because you think they should. This is my fucking life. I decide."

"Oh, please. How much longer were you going to go in there and giggle? Sometimes you gotta just go for it, Tatti."

"Fuck you, Izzy. Maybe I liked it just the way it was. With giggles and free lollipops and wondering if anything was ever going to happen." She just rolled her eyes. "I don't need you to do my bidding for me. If I'm going to go for it then it'll be my fucking decision."

I left her sitting at the bar and found Damian in the hallway still waiting his turn for the bathroom. When the handicap stall opened I invited him to share it with me. He kinda looked at me funny. "Oh, does that freak you out?" I asked. We took turns peeing in front of each other and then I pushed him up against the wall and kissed him like I'd had a couple of nine percent Belgian beers and gave very few fucks.

We dated for a couple of months. He was thirty-eight at the time and I was twenty-two. He worked construction on the days he wasn't slanging ganja, and the first time he came over to spend the night he brought a backpack with everything he'd need in it for the next day. "What's that?" I asked when he plopped it down on the floor beside him, knowing full well what it was.

"I have to be up early," he says. "I packed a bag to stay the night." So practical. So presumptuous. So grown-up. I could have puked.

My stomach turned as he proceeded to watch me finish the paper I was writing for an English class at Santa Monica College. "This is gonna take a while," I remarked. "I still have four pages and a bibliography to get out. You can, like, chill or something. You don't have to watch me."

"Nah," he says. "I like watching you work. Read me a little something."

After bullshitting about Hemingway or some other asshole, I looked up and he had this big-ass grin on his face. "Wow," he says. "My girl is so smart."

What a gross exaggeration. *My girl.* At what point after sleeping with someone do you become their girl? Ugh. That and a backpack. In addition to being sixteen years my senior, it bothered the fuck out of me that he'd decided all these things without me knowing. Having a crush is one thing, but if the full extent for a year of getting to know someone only includes the formal exchange of medicine for money and the occasional smile and free lollipop, you don't get to decide so quickly that you want to be with her. Furthermore, after a month of dating you don't get to call her your girl, and if you're sixteen years her senior you should know all of that before she does.

Sometimes I'd actually find myself kind of enjoying him. Maybe it was just the attention after Skylar, or maybe it was the sexual adoration you only really get with older men. To be fair, when he'd tell me about bouldering and books on Mt. Everest he'd light up and I'd think, "Oh! He's just kinesthetically intelligent. I read about that in Psych class." But then he'd drop in something like, "You should come out to Joshua Tree and watch me climb," and I'd throw up a little in my mouth.

When I was high, which was more or less all the time, my heightened sense of awareness would send my mind reeling and make my skin crawl around him. I'd take little ghost breaks in between seeing him to catch my breath, until enough days had passed that I'd start to wonder what the fuck was wrong with me and why couldn't I just chill and enjoy myself with this nice dude who obviously liked me a great deal. So I'd call again and pretend that I had been super busy. He'd buy it enough to equally pretend like everything was okay. Things would be fine until he'd try his luck like, "Let's get a room at The Standard this weekend and do a little role playing." Then I'd go all Houdini on his ass, and the cycle would start all over again. As if I didn't have enough things to be totally grossed out by, he also lived in the Valley. He'd argue that it was the only place he could rent and have a proper house for his tools and a grow room. But it wasn't even reasonable Valley, like Sherman Oaks or Studio City. It was *valley* Valley, like north on the 101 past Reseda, which, coming from the Westside, was practically against my religion. It was never gonna work out.

He wasn't a bad dude, really. Any girl out there who drinks Starbucks, smokes weed, and spends at least twenty minutes putting on makeup in the morning would be happy to have a man like him, I'm sure. He was kind. And handsome. And he had a truck and could build things. But we were just in different places. While he was pushing forty, waking up before sunrise to work construction, and looking for a girl like me, I was in my early twenties and I wasn't looking for shit. Not from any dude.

But I'll tell you what really did it. The night we all went out to celebrate my acceptance to Mills College he met my friends. I wore this insanely short button-up red dress. He very easily fit in, chatting up even the most skeptical friends who still hadn't gotten over Skylar and I breaking up. He kept looking over at me in that dress like I was going to be in big trouble later. I was probably about seven fingers into a bottle of Maker's when he pulled me down onto his lap and I told him that his nickname, Dami, sounded like "give me" in Italian. We went back to his house that night and he proudly showed off the loft bed he built himself inspired by the one Skylar'd built me, right before he made me pay for the red dress. I woke up the next morning naked in a whiskey haze in the fucking Valley, in a fucking loft bed that wasn't Skylar's, and this fool rolls over and tells me that the very first time I walked into the dispensary he turned to the owner and said, "That girl. That's the girl I need in my life." Then he said something about me leaving for the "Gay Bay," and then it was all, "I'm at a place in my life where I'm looking to settle down."

*Well, of fucking course you are, you forty-year-old man, so what the flying fuck are you doing with me?*

He kept at it too, like he was serious or something. Like if I let him keep talking he'd propose like that, naked in a counterfeit bed. My asshole clenched. And then he said it again: the Gay Bay. He couldn't just say Mills College, or Oakland, or even San Francisco. He just kept calling it the Gay Bay like some kind of homophobic meathead who felt betrayed because I was leaving him, so he teased me in all his maturity about the place I was moving to.

I laughed nervously. "You know your nickname means 'give me' in Italian?"

"Yeah." He rolled his eyes. "You told me that last night."

I shut right the fuck up after that. I didn't owe him shit.

"Whatever," he relented. "It's not that far. I could load up my truck and come see you in the Gay Bay, and we can make a weekend out if it."

I don't even think I responded. I only answered his calls for a week after that as a formality. And once I fell in love with Judah: Ghost Town 3,000.

The next time I saw him was about twelve years later. Venice had become the sort of place no one who grew up there could afford, and fucktards with ID cards strung from lanyards around their necks went from calling it Dogtown to Silicon Beach as they argued about what the best restaurant on Abbot Kinney was. Eddie was long gone. He told us he was going into the hospital for a routine procedure involving his swollen and enlarged testicles and ended up very, very dead. All the doctors could say while still honoring his confidentiality was that he had been very sick for a very long time, and there was nothing routine about what brought him into the hospital in the first place. Dahlia had lost her kids to the system a few years back, and the last time I'd seen her she looked like a ghost with missing teeth. I barely recognized her. The Chevy was gone too. I'd finally traded it in for a car you didn't have to pump three times, throw salt over your shoulder, and say a silent prayer to start up. Recreational ganja was legal, and the dispensary was still in business.

I drove by one day in my early thirties wondering if it was actually possible that this fool would still be working there after all this time. Wouldn't you know it? I walked past the security guard with just a California drivers license, and motherfucking Damian was on the other side of the door looking old AF. Like gray hair, in his fifties and shit. And you wanna know the first thing that came out of this fool's mouth? This fool looked at me through sun-weathered skin and said, "You were the love of my life. You know that, right?" I just laughed and shook my head. "Wow," I smiled. "That's... really something." He handed me a lollipop, giggled something about the one that got away, and asked me what I'd been up to since college. *A whole lot of nothing.*

"I don't know." I shrugged. "A lot of shit, I guess. It's been a long time. Where do I even start?"

"Well, like, are you still writing?" he asked me.

"I guess. I'm writing this book, or whatever."

"Oh, yeah? Is that what you do now? You're a writer?"

"Um, yeah. It's been twelve years. I have, like, three Pulitzers by now," I bantered. "Nah, I'm a fucking nanny, and I still live with my mom."

"Yeah, Venice is fucking expensive," he added. "Well, I wrote a book."

"Fuck you, no you didn't."

"Yup. I'm a published author."

"Oh, fuck. Really?"

He busted out his phone and showed me his book. It's about bouldering, and you can get it on Amazon.

"Wow. That's…really something," was about all I could manage.

Then he goes, "We should catch up. Go for a beer at The Otheroom for old times' sake."

"Yeah, yeah, for sure."

*Let's do that right after I fucking kill myself.*

# CHAPTER 29

YOU KNOW HOW, LIKE, in the *Twilight* series Jacob thinks he's imprinted on Bella only to find out later that while his werewolf pheromones were on point, his mind made up this whole false narrative to explain the inextricable link he actually had to her yet-to-be-conceived child? Well, falling in love with Judah was kinda like that, without the vampire child bit, and as soon as you are finished judging me for having read the entire *Twilight* series I'll elaborate with another pop culture reference. You see, when I fell in love with Jude, I zinged hard, à la *Hotel Transylvania*. It was a sensation so undeniable, so all-encompassing, that I was sure I was Joan of Arc reincarnate and the Archangel Michael himself had just whispered the name "Judah Levantine" in my ear.

We were in his parents' kitchen. His father was there, standing by the refrigerator with a cup of coffee in hand. Mr. Levantine was the teacher that saved my life in high school and never knew it, and there he was, standing in his kitchen in the house he'd raised his family in. I was no longer his student, but the girl who was dating his second-born son. Judah's mother was there too, standing over the stove stirring.

Mrs. Levantine taught at Santa Monica High as well. The Levantines were the quintessential Santa Monica couple, and I'd been looking up to them long before Jude and I ever began. We stood together in their kitchen before it was remodeled and Jude made a comment about something they'd casually mentioned that hit him deeply. Something about needing a minute to really feel it, and his parents shot him a look they'd probably been giving him his whole life. A look that said, we don't want to discourage you from being as sensitive as you are, but enough already.

Jude tried to play if off like he hadn't caught it. Like it hadn't struck him across the face. I watched him open his heart with deep compassion for the people who had raised him and who loved him so, even in the face of his suffering. I looked deep into his eyes that strained under the weight of all the things he could see in a nanosecond, and I saw right through them, around the planet and all the way back to me on the other side of the kitchen. Those familial subtleties that cut to the core as they bind us with love. The ones that say we love you for who you are but we are also afraid for you because of who you are. I knew those. I had those. And I knew the full extent of that one, seemingly small cut; as if I was the one they'd struck. Right there in that moment I was Jude. It was more than empathy. Total relation. Total immersion. There's got to be a word for that in English because just love doesn't come close. Affinity, maybe? True affinity? Anyway, I called it marriage. It didn't matter if we never signed papers, it didn't matter if the invitations had never gone out. It didn't matter that he had never asked. It didn't matter if he died the next day. We were married there in that kitchen, his parents as witnesses, in that moment. Forever.

It took me a solid ten years from that moment to gain any neutrality when it came to Jude. He was mine forever. Some *Love in the Time of Cholera* shit. He had fully imprinted on me, and no matter the distance I was sure that one day we'd be together again. I wrote him letters I never sent. Sometimes every day. Just to get through the days without him. I put everything into Jude. All the multicolored, bright, delicately designed Easter eggs into the Levantine basket. All into that beautiful creature who couldn't hold it. Who maybe wanted to, but just couldn't.

Next to Ms. Willow, Jude's father was my all-time favorite teacher in high school. He was the kind of teacher that spoke to you as if you were the most intelligent, mature, graceful human being that he'd ever been faced with, and so in turn you'd do your utmost to become just that, if only out of respect for such a man. I'd wait until class ended to tearfully ask him questions about coincidence and The Great Mystery, and he'd exhale deeply through his lips, shake his head, and ask me how I knew I could ask him these questions.

I bet at some point every one of his students thought they'd received special treatment from Mr. Levantine because he was just so damn cool, but I'm sure I actually did. He had a couch at the back of his classroom that we could sit on during the first ten minutes of music he'd play to set the tone for whatever would be explored in the lesson that day. For ten minutes out of the day you'd get to be treated like an adult. Not sit-in-your-assigned-seat-and-shut-the-fuck-up. Not raise-your-hand-if-you-have-something-to-say. Ten minutes of improvisation until he'd make sure the sound receded so expertly from the stereo we dubbed him Master of the Fade. Then you had about thirty seconds to find your seat before you could tell you were taking advantage of his coolness.

And believe me, you didn't want to make Mr. Levantine feel like you were taking advantage. His disappointment was the kind of thing that would haunt your heart all semester. Everyone would saunter to their assigned seats, except for me. There were certain days that last semester of high school, certain songs he'd play, during which a certain darkness that, once touched, couldn't be faded out in thirty seconds. On those days I couldn't move from the couch. Mr. Levantine somehow knew this and would just leave me be, let me move at my own pace, let me decide when I was ready to pull myself together enough to be in class again. He never ever looked disappointed in me. I don't know if it was because of what I was writing under his tutelage, or the kinds of things I'd say in class discussions, or if it was just because he knew that I hung out with his son's friends, and he knew what it meant to be a young girl around the DC boys. I don't know why, but Mr. Levantine gave me the kind of respect and autonomy at sixteen that no one else would.

•••

I'D ALWAYS KNOWN JUDAH peripherally, always wondered what it was like to be him. To have a father like Mr. Levantine. Jude was in DC, but in a way that was unlike any other. He somehow managed to never be around late at night when anything went down. He was in an underground hip-hop group, and even if we'd all gone out to one of his shows he'd rarely be around after. I always liked Jude, but I figured that he probably thought the worst of me on reputation alone.

So it was December 28, 2005. Maurice had a birthday party to celebrate his thirtieth. Maurice had rented two vans for the night and we all met at Nico's in Culver City before heading out to the City of Industry, or some such place, to go go-carting. All of the old faces were there. The Drinking Crew was still going strong more than fifteen years after naming themselves such. I wasn't much into going that night, and dressed like it. Just jeans with turned-up cuffs, an orange thermal, and some blue Sauconys. I don't even think I showered. Not feeling super great about being alive, not super stoked to spend an evening with the boys, not super good at saying no to Isabella yet. She did the whole "come on, Tash," and I did the whole "fine, fine," and we piled in.

Ours was the first van to get there. Isabella and I threw down some Jameson, jumped to the front of the line, took about forty-seven selfies with her digital camera, and raced the track with total abandon until she got eighty-sixed for slamming into the other cars. This was around the beginning of the time when Isabella and I'd be drinking and at a certain point she'd go to the bathroom and come back weird—angry, agitated, paranoid, but swearing she hadn't taken anything. I knew she was lying, but Izzy was known for lying. I was her best friend and certainly no prude. Why would she lie to me about drugs?

I jumped off the track as she was in a shouting match with the manager about their service. "I'm a manager myself," she slurred, "and I've never been treated so poorly in my life. My party is bringing in hundreds of dollars tonight and..." blah, fucking, blahzie blah.

I wasn't in the mood to play Babysit Isabella, so I just disappeared to the back tables with a New Castle to wait until the night was over. That's when Jude said, "Hey, Tash. What's up?"

I wanted to turn and ask him how he knew he could ask me that, but instead I just told him exactly what the fuck was up. And he listened. Really listened. With an ear the likes of which I'd never seen. When I got to the heavy parts he took a deep breath and exhaled audibly through his lips, "Oh, Tash," like he just needed a second to really feel it before I went on. I didn't tell him everything. I didn't tell him about the years before with those boys. I just told him about losing a grip on Isabella, about being tired of agreeing to be places I truly don't want to be, about feeling like I'm under obligation to attend these sorts of things but not knowing why, about wishing I wasn't bound to my past and a van, and I could just say fuck it and bounce.

"I know what you mean," he sighed. "I didn't want to come either, but I have this idea that I'm obligated to these sorts of things too. That it's more important for me to get out of my head and to be social right now, so I force myself into what is really uncomfortable in order to just do something different. But the truth is that I've spent most of the night with these people I grew up with feeling like an outsider, and just wanting to go home too. Maybe this is just the universe pushing us outside of ourselves into something greater. Anyway, if we have to be stuck here tonight, at least we've found an ally and be can be stuck together, with someone who understands and who will listen."

We stayed like that for the rest of the night. Stuck together with someone who will listen. When our friends were inevitably thrown out for doing blow in the bathroom, we hopped into the same van together and went to the Acapulco down the road. When the band started to play salsa hard and fast, Jude asked me to dance. "I'm not so great at salsa," I misled. "Me neither," he smirked, but we were both only telling half-truths, and goddamnit if the two of us didn't manage to have ourselves a good time, discovering an ally on the dance floor thirty miles away from the city we grew up in, surrounded by the coked-out people we'd always known, in a fucking Acapulco.

When the band folded up their brass, and the lights came on, we were still on the dance floor, only now wishing we weren't bound to vans headed home. Isabella, damn her, insisted Jude ride back in our van. We both blushed, asked The Great Mystery to send a blessing to Isabella, and threw tobacco into the wind before we climbed into the back of the twelve-person van side by side. We talked about Brazil mostly. About bossa nova, and the Tropicália greats. Caetano, Jorge Ben, Bethânia. He knew them all. He'd spent his semester abroad in Rio. Spoke Portuguese fluently, told me about all the fresh hip-hop coming out of there now...how all the cats were throwing back to the greats in both hip-hop and bossa nova. The next generation of subversive Brazilian musicians universalizing sound.

Judah fucking Levantine. I should have known.

We said goodbye outside of Nico's Culver City house with a deep embrace, and a deep breath so we could take a moment to really feel it. It probably would have ended there if Isabella hadn't opened her big fat mouth and insisted we exchange numbers. We were both hopeless. A few nights later, the new year upon us, Jude gave me a call. And on the insistence of Isabella, we met up with him and Pete. In a southside corner of Santa Monica, Jude and I watched 2006 crest the ridge in his childhood bedroom, in deep embrace, and deep breath exhaling into each other through our lips. Just kissing.

Well into the afternoon the next day, heavy and hungover, we stirred in his twin-sized bed. Uber Eats wasn't even a seed in its mother's womb and we joked about some sort of breakfast delivery service. Wouldn't that be nice. We could make millions. Jude got up to get us water and returned with his hands over his mouth, eyes smiling. "Tash. You won't believe it. You have to come with me into the kitchen." I covered myself in the button-up he wore the night before, just like they did in the movies, and moved down his parents' hallway feeling altogether glamorous, curious, and totally juvenile. There on the kitchen counter was a simple wax-covered paper plate fixed for breakfast with a note. Some angel neighbor woke up in the New Year, clear-headed and bright-eyed and thought, "I'd better fix Jude a plate today in case he had an awful good time last night." We carried this gift back to his bedroom, in joyful disbelief at the glory of the morning, and fed each other sliced melons and pan dulce before collapsing back into the tangle of slumber.

When we did finally rise properly, the sun had already set. "Come on, Tash. Let's get some proper food," and we eased our way into his car to Thai Dishes on Wilshire and Twentieth. You know, like a date. I was utterly uncomfortable. Not ten minutes prior we were brushing teeth together, shoeless in his parents' downstairs bathroom. Now with white linens, chopsticks, and folded menus a table apart I lost all heart and body and became one giant throbbing brain. Full of thoughts, I fumbled through his questions. Normal stuff, you know, like "I like you and want to get to know you" stuff.

I avoided his eyes, gave him half answers, said something stupid about not needing to fill the space with conversation. "We don't have to do this. Maybe this is just a hookup, and I'm fine with that. I can do that. We don't have to pretend like we are on a real date."

"I'm not pretending," he says.

By the end of dinner Jude was right in front of me, but reaching him felt like an ocean voyage. When we got to goodbye at the threshold of the Levantine house we hugged and I didn't want to let go. I didn't want it to be a hookup. I didn't want to ever lose him.

"Let's go for a walk," I offered. "I don't know what happened to me over dinner. I'm not ready for this to end. Not like this."

He nodded and we walked the south side of Santa Monica, hand in hand, and it all came out. The opposite of insecurity. I told him everything.

Everything he'd wanted to know over noodles and rice. Everything he hadn't thought to ask. I landed harbor and burned the boat. Told him about Skylar, and Mills College, and Isabella, and Dahlia, and needing to move away from it all, but being terrified I was abandoning those who needed me most by doing so. Told him about the baby, and the shame, and about all the dreams I'd barely managed to hang onto. He exhaled deeply through his lips as he listened.

"I know what you mean, Tash. You and I seem bound by a sense of duty to this place, even when we feel like it is hurting us the most. But maybe it's the act of leaving the village that will save it. The trouble is that we've all lost touch with the rites of passage of our ancestors. There's no proper initiation into adulthood, and no preparation for that initiation, and as a result we're left out here struggling through this inevitable shift alone, with no community support, no real knowledge of how to do it, no guidance. Nothing but the instinctual need to move forward. So maybe we make more mistakes than are necessary, and it takes longer than it used to. Or maybe we never properly make it through into our adulthood at all. But don't get down on yourself, Tash. You're just in your initiation, and I'm in mine, and we're doing the best we can with what we've got."

When we reached his parents' front door for a second time we were back to barefoot brushing teeth in the bathroom. We embraced and he thanked me. "That walk was a stroke of genius. And I've got your back, Tash."

It's impossible not to fall in love with Judah Levantine. I dare you to meet that man and try. Try to keep your heart closed in the face of all that compassion, all that sensitivity, all that kindness and consideration. And then listen to his music. Listen to his lyrics. Listen to him talk about race and space. The prison of our minds. Ancestral wisdom and the galaxy of the unknown. The glory of John Coltrane and the power of true healing. The need for apocalypse support groups. The collective struggle to recognize, and to administer our gifts, all in one short life. Listen to all that to the beat of the boom bap and you'll see. You'll see how I was on that doorstep. Lost and found in the power and the glory. In the space where romantic love and godly love become one, then two, then none, then one again. Try as you might to resist, your heart in sweet rebellion will unfold, and the love you have for that man will be an afterthought as you fall so deeply in love with the worlds around you, you'll swear you're rising. You'll love yourself in a way you never thought possible. And then suddenly everywhere you look you'll see yourself surrounded by kin. Every man your brother, every woman your sister, and you'll see the spark of the divine behind all those eyes. Those eyes. Your eyes. They're the same thing.

Judah Levantine is an angel among men, but he is also a man. He's just a man. And I've had so many men before. In very many ways, he's just one more.

•••

IN THE BEGINNING THE feelings were undeniable, but so were the facts. I was leaving, moving to Oakland, for at least two years. Jude didn't know how to be in a relationship without it falling apart. I didn't really care to think about the facts that much. My heart had launched itself into the abyss and my mind was keen to follow. I thought it better not to have discussions trying to figure everything out. Love was love, and the Great Mystery would sort out the rest on our behalf. Jude wasn't having any of it. He spearheaded every meeting and discussion on what was best, safest, healthiest for us both. I came to loathe the very notion of those three things. He'd draw the lines on partnership, commitment, and sex, saying things like, "This isn't a real relationship." I did my best to convince him that he could break through the trauma of his past, that we could hold whatever wounds still existed, mending them together in partnership. The very fact that our deepest wounds were triggered by each other gave me hope that we could grow more than we ever had before. That we could become our truest selves through this process of deep healing, so long as we did it together. Together. I was a damn fool.

We would discuss these things for hours, Jude and I, phones off, face to face, until sunset became twilight became night became *la madrugada* became the dawning. Real marathons of heart and intellect. An intimacy unmatched. By the time I left for Mills we "agreed" that it was healthiest to allow the physical space to dictate the space we were taking in our "not a real relationship."

The night before I left for the Bay was the coldest night I'd ever spent in Los Angeles. I had some people over to the house for a goodbye dinner. Skylar was there, of course, and Izzy, and my family and a few other people who were close then. Jude didn't want to come, said it wouldn't be right, us not being in a real relationship and all. I practically begged, and in the end he relented. Well after the food was finished and the guests had started leaving, here comes Jude. We sat together on the couch in the garage without insulation, deep in conversation, and the temperature outside dropped to thirty-one. I pulled the comforter down off of the loft bed, trying to make him comfortable enough to stay. Trying to stop the night from ending. Skylar opened the sliding glass door of the garage we used to share and found Jude and I sharing a blanket on what used to be our couch. He stood in the doorway in his full-sized wool coat and hat. Scarf and gloves.

"Hey, Tash. I just wanted to say goodbye. I'm gonna walk home."

"What? In this weather?" He shrugged.

"Do you want a ride?"

"Nah," he said. "I'll walk."

"But it's freezing out there!"

He just shrugged again and we hugged. "Good luck up there, Tash."

It'd been a year since Skylar and I'd split. One of us was bound to find someone, but the logic of that didn't matter and I felt all his pain through that wool coat as he hugged me. When he left the weight of moving away slammed through my body and I collapsed on that couch. Jude bristled uncomfortably with empathy.

"Go to him, Tash. I should probably get going anyway. I probably shouldn't even have come."

"No! I'm glad you came. This party was as much for you as it was for him. Please don't go! You could stay the night."

"Tash, I don't think that's best for either of us."

"But we could have one last night together! What would be so wrong with that? Please! It's freezing and I'm sad. Just stay. Please, just stay."

"Oh, Tash," he took a deep breath and exhaled through his mouth. "I don't think that's the healthiest thing for me right now. For either of us. But I'll stay a few more minutes."

•••

FOR THE TWO YEARS I spent in the Bay our "not a real relationship" progressed in much the same way as it did that cold night. Jude stayed focused on what was best, healthiest, safest. Deciding for us both. I stayed focused on the absolute abyss and the irreversible discontinuity of our love. We broke up and got back together every couple of months.

The panic attacks came back with the vengeance of 1,000 burning Arabian suns. Like fall on the floor, paralyzed, I'm gonna fucking die attacks. If I was really lucky, Skylar would call in the middle of one, and sometimes I'd fall with my phone in hand, and I'd have enough strength left to push the talk button. He'd tell me how to breathe. When to inhale, when to exhale. Skylar would stay on the other end of the line for however long it took until I could speak again.

I stopped eating. Not because I was too lovesick, but because I'd get so caught up in what was best, healthiest, safest, I couldn't decide what to eat. I'd drive to Berkeley Bowl and stand frozen at the entrance as people in shopping carts swerved around me. I couldn't even decide if it was better to get a shopping cart or just a basket, and I'd stand in between the sliding doors like an imbecile talking myself out of every possible item of food that popped into my head that I might want to eat. Whether the apple was local enough, whether the peanut butter was too caustic, whether the plastic lining of the bag of tortilla chips had leached too much poison into the questionably organic corn. I'd sit in front of Berkeley Bowl for an hour, just trying to decide something, until all I could decide was to drive back home hungry and empty-handed. Then Skylar would call.

By that time he'd moved up to Santa Cruz for school and I'd ask him what he was eating. What did he make for dinner last night. What he was having for lunch today. How he knew what to choose. He'd tell me to hang tight, and in an hour or so he'd be at my door and we'd go to the store together and he'd say, "Today we're just gonna buy whatever you want. If you see something and your first thought is 'I want that,' we're buying it and you're gonna eat it no matter what."

We'd buy organic pop tarts, and stuff to make pizza, bottles of beer and soda, cookies and chips and salsa, and I'd start eating. Then we would make love. I'd cry, tell him how much I was dying inside without Jude, and Skylar would just hold me, tell me it was gonna be okay, and for a little while I'd feel better. Better enough to get up in the morning and go to class.

When Jude and I would try to be together again a few months later he'd never understand how I could be in love with him and sleep with Skylar and then he'd tell me it wasn't safe for him. I eventually saw the futility of explanation and started lying about seeing Skylar altogether, even if Sky and I just went to lunch or something, just so Jude wouldn't break up with me again before we even had a chance to be together. By my final semester I'd finally convinced Jude we could be partners, like in a real relationship, and we made love and my vagina caught fire. Not in a passionate poetic way, but as if I'd douched with battery acid. It was a rough night. The next morning as I finish packing my car for the final semester in the Bay, Jude and I hugged with the promise of forever, and he asked me if there was anything I was hiding. My conscience got the better of me and I rendered a reluctant full confession. I told him about the times with Skylar when we were apart, and about Chantelle, and that boy named Javier that one night. And that was it. I knew Jude would never be mine again.

Over the next ten years I saw at least a dozen doctors. Doctors at the university who were heavy-handed with sexually transmitted disease medicines, despite negative tests. Doctors at the clinic who assured me it was just a bladder infection, a yeast infection, a urinary tract infection, and were heavy-handed with antibiotics, despite the negative cultures. Specialists who poked, prodded, and shoved tubes up my urethra, heavy-handed with attempts to rule things out. More antibiotics. Prescription diets. No nightshades, not too much salt, no sugar. Daily diaries to monitor pain levels, stress levels, misdiagnosed, undiagnosed, over diagnosed. Creams, essential oils, loose-fitting clothing, oatmeal baths, vaginal steams, and still every couple of months with no obvious pattern my vagina would turn into Vesuvius. It would go away for a year then come back without respite for six weeks.

Thousands of dollars I spent on my broken vagina, and all this time Jude wouldn't see me. It wasn't safe. Wouldn't process with me. It wasn't healthy. Would insist I stop leaving flowers on his car in the middle of the night. It wasn't best. I laid the foundation for the second part of this book in the time it took Jude to come around, to feel safe again in my presence. All those men, and a couple of women, I loved them all in my way, most sincerely, but I didn't fall in love with a single one. That had already happened. That part of my heart was already occupied, and I wasn't about to evict Judah Levantine for any one of them. This was *Love in the Time of Cholera* shit, remember? Fifty-one years, nine months, and four days it took for Fermina Daza to come around. Life is short, time flies, over in the blink of an eye, right? What's half a century between lovers? I could wait.

When we began courting friendship nearly a decade later, I wasn't the same Tash. Even when I couldn't imagine a moment without him and wanted to profess my undying love, I'd take a breath and think of what was best, healthiest, safest for me. I wasn't so terrified of life anymore. I was still alive. Even in the face of unparallel emotion I knew that shit wasn't so critical.

"Do you still love him?" our friends would inquire.

"I'll always love him. Our spirits were forged in the same fire," I'd say.

"Do you still want to be with him?"

"Meh," I'd shrug. "We made terrible lovers, and it's taken me ten years just to get him to call me back when I leave a message. But now we're friends, you know? Like not just friendly. I mean true friends. And I have that forever. I've gotten what I always wanted, even if it looks nothing like what I originally thought. And I'll be damned if I'm gonna fuck that up with romance."

# CHAPTER 30

Sexcon 2007 was the sort of party you inevitably end up at if you go to college in the Bay Area. Born out of queer theory in the birthplace of free love, it was one of thousands of parties of its kind that features live performances, artists, demonstrations, and discussions on all things non-heteronormative. We gathered tightly into the north-facing South Berkeley bedroom as the Mistress unzipped her suitcase and tiredly unpacked the whips and paddles she'd brought for the night. She wore black fishnet stockings with the kind of thigh-high boots you'd find at the Goodwill on Haight and Ashbury. Cheap, made in China, scuffs on the sides, platformed for effect—that kind—with a police costume that comes in a plastic bag, and a black layered wig to boot. She didn't seem to be all that into it. The persona, the instruction, the questions we lobbed at her. Standing awkwardly, sinking into the bedroom carpet in heels designed for the stage and adjusting her wig, probably thinking about what she was gonna microwave when she got home that night, she asked if there were any volunteers.

My roommate Petra shot her hand up and giggled her way over to the wall. Petra in a short dress and knee-high boots stood with both palms flat against the bare white wall, unmoving as the Mistress labored on technique, the effect of different materials on the flesh and the mind, and how to create the illusion of control. "When you have exposed skin like this," she said, tapping Petra high on the thigh, "always start with the paddle to build trust." She commenced with a gentility that was swift and self-assured, but as the room began to awaken with the splat of the paddle on white flesh, thoughts of microwaved burritos gave way to the electrifying erotic static in the air. The Mistress went from "building trust" to spanking the shit out of sweet Petra until rosy turned purple turned blue. I grabbed my Canon Coolpix and sandwiched myself between the white wall and Petra's straddled legs and began to shoot with abandon.

I think some folks pretend to like BDSM because they think it makes them sound interesting and sexy. Then there are others who gravitate toward it because they have a bottomless itch right in their shame region that's dying to be scratched. Still, others go in for the pure ecstasy that lies inside the transformation only pain can create, that profound peace that can only be reached when you push to the other side of your limit, the other side of too much, the other side of the safe word. Some just like to watch, and some folks have a deeply curious nature that lends itself to an exploration of all things. But Petra? Petra was down. Those digital pictures I managed to squeeze out of her face were portraits of pure bliss. A tear in the corner of her eye, a full smile exposing wine-stained teeth, her cheeks flushed like coming in from the cold. P would have stayed there all night if the Mistress hadn't insisted she stop being a greedy little slave.

I took a seat on the carpet next to the futon loft bed, and Petra sort of crouched beside me, doing her best to "sit" as the Mistress asked for another volunteer. This sweet little gay boy in tight jeans, white Jack Purcell's, and an Abercrombie button-up raised his hand so sheepishly you'd swear it was rehearsed. The Mistress brought out the flogger, and brushing the strands of black leather through her stubby fingers, she smiled, "Anyone else?" Another boy, too gorgeous to be straight, scruffy enough to pass, trucker hat, full beard, and dirty Vans kinda shrugged his hand up. Abercrombie assumed the position as the Mistress surrounded the scruffy one's sturdy body with hers, taking his hands as if she was showing him how to tee off. They swung the flogger in tandem to contact. Both boys stiffened straight-backed as a spark of lust and passion shot across the room.

I looked instinctually behind me to see where the fire was coming from and caught the eyes of the adorably skinny, light-skinned Chipster who had been burning a hole in the back of my head. The expression on his face was an identical match for mine. Delight, shock, excitement. He stretched out his hand, this young stranger, and I took it as the primordial chaos of Eros continued to sacrifice lambs for the feast before our eyes.

Dominance and submission was a blurred line. A flipped coin. A ballet on a hair-trigger. The two boys in front of us, each more frightened than the other, kept up their display, shaking and unsure until the Mistress took mercy on them and said, "Well, why don't you introduce yourselves to each other before you continue?"

The boys shook hands and we all joined in their laughter at the absurd formality. All the while the stranger and I holding hands, partnered in eroticism. The boys were at it again with about a dime's more confidence, and with each new whip of leather the dime multiplied in our eyes until it was raining silver Roosevelts in that tiny college room. With every strike the scruffy one would caress Abercrombie with such tenderness you couldn't be sure if it was his sub or himself he was trying to soothe. Each energetic shift on display, subtle or not, launched through sweaty palms and sparkling eyes until the stranger and I found ourselves in golden tears of galactic desire. Riding comets between Neptune and Uranus and shit.

When it was over and we hadn't aged a bit, the stranger and I embraced, electric blue, like we were old lovers. "My name is Javier," he said.

"Natascia. I am Natascia."

"Wow," he breathed like my name was made out of toothpaste. Pepperminted and So Fresh. "So how about it, Natascia?"

"How about what?"

"Come upstairs with me?"

"Maybe some other time."

"Some other time? Fuck time. Were you not just there with me? In the stars? Time is an illusion! There's only now!"

"Nah, this isn't going to work on me tonight. What we had was enough."

"Ugh. Will you give me your number then?"

"Fine, fine," I rolled my eyes, already resenting him for making it all so profane.

I looked over at Petra like it was time to go, fast. She took my hand and we piled into Noelle's car, back up to the ivory hill in the ghetto of East Oakland, to our apartment on campus at Mills College School for Women.

"What happened between you and that boy, Tash?"

"What do you mean, P?"

"What do you mean, what do I mean? You were both glowing, heating up the entire room. Why didn't you go home with him?"

"I don't know. I don't want to have to explain myself to Jude."

"Wait, are you two back together again?"

"No, but it won't matter. He'd never understand."

A few weeks later Petra and I went to see Cake perform at Hertz Hall in Berkeley. It was right after Jude emailed that he thought it was best for his process to not have contact right now. I thought it was best for my process to drink a bottle of Jägermeister and call that one boy from that one night. He took BART to Ashby and walked up to The Graduate on Durant to meet us for a pint after the show. We made it through half a beer before I got impatient and took him to the twin bed of my college room high on the hill. When he took his shirt off I was stunned by the most beautiful paisley tattoo in sapphire blue that cascaded from his neck down to his left wrist.

It turned out to be the only breathtaking thing about him.

I dropped him off by the Berkeley Flea Market the next morning. We kept in touch some. At least up until he told me he worked in "fragrance," which upon further investigation translated to working retail at the mall. That was a wrap forever on that. Not because I'm shallow, or whatever. But because if I slang shirts at Forever 21 it doesn't mean I work in textiles, okay? Don't be a douche.

Several months later Jude and I were doing our best to partner each other again, and I got an envelope in my PO box on campus. Inside was a CD-ROM with Sexcon 2007 and the photographer's name printed on it. I ran up the hill, turned on my Dell laptop, and shoved it into the disc drive. Photos from that one night in South Berkeley. The ones I had taken of me nude on a ten-foot crucifix in the room adjacent to the demonstration by the Mistress. They were beautiful, vulnerable, erotic…just like that night. But the disc didn't just have photographs of me like I was promised. The photographer included shots of everyone who had volunteered to be on the cross that night. After flipping through a half dozen, I open the next file, and there's Javier, the stranger with the sapphire paisley tattoo. Stark naked. Beautiful, vulnerable, erotic…just like that night. I smiled. The two of us. That night. Uncorrupted by sex. Moved. Exposed. And free.

# CHAPTER 31

Hooking up with a girl is just like hooking up with a guy. I don't care if you both have vaginas. It feels the same when she doesn't call you the next day. Or the day after. Or the day after that. At least that's the way it was with Chantelle.

We had the same Intro to Ethnic Studies class at Mills College. It was one of the few classes that held more than twenty students at a time. About forty of us lumped together awkwardly in the medium-sized lecture hall to hear the professor fall in love with the sound of her own voice singing tunes of colonialism and cultural appropriation. She wasn't big on class participation, but I wasn't big on paying $33,000 a year to be lectured to through freaking PowerPoint and said as much one morning after watching a series of images highlighting the similarities between anti-Muslim advertising campaigns for the army and Hollywood movie posters depicting "terrorism." The sheer magnitude of inception was as uncanny as it was disturbing. I audibly guffawed, along with many of my classmates, and then I lost it.

"I'm sorry, Professor, I know this isn't a discussion class, or whatever, but I can't do this. We all just laughed at some of the most grotesque displays of violence and dominance and desperation, and I'm ashamed of myself. I'm ashamed of all of us. And I get it; we get bombarded by this shit everyday out there, and then we dissect it in the ethnic studies department, but look at us. We're becoming desensitized to it. I mean, come on. What's the use of studying it if we don't also discuss ways not to become desensitized? To not dissolve in the face of all this suffering and laugh? Am I alone in this?"

Chantelle raised her hand and spoke first, then Mary Jane, and then it was off. The discussion took up most of the rest of class. Our professor was not impressed, but after that day when Chantelle and I would walk by each other on campus, she'd hold my gaze just a little too long for friendship. She eventually made me give her my number, and when Medusa came into town we had our first and last date in an upstairs club in downtown Oakland.

Chantelle wasn't all that into underground hip-hop as far as I could tell, but Medusa's power is undeniable. You really don't have to know what you're getting into before you realize you're already a fan. We walked into the club, and thank God it was all ages, because it turned out Chantelle was barely twenty. I ordered a double Makers on the rocks. Chantelle ordered a chamomile tea. The bartender and I exchanged a micro-look, both stunned by the audacity of a bedtime beverage half an hour before the headliner. He opened his mouth as if to say you gotta be kidding me with this shit, but then thought better of it, shrugged to no one in particular, and said, "Let me see what I can dig up." After disappearing into the back kitchen for a few minutes, he came back with a fucking teapot, a big-ass teacup, and a saucer.

"Do you have honey?" she asked.

I paid the tab, now committed to sitting at the bar while this beautiful but extremely young girl sat waiting for some dried flowers to steep and some boiling lava water to cool. I ordered another double Makers rocks in the time it took her to finish, left a huge tip for good measure, and tried not to take anything personally as I contemplated my life decisions up to this point.

Medusa came out sporting a bleach-blonde Afro, gold doorknockers, a camouflage jumpsuit, pristine high-top Timberlands, and murdered it. Chantelle was clearly enjoying herself, but all I kept thinking was how much I'd rather be at that show with Jude. I hadn't heard from him since he'd left a few months earlier for Canada to record some music and isolate himself in another deep process that didn't include me. When the show ended the Fuck It took over and I went back with Chantelle to her tiny dorm room in Ethel Moore Hall. She turned on the electric kettle, more tea, and we went at it while the rooibos went cold on the bookshelf.

The next time we had class together I picked fresh lavender from the gorgeous craftsman I moved to that Petra's dad had bought for her so she didn't have to live on campus anymore. I wrapped the stems in pink sewing thread tied with a bow and sat in class in front of Chantelle like a *stunad* as she proceeded to ignore me for the duration of the PowerPoint light show. When our professor was done lecturing on the evils of globalism,

Chantelle walked out without looking at me, and I, like a big old dummy, grabbed up the fresh-cut lavender wrapped in pink sewing thread tied with a goddamned bow and walked out behind her. By the time I gathered the courage to open my stupid mouth we were past the Mary Atkins Center, clear across campus. All possibilities of looking cool had dissipated across the two acres we'd traversed like that.

"Hey," I called out. "You ever get the feeling like you're being followed?"

She turned and gave me a sideways smile. I handed her the lavender like some sort of Sapphic salvo, and was all, hey, I like you, as I stood there with my thumb up my ass. But she kept on ignoring me for the rest of that semester, and by the next one she had a girlfriend.

During my final semester at Mills College in a class called Outside Poetry Movements, Chantelle and I met again. "I didn't know you were such an amazing poet," she said after class the first time I shared. I rolled my eyes at the obvious flattery that fell flat.

"To be fair, Chantelle, you don't know anything about me."

"Maybe you could help me with my poetry one day."

"Oh, you write too?"

"I try," she offered. Then I couldn't shake her. All of a sudden I'd become interesting to her, useful. Would I come to such and such poetry slam? Could she come over after class to read me what she was working on? Could I give her some notes? Help her write poetry? What an absurd notion, helping someone else write poetry. I mean, don't get me wrong, we can all learn how to become better writers, but I'm kind of a traditionalist when it comes to talent. You've either got it or you don't.

Chantelle came over one evening after class to read me something she was working on called "The Girl with Green Eyes." The next forty-five seconds that passed from the proclamation of that title until she looked back up at me are forty-five seconds of life I'll never get back. Then she goes, "So...what do you think, Tash?"

*I promise you, you do not want to know what I think.*

And just when I thought that nothing could make the moment more dreadful, more strained, more awkward, she smiled and said, "It's about you, ya know."

Any grasp on decorum, the few pink threads of manners I was holding onto unraveled, and I laughed in her face.

"What's so funny?"

"Uh," I say, sarcastic as fuck. "Look at me, Chantelle. Really look at me." She still didn't get it. "Are you colorblind or something?"

"Not that I know of."

"Dude. My eyes are unmistakably blue."

Both of us were gassing with total abandon at her and that poem, full of false sentiment, forced eroticism, and bullshit.

"What, did you write that on the way over here?" I asked.

"Well, I guess I ruined my chances with you, huh?" she giggled.

We were friends after that. How could we be anything else? We stayed friends through the semester and after graduation. I moved back to LA after failing miserably to land a full-time job while the banks were being bailed out. She'd come down to South LA to visit family and stop over in Venice to hang. She still tried to date me, bringing single roses and shit, but it wasn't happening. When I'd go back up to the Bay I'd hit her up for coffee, or lunch, or a couch or something. You know, like friends do.

The first time I stayed with her she was already collecting disability. This good-looking, young, strong black woman who was passionate about union labor and Audre Lorde, who loved nothing more than to get up early in the morning, put on a tie, and spend the day in her very own office getting jobs for other people, who took a tremendous amount of satisfaction in being helpful. This woman who had dreamed of a professional life, a career, and a desk job, opened up about the periodic total paralysis of a still undiagnosed disease. We went out that night to see some spoken word. She wore tight black jeans with turned-up cuffs, a plain white T-shirt with rolled sleeves, and tucked her natural hair into a faux pompadour. I wore high-waisted extremely tight banana-printed shorts with a long-sleeved black fitted crop top and knee-high, lace-up, tan leather boots. We were both standing in front of her bathroom mirror, checking each other out, and she handed me a stick of Cover Girl Lip Perfection called *Hot Passion*.

"Here," she said. "Put a little red on."

Namazzi and Helena were there with us too. Helena and I were still keeping what we'd done with each other the week before a secret from Namazzi, and things between us three were still copasetic. There's a picture of the four of us that night, having a stupid good time, looking young, happy, queer, and gorgeous. There were a lot of pictures that night. Polaroids at the club and selfies on the dance floor. Chantelle couldn't drink, but she made sure I did. Later, when we got back to her apartment and Helena asked about the sleeping arrangements, I sent her into the guestroom with Namazzi and tapped her drunkenly on the shoulder when she asked where I'd be sleeping. "I'll be in bed with Chantelle."

Helena looked at me through heterochromatic eyes and said, "I thought she had a girlfriend?"

I gave her two baby blues back to the dome and said, "That, my dear, is not my problem."

The next morning, bleary-eyed, her body entangled in mine, I tried to focus my lenses on the handmade posters surrounding her bedroom. Affirmations and aspirations in Magic Marker and Sharpie. Long-term goals listed in descending order: going back to work, the gym, getting off disability. Short-term goals: showering without help, walking to the front gate and back unassisted. Staying positive: gratitude lists, gardening, meditation, watching documentaries.

"Good morning, my Italian beauty," she stirred.

"Oh, Chantelle, you've really been going through it, huh?"

"Yeah," she sighed. "I don't know." She looked up at the posters, shrugging. "It could be worse. At least I can walk again. And having a garden helps."

We all went to Mother's for breakfast that morning and she told us about her amazing girlfriend, Naima, and how supportive she'd been through all of it. Namazzi, ever the meddler, opened her mouth. "Girlfriend? So, like, do you two have some kind of agreement that accounts for you and Natascia last night, or what?" Chantelle and I shot each other a bashful glance.

"She's a musician and she's on tour a lot," Chantelle reluctantly responded.

"Uh, huh...so?" Namazzi goaded. "Does that mean you have an agreement?" Namazzi never knew how to quit.

Chantelle shifted in her seat. "So, we don't sweat each other about what happens when she's out of town."

"What do you mean, like you have an agreement to open the relationship when she's out of town? Is it an explicit agreement?"

Chantelle looked up at me, smiling uncomfortably. I cut in, staring at Namazzi, "Well, whatever their agreements, I'm sure it's none of our business, Namazzi."

"I don't know, Tash. It seems like it would be precisely your business." *And she wonders why Helena wanted to keep us a secret from her.*

"That may be true," I said, gritting my teeth. "But that doesn't make it your business by default, so let's just drop it, yes?"

"Fair enough," she gave in.

We paid the check and went back to Chantelle's to pack up. When we said goodbye at the top of her driveway, we kissed deeply in an embrace. "I'm glad you found someone who has your back, Chantelle. And I'm always here for you."

The next time I was in Oakland she and Naima were out of town together, but she gave me their place for the weekend. I bought her some flowers and lavender essential oils as a thank you.

A few months later I was back in Oakland and we kept trying to meet up. Maybe for coffee, maybe for a drink, maybe for lunch. A lot of "okay, I'll call you back in an hour or so" that amounted to nothing. Eventually I had to catch a flight home. I've hit her up on Facebook since then, called and left messages, sent numerous texts. Nothing. Years later when I was diagnosed with Hashimoto's disease, severe adrenal fatigue, a cocktail of hormonal imbalances, and a couple of herniated disks, I thought of Chantelle. When I could barely get out of bed or even move without experiencing severe pain for nearly two years, I thought of Chantelle. When it got so bad I didn't recognize my own face in the mirror; when I didn't exactly want to kill myself, but I just didn't want to live anymore in constant pain, I thought of Chantelle. I thought of her naked in bed, surrounded by her homemade posters, shrugging and saying, "It could be worse."

It took about five years to come out of the woods with all of my maladies, but honestly, it could have been worse. I still haven't heard from Chantelle, though, and unless this book becomes a bestseller, I expect I never will.

# CHAPTER 32

In 2001 Avi Feinstein and I were comparing senior class polls over a lunchtime joint. "Who'd you put down for Best All-Around, Avi?"

"You," he answered. "You and me."

Huh. I never figured myself for best all around. Avi for sure, but not me. Never me. But Avi said it like a given, like who else would he put for Best All-Around?

•••

My first week back in LA after Mills College, Avi, Spencer, and Ford moved in together in one of those semi-commercial, heartless, stucco tower apartment complexes in Culver City. It'd been years since anything remotely resembling high school held my interest, but there I was, unemployed and living with Mom again, so I figured what could it hurt to hang out with high school friends? I met Helena for the second time at their housewarming party and we really hit it off. Someone snapped a Polaroid of that very moment. She and I sitting on the couch by the balcony, both illuminated in the light of kindred spirits, deep in recognition—but that's another chapter altogether.

Avi and I had a long conversation that night, too, on the balcony about the state of the recession. He'd miraculously landed a job with a record label and managed to not get laid off during the crash. I was lamenting brokenness personified, flashing my EBT card and financial dependence. "Where you are right now is not your fault, Tash. And you'll get a job and your own place again. Give it some time." Best All-Around. You and me.

We hadn't really kicked it since high school, but we'd always gotten along so well, apparently holding each other in the highest regard. He started inviting me out all the time. Dinners, bars, parties. Anytime that gang was together he'd take it upon himself to include me. I felt special when I was with those guys. Lucky, bright, equal. We'd been cool before, but my head was so far up my ass in high school, I just never thought any of them had a real interest in me. I was a total burnout. A smart burnout, but a burnout nonetheless. They were hyper-intellectual, talented, and witty as all get out. While I was doing blow in bathrooms they were studying for the SATs and taking AP Spanish and shit. Artists, musicians, wordsmiths, student council members. We sort of all came together over ganja, though. That was level ground.

Senior year after buying PJ a three-foot bong for his birthday, we informally referred to our haphazard gang at the Varsity Bong Rippers (VBR for short). Still, aside from getting high at lunchtime or seeing them at parties on the off night I wasn't kicking it with Dali or the DC boys, I was kinda on the outside. When PJ and some of the other guys started a group called Artists Anonymous and asked me to be in it I was beyond flattered. I went to one meeting, maybe. I don't remember. I hadn't really kicked it with anyone in my grade past middle school, but that first semester of my senior year, before moving to Italy, there was VBR, and Artists Anonymous, and even though I felt like I was on the outer edge of the perimeter, it felt nice to be included.

Eight years later I was on the immediate call list. I still felt like I was on the outside looking in, but Spencer kept trying to make me laugh, Avi always wanted to know how I was getting along, and Ford's bluegrass jazz revival band always had a show or something we could go to.

We went out to the Circle Bar on Main Street one night. Someone was having a birthday. I was with the non-burnout cool kids, so fuck it, Circle Bar, sure. I could stomach that place for just one night. They played music from a decade ago and we danced. All of us. Together. And then it was just Avi and me. We kissed. It wasn't half bad.

He spent the night that night with me in the garage. We kept all our clothes on, just kissing like we were in high school again. I was tense about ruining our friendship. In the morning I offered to give him a ride home and he kissed me and replied, "Nah. I think I'll enjoy the walk. It'll give me a chance to think."

Maybe a week later I went over to their apartment. Sat on the couch with Avi as Ford and Spencer played on the Indo Board and tried to outwit each other, quoting scenes from shit movies like *Air Bud 2* and *Beverly Hills Chihuahua*. Spence was always partial to movies that featured animals in heroic roles. Ironically partial. You know, just another night at their apartment in Culver City or whatever, drinking beers. But then everyone started going to bed. I went with Avi into his room.

"I don't know what this is, but your friendship is important to me, and I don't want to lose it over sex," I implored.

"Agreed."

Yet the moment we got started was the moment we lost it. I don't think I spent the night. Or if I did, I certainly didn't want to. I hit him up a few days later to check in. Just to talk about what went down. "Hey, Tash. I just found out my mom has breast cancer. You're right, we should probably talk, but I just can't right now."

Avi's mom fought hard for the next five years. When she died, I spent the afternoon babysitting Avi's niece so everyone could be at the wake together. Avi and I didn't really talk again. Not like we used to. When we did talk or see each other it was always strained. I drank more at Ford's band's shows, and when Spencer and I finally started our affair, I began hanging around again, but it was never the same. By the time PJ died from a heroin overdose nearly fifteen years after we bought him his first bong, in one way or another I'd managed to fuck up friendships with all three boys in that apartment. If we had a revote today, I don't think a single one would write me down for Best All-Around.

# CHAPTERS 33 AND 34

AROUND 2005 THE GAY bar on Channel Road called The Friendship turned into the über-hetero douche club called The Hideout. I'd just broken up with Skylar and was trying to remember who I was before him. The night started at Dahlia's, digging through her closet trying to find something to wear, something sexy, something hip, something that didn't make me look like I was someone's girlfriend. When I laid down with three-year-old Logan to read him a bedtime story I was in an ill-fitting handkerchief short skirt with far too much pattern, a camel-colored faux cashmere sweater with an oversized turtle-neck, some cream-colored stockings, and my tan, knee-high, lace-up boots from Italy. By the time he'd fallen asleep, Dahlia's patience for me to try on another half-dozen outfits had expired.

"I look fucking ridiculous, Dali."

"Who cares? You look fine. Let's just get the fuck out of here before Wanda changes her mind about watching him."

We pulled into the Rite Aid on Lincoln and Lake and pulled back out with a bottle of Jim Beam and a Coke. By the time we hit PCH there was mostly just Coke left and I thought, "She's right, you know. Who fucking cares?"

I never knew how those impromptu high school reunions happened. It was usually around wintertime, summertime, spring breakish, and all of the sudden you'd show up to a bar you never go to in the off-season and everyone you don't really want to see is there. Kinda like it used to be going to the promenade in the nineties, except we were older, and alcohol was legal and expensive. I drank a few beers and chatted with people I didn't give a shit about anymore until I spotted Spencer Bloom in double across the room.

"Hey, Tash!"

"Hey, Spence! You know, I had a big fucking crush on you in high school and was always too chickenshit to do anything about it."

"You're fucking with me, right?"

I smashed my lips on his. "Not fucking with you."

It got hot fast, and we stayed like that, pushed up against the wall at the old gay bar until the lights came on. He tried to get me to stay or go with him or give him my number, or something. I laughed and waved goodbye. *Better quit while I'm ahead and conscious.*

A few months later Avi was in town from Argentina and had people over at his parents' house. We drank Fernet-Branca and Coke in a mansion north of Montana and I tried to convince myself I belonged there with those well-adjusted people and not pissing booze in a back alley with Dahlia and who knows who. High school all over again. Spencer was there, being Spencer. Charming, sassy, and delightful. I was all clammed up, dropping the wit ball every time he pitched it. Still, he showed a lot of grace that night, displaying interest but not too much. Nothing creepy or strange. Certainly nothing to warrant the suspicion and disdain I shoveled his way when he walked me to my car and asked if I wanted to hang out.

"Hang out where? Your parents' house?"

"Uh, yeah," he scoffed uncomfortably.

"And do what, exactly, Spence?"

"I don't know, Tash. I'd just like to spend more time with you."

"You mean you'd like to fuck me?" *Jesus, Natascia.* "No, thanks. I'm good, Spence."

Whether it was the case or not, I couldn't stand the possibility Spencer just wanted to fuck me, and for a reason that still eludes me, that thought generated a resentment I was constantly at odds with every moment I passed beside him. He was too smart. Too clever. Too charming. If I couldn't be his, I don't know. I think ultimately it meant that I could never be any of the things I thought of myself on a good day. Reject him before he could reject me. Textbook playground. Does it get any more basic bitch than that?

So now we're back to post-recession 2009. Overqualified and underemployed, bartering food stamps for rent in my mom's non-insulated garage. Bridget and I had been friends since we were little at camp. We first met when she climbed up on my bunk bed one winter camp and proclaimed, "I'm Bridget! I'm on a sugar high!" In 2009, she was also living at her mom's about half a mile away, sitting on a master's degree, begging for jobs at various retail outlets, and being degraded by Sunday family dinners and chore charts. Other than searching for jobs we didn't want anyway, and stressing out about having no money, B and I didn't have shit to do. We spent most of that year riding bikes around the neighborhood looking for some trouble to get into. Something to drink. Some boys to party with. One of those nights we ended up hanging with the dudes from my grade and when the night was a wrap and I made noise about wishing it weren't, Spencer suggested the three of us grab a bottle of champagne and head to the beach. B wasn't super into the idea, but I wasn't going to risk Spencer alone, so she obliged as a favor to me because that's what besties do. We took turns on the shoreline somewhere north of Station 26 drinking the Moët I convinced him to buy us.

The unfortunate thing about being a redhead is that your emotions are just as transparent as your skin. An "everything is fine, I'm fine" from Bridget has a passive-aggressive weight greater than or equal to a blue whale landing on your forehead. Even if she's mostly fine, despite her best efforts to conceal it, the .000001 percent of her that isn't fine is all "SEVENTY-SIX TROMBONES LED THE BIG PARADE!!!" Poor old B is like the princess and the pea when it comes to being annoyed, and with the champagne nearly empty, Spencer and I enraptured with one another, and the post-midnight breeze from the bay not getting any warmer, if I didn't figure out how to get Bridget in, the night would really be a wrap. Somewhere in all this Spencer decided to kiss me, and when he kissed me I grabbed her. *If this is gonna happen it's gonna be memorable. And if he's going to reject me, he's going to have to reject us both.*

She really wasn't that into it, but who would be? I was third wheeling her hard, and to her credit as a friend she let me. I pulled her underwear down, telling her to just relax and try to enjoy it right before I drunkenly kicked sand into her vagina. Then she was pissed and I had to plead with her as she walked away. "Please, B. I'm crazy about this dude and I need you tonight. I can't do this alone. Please, just come back with us to the garage. I'll owe you one."

"Fine, Tash. Fine."

When she finally gave in, she gave in all the way. The three of us burned pretty bright on the loft bed Skylar'd made me, taking turns being the center of attention. It was all fun and games until it came time to watch the two of them together. It was all I could do to not murder them both in a jealous rage. His body in hers. *Is she even enjoying it, or is she just pretending for our benefit? Does he like her more than me? Do I repulse him? Look at them! They're not supposed to be enjoying this!*

I don't remember much past the jealousy, other than turning away and falling asleep while they continued. I do remember waking up in the morning in the middle of the two of them. Spencer along the wall reaching out for me trying not to wake Bridget, and Bridget at the edge with her back to both of us pretending she was still sleeping. Our kissing got to the point of too obvious to ignore and she "woke up" hungover, disgusted, and pissed off. She got up and gave a forced goodbye that sounded a whole lot more like, "I hope you two assholes are fucking happy now."

The moment the sliding glass door closed Spencer held me and joked, "I thought she'd never leave." My whole body shuddered in ecstasy as I realized he'd kinda meant it. Then he turned 100 percent adorable as he put his chin in both palms, lying on his stomach with his knees bent, feet in the air...

"So...what was your fourth grade teacher like? What was your most embarrassing moment? Have you ever been in love before?"

I blushed, and answered with some quip about my first childhood crush. We spent the morning together like that, trying to outwit each other, a banter in half-truths about our deepest fears and desires. He might've even told me he really liked me. I might've even allowed myself to believe it for a few minutes. He said that he'd never been in love before, that he wasn't even sure if it was a real thing, and even if it was he was pretty sure he wasn't capable of it. Not in a self-deprecating way, or anything, but in the way that some people's brains just aren't wired for hypnosis.

We made love all morning and it was sweeter and sadder than the night before. We slept with each other for a while after that, but the curse of resentment never really left us. Each time, no matter how much I was enjoying myself, I'd do something to fuck it up. One night we were on the beach just the two of us and I tried in earnest to have a conversation about what we were doing with one another, basically soliciting the possibility of a relationship, and I looked him dead in his eyeballs and said, "You know, it's crazy. I don't think about you at all when you're not around. When you're in front of me I just want more from you, but the second you're out of sight you just don't occur to me."

Yeah, I said that. I mean, it was true, and I was sort of fascinated by the fact that Spencer was the only dude I'd ever had romantic notions about that I didn't privately obsess over, but if I was trying to be this dude's girl, telling him that he wasn't in my thoughts wasn't really the move. One time we were lying in his bed together in the morning and started arguing about self-defense. I took the position that killing is wrong, in whatever form it takes, and even if someone had a gun to my head and the only way to live was to kill them I wouldn't do it because then I'd have to live the rest of my life having taken someone else's and it wasn't worth it. He strongly disagreed, and what began as a hypothetical philosophical exploration turned into an overly emotionalized argument about the validity of the other person's worldview. I got dressed in a huff, told him to go fuck himself, and left.

But it wasn't all me. It wasn't all my fault we didn't work out. Sometimes Spence would hit me with these totally inaccurate assessments on how I viewed him and I'd think, I didn't generate that. I couldn't have. Like the night I'd gone to visit him while he was still tending bar on Venice Boulevard and told him about the time Bridget and I played Marry Fuck Kill with him, Avi, and Ford.

"Oh, please don't tell me this, Natascia. I don't want to know how fast it took you to kill me."

"What? No. Kill you? Are you fucking kidding me? I killed Ford. I already fucked Avi, so that was easy, and I don't know. Maybe it's totally fucked up. I like Ford and all, but I'd fucking kill myself if I had to marry him. But you and me? I could be happy with that. Even if we fought all the time, you're the only one I could marry and feel like it I stood a chance at being happy in life."

He didn't believe me. He didn't believe me, and I didn't believe him. That's how we carried on for a couple of years. Sort of just hate fucking our projections of rejection on one another.

# CHAPTER 35

GENERALLY SPEAKING, NOTHING GOOD ever comes from a night at The Daily Pint, and more specifically nothing good came from Halloween night at The Daily Pint 2009. I was dressed as a skeleton for the third year in a row and he was dressed as one of the dead football players from Beetlejuice. We both had our faces fully painted. He had a massive, gorgeous Afro picked out to the extremities. Our painted eyes locked. He told me his name was Juan. I let him have my number.

He called and we joked about not knowing what the other person looked like under all that paint. He picked me up one afternoon and said, "It's so nice out, let's grab a beer by the beach." When he pulled up to Cabo Cantina on Washington Boulevard my eyes rolled into the back of my head and more or less stayed there as he bored me with stories of fantasy football and growing up somewhere irrelevant in LA. On the way back to my house I was in the middle of answering one of his asinine questions when he leaned over and full-tongue kissed me mid-word. Ugh. The audacity.

He kept calling. Like all the damn time. I kept turning him down, not picking up, not calling back. He kept not getting it. Like a debt collector. I finally just said fuck it and one Tuesday afternoon I let him come to the garage and when I was done, he kept wanting more. "Let's spend the day together," he said.

"Uh, I have to leave for work, or something."

One afternoon I was walking off a bean and cheese from Holy Guacamole with Isabella on Main Street, and I looked down at my phone to the unsaved number blowing me up. This is getting out of hand, I thought. Enough already.

"Juan?"

"Hey! What's up? How are you? Where are you?"

"I'm fine. I'm on Main Street."

"Wow! I'm in Santa Monica too! With some friends. Where are you gonna be? We can come and meet you! I miss you!"

"Juan, listen to me very carefully. I don't like you. I have no interest in you, or in ever seeing you again. Please. Stop. Calling. Me."

Izzy's mouth was agape as she watched me wrap that call. "You're a real bitch, you know that?"

She was probably right, but you know what?

It. Did. The. Fucking. Trick.

# CHAPTER 36

GORDON WORKED WITH BRIDGET at Top 2 Top. My girl had a master's in Anthropology, and had worked on excavation sites in Greece, but the only job she could get in 2009 was slanging running shoes to housewives in Santa Monica. Damn recession. Gordon was tall, extremely white, and extremely skinny in that unnatural I-run-long-distances-our-bodies-weren't-evolved-to-sustain way. He once fitted me for a pair of Brooks that were singularly responsible for the shin splints that followed and still plague me to this day. Turns out my feet aren't pronated in the least, Gordon, so thanks for your expert retail advice, bro.

There was a group of them who worked together, lived together, and who'd wake up at four in the morning to run Mandeville Canyon together. Bridget started kicking it with these dudes all the time. She ended up dating the brother of one of her coworkers. He was a real dud. They all were, but B was my main squeeze, and if she was kicking it, I was kicking it. I even woke up once for a sunrise run. Gordon wasn't terribly attractive. Not terribly unattractive, but not that far off. All right in that sort of limited way for an off night.

I don't know why or how I ended up in bed with him. Damn recession. But, you know, he wasn't half bad. In fact, for a skinny white dude a stone's throw away from ugly it was shocking how good he was. So we did it a few unremarkable times more until he started dating someone he saved in his phone as "It Girl." They married a month or so later and I left for Germany to keep a pact with Skylar that resulted in the beginning of the end of our friendship.

# CHAPTER 37

SKYLAR AND I RETURNED TO Munich in 2009 to keep the drunken pact we'd made that first Oktoberfest together in 2003. No matter what our lives became, in six years we'd come back to Germany to be together again. In 2009, Skylar'd started dating Moira, and for some inconceivable reason, despite the warnings I'd given him after witnessing the fall of my relationship with Jude that he should be honest in every moment with her regarding his friendship with me, Skylar thought it was a good idea to wait until the day before I arrived to email Moira and let her know his ex-girlfriend would be joining him for the next few weeks in Europe. To be fair, even though we'd made the pact, I was on the fence about going until a couple weeks before the flight. You know, the Great Recession, unemployment, food stamps, etc. Getting on a plane to Germany to drink beer for the better part of a month wasn't exactly the most responsible decision I could make at the time, but the economy was fucked, there wasn't much I could do about it, and a pact is a pact. So I sold the fraction of what was left after the crash of the mutual fund I bought with the leftover money Nonna gave me before she died and hailed the Millennial battle cry all the way across the Atlantic. YOLO!

Johnny Pine kept emailing me about getting married when I got back, and would I rather live in Hawaii or Germany or some other place, and would I hurry up and let him know so he could put in the request when he reenlisted to be stationed there. And Skylar? Well, when Moira found out the night before I arrived, she lost it and broke up with Sky on the spot. Skylar was a wreck and took it out on me. I'd ruined his plan of avoiding the subject altogether by deciding in the final weeks to fly out. No amount of "I'm not mad at you" and "it's not your fault" could mask just how mad he was, and how much of my fault he made it. He treated me like I was a nuisance. Wouldn't even sleep in the same room as me. Wouldn't touch me, even in the friendly way you would an old pal. It was just like we were dating again.

Skylar drank a lot that Oktoberfest. I'd always been accused of being the lush in the relationship, but at the end of September in 2009 you'd have never been able to tell. I stayed sullen and silent. Someone had taken my best friend and replaced him with a drunken cocksucker who couldn't care less if I was around or not. After a week in Munich with Amos, Skylar and I rented a car and drove around Belgium, just the two of us, like we used to. I could tell he hated every second of it. By the time we were in Köln at the end of the trip it seemed like Sky had just about had enough of my ugly mug.

I barely drank that trip. Too many bad memories. Wolfgang who was nowhere to be found, our breakup after New Year's on the bridge in 2005, and now the ending of the most important friendship I'd ever had, I was for the first time in my life too depressed to drink. Skylar left Germany before I did, and he barely said goodbye. Things were never the same between us again.

In the days that followed before my flight out, I got two emails from back home. The first was Dahlia telling me that not only was she pregnant again but that Roberto baby daddy *número dos*, had been arrested while I was away and was in jail awaiting trial. The second email was from the Chaplain at Mills College whom I'd grown very close with, informing me that our mutual friend, Ruth, had walked into oncoming traffic on 580 near the Seminary Avenue exit, and had been struck square in her bones by another Mills girl on her way to class.

The last time I'd spoken to Ruth I'd already graduated and moved back to LA. I could barely follow her. She called me because she said she kept being called to, or whatever, and began raving about angels and the divine in all things. About how she woke up thinking about her friend Sarah and how that same day her server at Zachary's Pizza happened to be named Sarah and isn't that amazing. The great synchronicity of life was more or less the subject, but she could hardly form a coherent sentence between the laughing that sounded like crying, and the crying that sounded like she was staring into the eternal joke. I was just crying, plain crying, sitting in the parking lot of Aahs on Wilshire and Franklin, trying to be there for a friend that was a few planets away. I didn't know it had gotten so bad, but I knew there was no way to reach her. Nothing, at least that I could do. So I just listened. A month later she was dead.

I took a connecting flight the next day from Munich to Paris. From Paris to Los Angeles. From Los Angeles to Oakland. And from Oakland International Airport straight to the chapel at Mills College. I sat there in the pews beside the Chaplain as the organ wailed for Ruth. We held hands listening to friends and family tell stories. When the service ended, and the family went home, the Chaplain and I sat on the patio outside the Mary Atkins Center for Returning Students, and we shared a couple of cigarettes and a beer in private, away from the rest of the mourners and students who needed her. We spoke frankly about death and suicide. About Ruth. Neither of us could stomach the notion that people who take their own lives are cowards. We talked about the possibility, however taboo, that maybe, just maybe she'd acted bravely. That she'd taken the mercy life hadn't given her by walking into the freeway. That maybe she just couldn't live with the pain any longer, no matter what new method or medication the doctors tried. And that in a state of total mania she'd tapped right into the source and it consumed her, so she gave her life to God in the only way she actually could. That poor girl, the one on the freeway, on her way to class. The one who woke up that morning not knowing she had a meeting with Ruth and Death. She was the one to worry about. To send prayers to. Not our sweet, soft-spoken Ruth. She was home.

•••

I CAME BACK TO Venice Beach from Oakland a few days later. Isabella was dating this dude she'd end up spending the next phase of her life with. A local boy of the white conservative Venice variety, now a son between them. Before I'd left for Germany the two of them had tried to hook me up with Buddy Davis so we could all, like, you know, hang out. Buddy was cool. Used to hang out with PJ before he OD'd. A graffiti artist. Buddy and I had gone out one early morning together. I got halfway through my first official piece before SMDWP rolled up on us and we had to abandon our art and about fifty dollars' worth of spray paint beside the concrete creek in Rustic Canyon.

There was nothing between Buddy and I. Just an idea that wasn't even our own. When I got back from Germany via Oakland, the idea was mostly gone. Isabella and her dude were now a full-fledged couple and didn't need the excuse of a group hangout to be around each other. Still, she managed to convince me to go to Buddy's house on the north side one night with her to meet "the boys." I was kinda just numb and didn't protest. In his bedroom, lying in his bed, I started to tell him about Johnny Pine. He told me that while I was gone he'd started seeing this girl he "really liked." We shrugged. Did it anyway. And then we lay there, talking into the morning light. Before I left he reached over into his nightstand and gave me a silver ring with a green jewel. I wore it for a while to remind me of a life of bad decisions. A year later, after joining the cult and committing myself to slaying the fucking dark demons within I took that ring to the ocean at Breakwater and threw it in.

# CHAPTERS 38 AND 39

AFTER TAKING A COURSE called Women of Color in Social Movements in the ethnic studies department, I abandoned all possibilities of having a leisurely two years at Mills. I launched myself headfirst into the wonderful world of Liberal Arts, dedicated to getting a double degree in deconstructing the learned racism that lived like rot inside of me. It was a real dick move. I mean, I'd already spent four years at community college pursuing the fuck out of my interests. I could have just transferred into that expensive-ass school and enjoyed my life taking Photography and Book Arts and shit, but I was all, fuck it...I'd rather have an aneurism. I'd put in a conservative thousand hours in the study of psychology at SMC, and I'd like to say that the psych department at Mills put up more of a fight, but the truth was that it was pretty easy to convince my advisor that in my case an exception could be made to give me a degree with the minimal requirements. Regardless of the fact that no one in the department really knew me, I negotiated only one psych class per term, and I put all my focus into getting an ethnic studies double major before giving up my final semester after one too many panic attacks.

The ethnic studies department was blowing my little white mind on the daily. The hijab as a symbol of political resistance? Anti-vagrancy laws as a funnel into the prison system for the post–Civil War South? The continued legacy of slavery in professional sports? Fascism in the Zionist movement? The fuck out of town.

I met Mary Jane in one of those classes. She was the only other white girl in class, but if we were going on skin alone, you'd be hard pressed to identify one color. Mary Jane's body was like Joseph's Technicolor dream coat. Most of the white was covered with psychedelic tangerines and turquoise, bayou greens and lightning lavenders, thick black lines like three-ring binders snaked in ancient foreign wisdom around her legs and a Hebrew band that said Hashem knows what took hold of her other, non-sleeved arm. Branded, pierced, and colored, with pixie hair hellfire red and two jade half-dollars stuffed into her stretched lobes. Even at a liberal arts women's college, Mary Jane was hard to miss. After some impassioned rant on queerness and mixed races I must have been hard to miss too because she beelined to my desk the instant class was over. "Hey, I'm curious about what you said today in class. Wanna grab a coffee?"

*Oh, great. The two white girls in ethnic studies, thick as thieves.*

"I'm having a hard time in this class," she says, sitting on the lawn behind the main building, sipping a latte through a cardboard cup. "Do you ever feel weird as the only white girl in class? Like you are being held accountable for all the things white people have done?"

*Oh, shit, here we go...* "No, I don't personally feel like I'm being held accountable, but I get it can be rough unpacking some of this shit they call privilege, and facing what's been right in front of you your whole life, but you've been too blinded by your own whiteness to see."

"I don't know," she says. "Don't you think racism can go the other way?"

*Fuck me.* "What do you mean, Mary Jane?"

"I mean when I was in Ghana visiting my boyfriend I stuck out like a sore thumb and the people in the village treated me differently because I was white. I mean, I had to line up with the rest of them at the well to wash my clothes, and you should have seen the way these women looked at me."

"Okay...but I don't think that's racism. Racism is about the institution-alized oppression of a group of people. White people haven't been system-atically oppressed. They've been the systematic oppressors, so you can't re-ally call reverse racism on a group of women in Ghana wondering what a white girl covered in tattoos and plugs is doing vacationing at their well."

"What about Jewish people?"

"What do you mean?"

"I mean, the Jews were slaves, and were systematically oppressed around the world."

"Are you Jewish?"

"No."

"Oh, you just have Hebrew on your arm...I thought...well, um...being Jewish is complicated, and, uh...sure, our ancestors were slaves, but that didn't stop Jews from participating in the transatlantic slave trade. Or the fucking Palestinian apartheid. So, yeah, we have a history of oppression, or whatever, but you can't really compare the racism experienced by Jews in the US to the racism experienced by African Americans."

"Huh. I don't know. Don't you feel like what you have to say is less important because you're a white person talking about race?"

"I don't know, Mary Jane. As white people taking these classes we have to be extra vigilant and sensitive to the wellspring of thought from which our questions and discomforts arise. We are sitting in classrooms full of women who have been told they are less important most of their lives. I think we're just coming face to face with our own privilege, and we have to come to terms with the fact that in these classes what we have to contribute is not that fucking important." She went quiet. I felt bad.

"So," she looked at me. "Where do you stand on cultural appropriation?"

"Uh, in what sense?"

"Like if people get tribal tattoos and stuff. Like what if they really research a particular ritual and it strikes a chord deep within them?"

I shrugged. "I don't know. I mean, I get the inherent harm in cultural appropriation, but I try not to judge people on their past. We all do things that we may regret later on, and we hopefully all learn things along the way. Far fucking be it from me to judge."

She nodded, asked for my number, and despite our whiteness and questionable positions on various topics, we became thick as thieves.

I guess I liked her. Most of my life up until that point had been filled with obligatory friendships, people who had been around for years, shared a history and a neighborhood. Mary Jane and I had no shared experience, no personal history, not really any of the same ideas or anything like that. But I'd watch her sometimes get into these conversations where she'd be telling a story, and when she'd get to the part where the black woman said something she'd change her voice and her head and neck would go wild. Or other times when she'd just have to mention someone's Jewishness, as if it was a contributing factor into what happened, and I'd think, what the actual fuck? Did she actually just say that? Can I actually be her friend? But I don't know. She would also call me up in the middle of the night to see if I was okay, or she'd get on her bike in the rain and drive across the bridge for me if I was lonely and needed company.

Whenever Mary Jane wilded out I just didn't take it personally. Her shortcomings weren't mine. When everyone else would lose their shit about the overt racism in her arguments and would leave the room, I'd just stay and look at her bewildered and incendiary face and laugh gently when she'd ask if I thought she was wrong. I wouldn't fight fire with fire; I wouldn't take the bait. I'd just take a deep breath and speak to her like the beautiful intelligent person she actually was and remind her of the importance in accounting for your own shit before calling other people to account for theirs. With me, MJ would at least consider the error in her ways. And maybe, I don't know, was there an attraction there? "Is there something that I'm sensing between us?"

"I mean, I'm with Kwame and even though he's in Ghana we have an agreement to remain monogamous."

"Uh, yeah, but I'm not tripping, right? There's something there."

"I don't know, Tash. Even if there were, I wouldn't act on it."

"Sure, sure. I support you in your long-distance monogamous relationship, or whatever. I'm just asking if you feel this too."

Mary Jane ultimately transferred out of the ethnic studies department into political, legal, and economic analysis. She spent the better part of her time at Mills studying the cacao trade in Ghana and being chaste. Still, in the end, Kwame left her. Maybe it was the fact that they only saw each other once a year, or the fact that she didn't want kids, or the way she spoke of the people in his village while histrionically avoiding the term "uncivilized." Or maybe, just maybe, monogamy is an absurdity we all try to fit ourselves into to prove that our love is real and true. Mary Jane and Kwame were worlds apart. Seven piercings on your vulva or not, love doesn't conquer all.

After Mills she went to Mexico for the summer with her friend Hanson and got her Hebrew armband covered with Aztec art before she started her graduate studies at Columbia University. From my understanding, Hanson and MJ had been friends for over a decade. She met him during her piercing, stretching, suspending, branding, and tattooing years in San Francisco. They somehow managed to maintain one of those rare male-female friendships without having sex. At least until I came along.

I'd met Hanson a couple of times already. He'd come up to the Bay and stay at MJ's on the air mattress when he was in between countries or permaculture communities. Where Mary Jane was fire and brimstone,

Hanson was river water and clay. The gauges in his ears were twice the size of hers and contrasted deeply with his unmistakable whiteness. Hanson could talk for hours about indigenous irrigation systems, rainwater collection, and how to compost human waste properly. He was the kind of guy you'd expect to meet on a train somewhere, lounging beside his backpack in dirty socks and hiking boots, ready to tell you tales of his travels in South America and how the best night of his life was the time he'd gotten drunk with some such indigenous tribe in Peru who use their own saliva to process and ferment the purest alcohol. Hanson was the kind of dude you felt like you had to keep around in case of the zombie apocalypse. Like, in case you got through the worst of it and somehow managed to stake claim on a piece of land and all the canned goods have long since been opened and the threat of starvation and malnutrition have long since surpassed the threat of the undead.

I liked Hanson just fine, which is to say that I wasn't really attracted to him. Not at first glance—or second, for that matter—but I liked him just fine. Mostly for the ways he'd diffuse the occasional bomb that was Mary Jane. He'd known her longer than anyone else left in her life, and compared to the way he would skillfully listen, steady his breath, and keep an even tone in the face of the outlandish shit that would fly out of her mouth, I was a rookie. Hanson had a way of making all parties feel seen, heard, and valid that might've earned him an honorary degree in family counseling in a different world. While I didn't initially have an attraction to him, after several years of encountering him in passing I found myself totally surprised at just how sexy a man who listens can be.

Hanson and Mary Jane both came to visit me in the garage one summer after traversing the jungles of Oaxaca or Chiapas or some such place together. I'd gotten my first Brazilian that afternoon and wore my all-time favorite extremely short blue babydoll dress with tiny pink flowers on it. The three of us piled into their rental and went to dinner at Real Foods Daily, where I asked Hanson a dozen questions about being Type 1 diabetic. He told me how he managed it on a daily basis and how he would have a conversation with every woman he slept with about birth control and protection because he hated the disease so much he was determined not to pass it on to a child.

"Wait, so you've never had unprotected sex? Like, even on accident?"

"No way. I don't have sex on accident. And I always use protection."

"Always? Like what if the girl doesn't want to or is allergic or something?"

"Then I don't have sex with her."

Then an hour-long conversation on whether or not it is the duty of intelligent people to reproduce ensued over tempeh. After our overpriced vegetable dinner was split three ways, we all had the feeling like we didn't want the night to end. "I don't really do bars," he said, so we pulled into the same liquor store on Pico where Spencer bought us champagne that one night with Bridget. MJ threw down forty on a bottle of Woodford Reserve, and by the time we were halfway through it I started fishing for compliments in that self-deprecating kinda way. The let-me-make-you-laugh-at-all-the–things-I-hate-about-myself-until-you-adore-me shtick. Hanson started blushing and giving me the "no, you're so beautiful" spiel and I was all "no, stop, stop...go on."

When he told me what I had been doing to him all night in my favorite blue babydoll dress with the tiny pink flowers on it, Mary Jane got up to go to the bathroom in the main house and laughed. "Okay, you two. You behave while I'm gone now." As soon as the sliding glass door closed behind her, I looked at Hanson.

"What about Mary Jane?" he protested.

"Oh, don't you worry about her," I offered, brimming with bourbon. "I'll take care of her." When she came back in through the sliding glass door, sheepish and feeling left out, take care of her I did.

The night carried into morning with the three of us entangled, and not a stitch of latex between us. When Mary Jane and Hanson broke the seal on their friendship in the very same spot I'd watched Bridget and Spencer, not an ounce of raging jealousy surfaced. In fact, in that moment I couldn't have cared less about either of them.

# CHAPTER 40

Y OU'RE NATASCIA, RIGHT?"
"So?"

"I'm friends with Helena. I've looked at pictures of you on her Facebook page."

"Well, that's a helluva thing to admit to."

"I bartend here."

"You don't say?"

"Yup."

"Well, I come in at least twice a week. Gjelina's my new fave."

"Stay put, I've got something for you."

That was how we met. Me and the blue-eyed bartender with curly hair and a crooked smile who went by Jay. He brought a bottle of wine to the table with a plate of prosciutto, burrata, and peaches. "We're closing up soon," he says. "Stay put. I'll bring dessert. We'll talk."

So stay put we did. Me and MJ. Firm in our wooden stools at the community table, feasting with Bacchus on the fermented vine in the Elysium of artisanally cured charcuterie while the restaurant slowly emptied and the lights turned on around us. True to his word, Jay brought out a yogurt panna cotta with blackberries, the rest of a bottle of prosecco, and three spoons. We talked, all right. Boy howdy. Through the counting of the tills, through beers with the bussers and dishwashers, through the locking of the doors, through the parking lot on Electric Avenue, and right into the garage on my street.

It still shocks me to this day when I think of what happened next. I mean, this dude had practically set the stage. From what I could tell then, and what I came to learn about him later, Jay wasn't exactly the most scrupulous or modest of men, especially when he'd been drinking. Which was practically never not a factor. We kept talking a little, and we kissed some. Mary Jane was passed out by that time, but the dude who'd just spent the night coming at me with the swagger of two hundred horses, who'd just robbed another bottle of champagne from his job for the party to continue, couldn't quite get over the fact that she was sleeping in the loft bed right above us. "What about your friend?" he asked, looking up at Mary Jane, who was unmoving.

I shrugged. "She's cool."

"Walk me to my car. We'll do this another time."

It was the summer of 2010. A year where the summer actually passed us by entirely on the Westside. The first time the whole global warming thing could really be felt in the neighborhood. We spent the entire summer waiting for June gloom to pass. Sweating under the overcast sky, praying for the relief of the sun to break through, to lead us down to Station 26 like it had always done. But this particular summer no such relief was possible. Just sweat, and clouds, and fog. Endless grayscale.

We started seeing each other once MJ went back to Brooklyn. In the beginning it was always like that first night. The decadence of mushroom toast and smoked trout at Gjelina, the stumble of stolen bottles of half-poured bubbly on Electric Avenue until finally we'd reach the loft bed in the garage. It really wasn't as glamorous as I'm making it seem. It was good fun, sure, but it was the kind of fun you get playing five-finger filet. It's just a matter of time until someone's sweating off the hangover in the emergency waiting room. The first time we slept with each other was like two engineers playing chicken with the company freight trains. Neither of us would yield, and the next morning I awoke in the disaster of shrapnel and smoldering pyres, battered and bruised. *What the fuck was that last night?*

I sat back on my knees, my legs folded under me, and looked up to the loft bed where that beautiful young boy still slumbered, surrounded by torn sheets, broken condoms, and house plants with snapped vines and tossed soil. Everything ached.

We didn't say much when he woke up. Barely looked at each other. *Did he actually enjoy that?* I wondered, rubbing the back of my head with heavily bruised arms and shook a wad of hair loose. *Did I?* It was too dark. He drove me back to my beige Corolla in his blue one, and just when I was thinking I'd never like to do that ever again, "Touch Me" came on the radio. We rounded the corner on Redwood and Washington, and before I could even roll my eyes, Jay started drumming in perfect time. In the air, on the dash, the steering wheel, the window. Black curls flying, flailing, and begging for adoration. Every crash of the cymbal, double time on the snare, hi-hat, clutch foot on the base, ride, ride, splash. Fingers twirling drumsticks that weren't there. It was almost enough to get you to like The Doors again.

Jay wasn't the sort of boy you liked. Not at least if you cared about life. He was a vortex of shadows masked in charming intoxication. He wasn't the sort of boy you asked after. Not the sort of boy that if you did ask after you'd expect to hear anything good. Not boyfriend material, as Helena put it with a scoff. Not that I fucking wanted to know, you understand. Not me. Not that gray summer in 2010. I didn't fucking care either way if he never called me or texted me back. I wasn't a fucking idiot. I knew he'd never be my boy. He'd never be anyone's boy. We coulda been twins. We carried on some that gray summer that never came.

We carried on, until we didn't. Years passed.

By the time Helena came to live with me in my tiny one-bedroom on the south side of Santa Monica, I hadn't seen or spoken to Jay in damn near four years. He came pouring through my front door, black curls twice as long, fully bearded with cowboy boots and a black snap-collared top with embroidered roses on the shoulders. Helena and Jay hadn't seen each other in a while either, but the moment he walked through the door it was like she wasn't there. I tried to disappear into my room, give them space to catch up, but he kept including me in everything he was saying, shouting, "You know what I mean, right, Tash?" through the apartment like it was me he'd come to see.

"You'll join us for dinner, right? Say you'll come. Say you'll go back there and put on a dress. We'll wait."

I was still kinda mad at this dude for having more or less ghosted me, but the next thing you know I'm slipping on cowboy boots and a white short sleeved babydoll dress, looking like Dolly freaking Parton on her wedding day, walking side by side with Jay in his denim and black rose garb down Highland Avenue to Venice Beach Wines, practically hand in hand while Helena tried to keep up.

"I can't wait," he kept saying. "I can't wait until I can walk down a street I have no memories on." He'd leave for Austin a few months later, for a life that didn't include drumming, that didn't have a dysfunctional family, old friends, or memories of his hometown.

That night, over cheese plate and brut rosé, he told us everything in his heart. Everything he'd thought and felt about his life. Everything I'd always wanted to know from him. I wanted to think it was because Helena was there and they'd been pals for so long. It made logical sense, after all. Why else would he open up to me like that after so many years? I guess it was mostly because of Helena, but when he asked me to join him out front for a smoke and we were away from her ears at last, he told me all the dark things locked behind his crystal blue eyes. Staring into the abyss. Seeing your own end. "Please don't tell any of this to Hells. Promise me, Tash. She doesn't have the darkness like we do. She won't get it. And what she won't understand will just worry her. And I can't have that on my conscience too. I have to do this, Tash. I have to leave this place or I won't make it to thirty. I'll drink myself into an early grave or end up like James Dean, or something. I won't make it. Not again. There's nothing here for me but memories."

We embraced through brut rosé tears. Helena found us like that on the sidewalk with a face like how the fuck did I become the third wheel? Jay snapped back into full charm when he saw her. "Let's get out of here," he smiled. "Let's not let this night end. What should we do?"

"I've gotta wake up for work tomorrow," Helena scoffed. "It's already eleven."

"No, Hells! Don't go! Come on! We're young!"

"I've got a fresh bottle of bourbon at the crib," I piped up.

He beamed. "Ah, a woman after my own heart."

We walked back up the hill to my house and drank until Helena fell asleep on the futon in the living room, which only took about fifteen minutes. Jay and I comforted each other in the bed above while the bottle of bourbon lay empty on the floor below us.

The next few months I had him as I'd always wanted him: around. Sometimes he'd just show up at my house in the morning. Me, still in my underwear drinking espresso on the couch with Helena. He'd saunter down the steps to the backyard with the peppertree, uninvited but always welcome. Puffy and hungover, he'd collapse on the couch muttering prayers for breakfast. We'd get dressed and walk down to Venice Beach Wines, running into young girls he knew with big sunglasses and expensive clothing sized extra small. The New Venice. Jay would greet them in embrace, pouring out his charms and making plans for later that night. Then over orange juice and coffee he'd pull my legs up onto his and fall into my breast. Droplets of whiskey escaping through the pores on his forehead, curls a tangle. He'd hand me the menu. "What do I want?" he'd ask me.

"You want a breakfast burrito with chorizo," I'd answer, and he'd squeeze me with a sigh of relief.

"You know me so well," he'd exhale, and wouldn't move from that position until the server came. Then it'd be full attention and charm until she'd giggle and we'd end up paying for only half of what we ordered.

Other times he'd come over at the end of a night out with girls with big sunglasses and expensive clothes sized extra small. Down the steps to my bedroom window. He'd pry it open with both hands, and with only enough words to keep back the tears and the spins he'd fall into my bed. The midnight hour ours again. Helena asleep in the next room, never the wiser.

Our last night together was much like our first. Hostile, aggressive, slapping, pulling, scratching, both of us fighting for the throne. Gone was all the tenderness and the grace to acquiesce. Something snapped in him that night and I pushed back with all I had. Through the window, in the shower till the water ran cold, on soaked sheets. Neither of us climaxed that night. We collapsed—bruised, torn, sore—and gave up around dawn.

He hid under the blankets when Helena came in that morning to use the bathroom, waited until after she left the house to speak. "What the fuck was that last night?"

"You tell me, Jay."

"I didn't like that. Scared the shit out of me."

"I didn't like that either. I kept trying to get away from you, and you'd chase me down."

"I thought you wanted it. You kept fighting back like you wanted it harder."

"I didn't like that. Let's never do that again."

And we never did. He moved to Austin a few days later and made his way as an apprentice in the BBQ world. Jay eventually welded his own smoker and took off across the country to bring smoked meats to the people. I came across an article in *Food and Wine* magazine one summer with his picture in it. He's puffy and red-eyed under his full black beard and curls, but he made it to thirty. Still alive.

# CHAPTER 41

I DON'T KNOW WHY I was back at Billy's mom's house that day. It was the summer, I tried to tell myself. The phenomenon of Santa Monica, like the Bermuda Triangle. Countless ships lured in to their own end. The voiceless cries of mayday over dead radios. It was the summer. Billy's mom had a pool. It'd been long enough. I was just gonna hang out with my friends. Bygones. No big deal.

Genevieve was there. Disappearing with Nico. I wore a bikini, and feigned confidence. Patch was there too, and despite having rejected him after he tried to convince me that it was okay if we fucked because Jude was "totally over me," and I needed to "just get over it," Patch and I were still friends that summer.

He'd gotten a DUI and called Ricky—yes, that Ricky—after one of his court-mandated AA meetings to declare that he was serious about getting sober. The craters on the sea floor in the Santa Monica bay sucked me farther and farther into a loop where time and content just repeat themselves.

I waded up to him in the pool, and Patch, beer in hand, gave me the long, drawn-out "Taaaaaaaaaaaaaaaaaash!" I threw the obligatory "Paaaaaaaaaaaaaatch" right back and we embraced through chlorine and booze like we'd been doing since the nineties.

"You drinking again?" I asked.

He took a sip. "You know what they say in the program, Tash. It's progress, not perfection." Ninety seconds later V came out of Billy's old room rolling on molly and collapsed on the plastic chaise lounge, chewing her cheeks and asking if I wanted any.

Johnny Pine called from Oklahoma right when I was losing faith in all humanity, and I stole into Billy's old room for privacy. I sat on the mattress, listening to Johnny slur out another marriage proposal, and wondered what remnants of my ruin I might find if I pulled up the sheets to inspect the mattress.

V rolled into the room. I mouthed "Johnny" to her and rolled my eyes, and she handed me a red plastic Solo cup dripping with condensation and mouthed "vodka" right back.

By the time I got back to the pool I was sucking ice cubes. Maurice Milton smiled at me. I smiled back. He refilled my cup. I let him. V disappeared into Billy's old room with Nico again. Maurice pulled me into Billy's little brother's old room. Gone were all the WWF action figures. Gone was the twin-sized bed I'd faked my virginity to Cole on. Maurice pulled down the new Murphy bed from the wall and I just laughed. "Come on, Tash. It'll be fun," he promised. I closed my eyes and prayed Jude would never find out before asking Maurice if he had a coin in his pocket. He flipped it. Heads.

# CHAPTER 42

BRIDGET'S YOUNGEST BROTHER WAS conceived in total darkness, on a moonless night, in a field surrounded by spirits of the recently deceased. Still too stuck in the stupor of their former lives to finish their business, the spirits convened a perimeter around Maggie and George Swift, who themselves were in the throes of a union bound to its own end. As curling mist engulfed a final attempt to make it work, pathetic fallacy wrinkled time to foreshadow inevitable divorce. A lone coyote cried out in anguished longing for the return of its beloved moon, half a breath before being mauled by the last black bear hiding in the Santa Monica Mountains. In the very moment where the life of one creature means the death of another, an icy shot of hope reached out to the final willing egg. The majestic death rattle of Mother Nature. The circle unbroken in orgasmic grace. Nine months later, to the breath, Jordan was born. Cue the cellos.

•••

IT WAS THE YEAR of the Great Recession, and 2009 rang in like the slow descending tone of a slide whistle. In a time when a couple of college degrees and six bucks would buy you a pint at the Alibi Room (unless you were good with bartenders and then, of course, each night was all you could drink). In a time when unemployment spread like the black plague, and student loans were worn like fashionable albatross on velvet chokers. In a time when we should have been busy becoming young urban professionals, but the banks and the bailouts gave us no other choice but to become young urban degenerates, Bridget and I were ace number ones. Living at home with Mom wasn't where we saw ourselves at this point, but it wasn't without its perks.

All of the Swift kids were back with Maggie in 2009, only this time Jordan, the youngest, got his own room. "It's his time," Maggie would say. "The rest of you had your turn. It's not his fault that his finally came when everyone had to move back home." So Bridget and Victor shared the bunk bed in the back, while Jordan, despite being the youngest, had his very own room with his very own bed and his very own side-door entrance. Jordan had grown the fuck up since I'd last seen him as the sullen blond baby-faced camper.

Maggie's fridge had a seemingly endless supply of string cheese and boxed juice despite her three children being of legal age, and when we couldn't scrape enough loose change out of the couch for a bean and cheese at Holy Guacamole, B and I would gather snacks and hang with her mom in the living room to watch *Project Runway* until too early to go the bar became late enough. Netflix had just started streaming, but marathoning TV shows wasn't really a thing yet, so if Lifetime was playing last week's episode before this week's we'd settle in, stoked to get an extra dose of a reality where art, vision, and talent could still translate into money and fame if you were totes cool with working yourself sick while watching the dreams of your peers die around you. I'd like to say that the televised promise of young talent reaching for what dreams may come offered us some solace from our dismal prospects. I'd like to say that Tim Gunn's "make it work" tagline struck us in our heart of hearts as inspiration to squeeze more lemons with gusto to sell on the rag-tag street corners of our childhood homes. I'd like to say that for those sixty minutes or double that on a lucky day, we had a break from the bullshit post-apocalyptic economy we'd inherited from our parents' generation.

I'd like to say all that, but right when we were starting to feel like maybe someday we too could translate our intelligence into financial security, a commercial break would interrupt to remind us of all the shit we'll never be able to afford, zero percent APR financing or not. Then the long list of side effects for another antidepressant hollered at auctioneer's speed would follow. Nausea, diarrhea, applying for forbearance, trouble sleeping, panic attacks, dry mouth, over-excitement at finding a folded twenty in an old jacket, living at the mercy of your elders, an increase in alcoholic consumption, blurred vision, vomiting, sexual problems such as increased sexual desire and decreased orgasm. Ask your doctor if Zoloft is right for you. Whatever fantasy we were having in draped silks and tailored leather was no match for the flashing glow of 2009 pouring out from someone else's Costco flat-screen TV. Picking Cheez-Its and fruit roll-ups out of my molars, biding my time until the Alibi Room opened, caught between the existential angst of gratitude and resentment for our parents, I looked over at Jordan spooning up a Snack Pack and winked. By the next commercial break I knew that he knew that one of these nights I'd be by after the bars closed.

I snuck into his mother's house well after midnight. All the Swift kids with bellies full of broccoli and cheddar cheese lay safely asleep, save the dark one who was expecting me. Jordan and I shared a shockingly intimate loving embrace on a moonless night. He was younger and less experienced, yet it was as though for that brief moment the shape of his melancholy conformed to the shape of mine, or vice versa, and our bodies had known each other all along. When it was finished we sat on the step of his side-door entrance and shared a cigarette in silence. Placid in the still of the night.

It wasn't supposed to be like that. It was supposed to be forgettable. Regrettable. But it was good. Really good. Good enough to land him in the top five for a few years. It shouldn't have been as intimate as it was. Something moved through us. Some old married couple that'd recently passed. Him from a stroke, her from a broken heart, mounting our bodies for one final embrace before crossing over. Anyway, sitting there on the steps below the few stars the city lights would allow, I lay my head on his shirtless shoulder, way more comfortable than I ought to have been and thought, yeah…we should do this again.

Four years later and a lot of shit went down in the interim. Jordan had gone AWOL a few times. He'd had some trouble—with the law, with his meds, with his family—but he sent me a Facebook message and insisted on taking me out for my birthday. In the three years I'd spent "erasing my personal history" with the Intimacy Project, I'd distanced myself from Bridget and the Swifts and anything that reminded me of who I used to be. But at the end of 2013 my ties with the cult were beginning to unravel, and despite the collateral damage the Intimacy Project had inflicted on my former life, when I got his message on my twenty-ninth birthday, my rebel heart was all, fuck it. For old time's sake.

We went to the rooftop of some Hollywood hotel where the manager owed him a favor, and over painstakingly small bites of duck and toast we talked of the passing of time, the neighborhood, our families, and our feelings.

He'd changed a lot. Sort of numb around the edges like someone on the wrong dose of lithium. I knew right away I wasn't going to fuck him, which made being on a *date* date practically unbearable. If it were anyone else, I'd have bailed before dessert with some overly blunt statement about precisely how disinterested I was in continuing, but it was Jordan Swift sitting across from me under all those meds. In the parking lot under the hotel we said an awkward goodbye, no kiss. When he hit me up a few nights later I wasn't sure if it was a hell no, or a hell yes, so I was like sure, sure, fine, I'll meet you for drinks at the Alibi. He showed up in orange board shorts, flip-flops, and a hoodie looking a whole lot like a hell no. We drank dirty martinis and smoked Marlboro Reds and when it was time to shit or get off the pot I thought, meh, fuck it, for old time's sake, and we went back to my place.

At my one-bedroom in Santa Monica, the full moon shined down through the peppertree and lit us as we tangled up in each other like strangers. It was nothing like it had been before. No melancholy, no tenderness, no unfinished business of longing lovers recently deceased. Somehow the awkward fumbling had caught up to us, and four years after the fact, we finally assumed the roles of older, more experienced woman and inept younger boy. All the intimacy and nuance was gone, and in its place was the parasite of difference. I cared deeply for Jordan and still do, but when it was all done I couldn't bear the sight of him.

In the glaring martini morning, I watched the hours pass to *I Love Lucy* reruns in the waiting room of the Westside Family Clinic. Ignoring Jordan's texts of "I'm really sorry" and "is there anything I can do?" I popped the Plan B that took nearly four hours to get and decided I never needed to do that again.

# CHAPTER 43

I'D WANTED WARREN BENJAMIN for about four years. He was always the thing I looked forward to at any of Barry's camp parties. The hopeful thing, the exciting thing, the something different and new when being beside a very cold and aloof Skylar got to be too much. Camp parties were always great, don't get me wrong, but surrounded by the same old faces in the same old solid relationships beside your failed one didn't exactly stoke enthusiasm in the depths of me. Warren Benjamin was the antidote. Tall, darkish, and extremely skinny, just like I like 'em. He had a giant smile that barely held in his massive white teeth, and always wore a Yankees hat broadcasting New York in the sexiest way possible.

In four years I never really talked to him. Never really flirted with him. Never really let on that I was all that interested. I always just floated around whatever circle he was in. Like, if he was hanging out on the balcony smoking with a couple friends, I'd go on the balcony for a smoke too. But I wouldn't really try to strike up a conversation or keep one going or anything. I'd just awkwardly ask him for a light and then more or less feign disinterest.

I never thought I was pretty enough for him. When he'd occasionally bring a girlfriend around, I'd be positive I wasn't pretty enough. He liked the lululemon and Ugg boots pumpkin spice latte in the day, bodycon dress with stilettos and chardonnay at night type. Girls who cut themselves off after two drinks and go to bed before midnight. Girls whose bathroom counters are filled with products and grooming appliances. Girls who work in big office buildings and wear their hair in ponytails to go running, or worse, to the gym.

In December 2010, Barry and Rose finally tied the knot under an arbor in Palm Springs. I brought Bridget as my date, and Skylar brought Moira, who had the good sense to wear white to someone else's wedding. Just to show how much I was totally over it and really happy for them, I sat on top of Warren Benjamin in the hot tub and made out with him while he fingered me through steaming chlorine. Skylar and Moira retired shortly thereafter; Barry and Rose were back in the honeymoon suite in love forever; and at a wedding that ended too early because the DJ charged by the hour, in the shower in his hotel room, with no one but God as my witness, I fastballed the Warren Benjamin fantasy into the catcher's mitt of harsh reality. Forty-two notches on the bedpost became forty-three because other people getting married in public just really brings out the best in me.

•••

A PIECE OF UNSOLICITED advice in case you're just starting out, kids. If you have a fantasy about someone, or something—not a dream, mind you, but a fantasy—a shiny beautiful, effervescent little story in your head that comforts you on occasion when you need it most—hold dear to it. Guard it with everything you've got. And for heaven's sake, whatever you do, don't let it crossbreed with reality. Not only will you be sorely disappointed, but never again will you be able to go back and be soothed by it in the moments you need it most. Because it turns out that most of the time reality sucks a crooked, skinny, circumcised dick, but fantasy—fantasy just might save your life one day.

# CHAPTER 44

THE LUNCHTIME QUAD WAS bustling in that hushed, all-female, liberal arts sort of way. Six dozen voices being heard, six dozen ideas being shared, six dozen thought processes being listened to, validated, encouraged, seen. No one talking over anyone else. No one interrupting you to say precisely what you were saying in a slightly different way. No one competing for your attention or admiration. No one taking credit for someone else's thought. All sources cited. Six dozen women under cherry blossom trees in springtime bloom, drinking soy lattes and herbal iced teas, eating salads with grilled, wild-caught salmon. Discussing the medical impact of environmental racism, the political and economic impact of colonization in urban planning, the psychosocial legacy of cultural genocide, the generally agreed upon importance that queer theory plays in anything from education, to policy, to literature, to medicine. Discussing the next rally, protest, conference, open mic, film festival. Six dozen ways to get involved.

He was standing with all my new friends like he owned them, saying something about the injustice of having to fight the administration to accept his queer studies major as an independent study. I walked up cautiously, captivated by his confidence. He stopped mid-sentence when he spotted me. "I'm Mickey. Who are you?" Mickey had a way of making you feel like the world disappeared around you when he looked into your eyes. Like you were the most interesting thing in the room.

Mickey was dating some girl named Daisy and sleeping with my friend Rebecca, who was dating some other girl whose name I can't remember. Not everyone was totally cool with the arrangement, but everyone was more or less trying to be cool with it in that queer poly Bay Area kinda way.

I took to Mickey pretty fast, but not as a lover. I didn't dare. That shit was hella complicated, and in his world I was just a straight girl who was bicurious, which apparently didn't count as queer. Not that those labels ever resonated with me, but I didn't even know how to begin to explain myself, so the fact that I wanted to fuck him from the moment I saw him took a firm backseat to my total ignorance of all things queer.

The first time Mickey talked to me about transitioning he came out of the men's bathroom in the library holding his breast, pale with worry. "There's something there. I can feel it." As we discussed mammograms and biopsies, Mickey worried, "I don't know, Tash. Maybe this is just the universe's way of forcing me to make a decision about my breasts. Maybe I just need to get top surgery already and be done with it."

"Oh? What do you mean, top surgery?"

"I don't know. I don't really feel like I'm a man or a woman. I'm both, and I've been thinking about top surgery for a while. I'm just not sure if I need to outwardly present as male in order to feel more in alignment with who I am inside, or if I can keep my breasts and still feel like I'm both. And maybe this lump is just forcing me to make a decision one way or another. I just don't know, I mean. Is passing really all that important?"

"Whoa. I have no idea. But I'm here for whatever you need and decide."

We got closer over the next couple of semesters. When Skylar would come up to visit from Santa Cruz, I'd take him to where Mickey worked in the Mission, and the three of us would have a pretty good time. I even met Daisy, and not just through Mickey's endless lamentations. Natascia then would have never said this because she was all understanding and willing to give people the benefit of the doubt and not judge them and shit, but Natascia now just wants the sweet release in the letters and words of it: Daisy fucking sucked. Like bad. She wasn't even close to right for Mickey. I don't know who she is now, so I won't even pretend to presume, but back then Daisy was a soul-sucking, passive-aggressive, scheming sorceress of all things unholy. She didn't like me, and didn't fucking like her partner hanging out with me, but she'd give me a long-haired, round-eyed smile while she'd ask me the sort of questions that were masked in genuine interest but were designed to confirm whatever theory or position of power she was playing at the time. You know, like, "So wearing leather doesn't bother you as a vegan?" Or, "You look really nice in that top. Is it a feminist choice you're making showing that much skin?" The Daisy I knew then existed in a playing field where all movements of energy were either a win or a loss, and if you tried to show her you weren't playing her game, she'd up the ante. But Mickey meant so damn much to me at the time that I tried to get to know her at least enough not to lose him to the rabbit hole of Daisy's insecurities.

I had already graduated and moved back to LA when Mickey finally decided to go through with surgery. "I'm there, Mick. For whatever you need."

A week later I got in my Corolla, drove to Mickey and Daisy's apartment in the Mission, and buckled up for the long weekend. Mickey was a wreck, which by that point I'd grown accustomed to as his modus operandi, and Daisy was going out for the Oscar for Best Girlfriend in a Supporting Role. "We decided it would be best if you slept in my room," she informed me as I walked through their basement apartment door. "That way Mickey and I can have privacy while you help out."

"Fuck you and die, you uppity-ass bitch, I'm not the fucking help," is what I should have said. "Yeah, sure, of course, whatever you think is best," is what I actually said.

I was eager to spend time with Mickey and help him process all the anxiety he was sitting in, but Daisy wouldn't give us a moment alone. Any time we got close to the intimacy Mickey and I naturally shared, "Natascia, do you mind helping me with this?" or "Mickey, maybe it would be best if you went into the other room to do your meditation now," would come out of her thin-lipped mouth. I don't care how nice she was about it, no amount of acting the supportive girlfriend could mask just how wildly unwelcome I was. But I wasn't there for Daisy, or their relationship. I was there for Mickey, and I was determined to deal. Daisy be damned.

We woke at sunrise on the morning of the surgery. Mickey grabbed some sweet grass his therapist had given him that hadn't fully dried out and asked me if I'd come outside to do a ritual. "Do you think it'll burn even though it's not dried?" he asked nervously.

"It doesn't matter if it burns or not, or if the ritual is perfect or not. It's the intent behind the ritual that matters, Mick. It'll be all right."

We prayed together in the backyard as the sun rose. Three and a half minutes alone together before Daisy poked her head out to tell us to wrap it up and we loaded into Mickey's Toyota for the surgical center.

Daisy was a stick, a shaft, a beanpole. Unmoving as she put on airs of calmness. Speaking only to remind Mickey of some such thing or another.

Mickey was a wreck, a frozen leaf shaking in the wind, a little boy, a little girl, a woman, a man, racked with uncertainty, breathing with nervous resolve. The nurse came in to prep and asked Mickey to remove his shirt and sports bra. Then she looked at me and asked Mickey if he wanted me to stay. "Yeah," Mickey quivered. "She stays. Anything you have to say to me, you can say in front of her." My heart ballooned. My sweet, seductive Mickey sitting on the examining table, feet dangling over the edge, bare-chested and exposed. I used to fantasize about sleeping with him. About what he would look like bare-chested and wrapped in my arms. Strong, proud, self-assured, dripping with sensuality. When the nurse started marking his skin with felt-tipped pen, Mickey's whole body shook and he reached out for my hand. Daisy just about blew the world's quietest gasket.

"It's just the anesthesia," Mickey kept saying. "I just don't like the idea that I'll be under and unconscious while they're doing it. Like I should witness it, or something. I mean, I know I want to go through with it, I just don't want to be out when someone is removing my breasts."

"I'm going to give you three a few minutes," the nurse said. "You two try to calm him. The calmer you are going under, the calmer you'll be coming out."

When the nurse left, Daisy got up and held Mickey and gazed into his eyes and had her girlfriend moment. As I watched them embrace, the words "get out" formed in black smoke in the air behind Daisy and echoed all around me.

The doctor came in and Mickey went into full hyperventilation, trembling out questions about anesthesia in short, hurried breaths. "You're going to need to get control of your breathing before we head back there. You ladies need to help calm him."

I've never felt so useless and out of place. We did a few rounds of deep breathing and said whatever words of encouragement we could muster in that moment, knowing nothing of the strange courage Mickey was facing. And after what felt like not enough time, Daisy and I were ushered into the waiting room to be alone together for the next three hours—minimum.

Mickey finally came out of anesthesia to the tune of halle-fucking-lujah. "Tash!" He said as I walked through the door. "Tash," he cried, covered by a hospital gown and a labyrinth of tubes. "Tash," he breathed as he reached for my hand. "I saw Leslie!"

"Leslie Feinberg?"

"Yeah! Leslie came to me and welcomed me and told me I was going to be okay. You're right, Tash. This is my initiation. This is my initiation." And Mickey's eyes fluttered back into induced sleep beckoning him to forget. "Tash...Leslie...you were right..."

Maybe a half-hour later we managed him into the car and back to their underground Mission apartment. Daisy turned to me and told me to "take the rest of the day off and be back for dinner" like I was their house boy. And stupidly, because I'm a sucker, when I was on my way back from Berkeley, I texted Daisy to ask Mickey if he wanted me to pick him up anything from Café Gratitude. I got a reply to the tune of $100 worth of raw vegan food. When I handed it over and not a dollar was offered in return, do you think I just stood there and took it? Well, yes. Yes I did.

I managed to squeeze in a three-minute goodnight with Mickey that last night and I snuck out the next morning before anyone was awake. I didn't even pee before I left so no one would hear me. I left a note on the table as the sun rose and hoped it would be enough.

About a year later, when the scars from top surgery had healed, when Daisy was finally out of the picture, when Mickey started going by male pronouns, he came down for one of his drive-by LA family visits. I hadn't really seen him since the surgery, and each time we spoke on the phone his voice was an octave deeper. I saw the full effects of hormone therapy until that evening. When I got to the restaurant, the boy I met up with made confusing pronouns a non-problem. But more than the obvious physical changes, I was totally unprepared for the psychological transformations my friend had gone through. I knew that testosterone changed things like facial hair and voice lowering and stuff like that, but I had no idea this shit was gonna turn my very woke friend into a fucking bro.

I didn't really see it until he started telling me about going on this cross-country trip with some girl named Iris, and I was all, "So, is Iris your girlfriend?" and he was all, "No, I don't even like her. I mean, I'm pretty sure she's in love with me, but I'm just trying to fuck. What's the best way to tell someone goodbye, we had a nice summer, thanks for sucking my dick?"

If this were anyone else, I don't know. I mighta said something about how callous that sounded. And I get it, you know. I have an older brother, I grew up around boys who would forget I was in the room, and would speak about women like they were pieces of meat while telling me I was cool or different or whatever. But this was the person who'd single-handedly created a queer studies major advised by professors in the women's studies department at Mills fucking College. I wasn't gonna soapbox feminism to him in a vegan restaurant in Culver City over French fries covered in cashew cheese and fake bacon. I just sort of nodded and smiled.

A few months later he was back in town and we met in WeHo. I guess he'd sorted out the T or his body got used to it or something, because he seemed much more like the Mickey I knew, and over coffee we finally got into a frank conversation about why I bailed that morning after surgery. By the time I pulled up to his parents' house in Beverlywood, I'd more or less confessed that I'd always wanted us to be lovers but never really knew if the feeling was mutual or how to initiate.

"Okay, Tash. I'm going to do something and if you don't like it, just tell me to stop." He leaned across the center console and kissed me. It was exactly how I'd imagined it would be. Extraordinary.

"Spend the night with me," I managed in between breaths.

"I'm going to go inside," he replied. "There's a lot to process here. Let's take time to sit with this and we'll meet up tomorrow. I need to call Iris and let her know what's going on."

"Iris? I thought you didn't even like her. You're together now?"

"No, but we have an agreement that if we are going to sleep with other people we discuss it beforehand. And I feel like I've already violated our agreement."

"Uh, okay. So you're not spending the night?"

"Not tonight, Tash. I think we both need to process this."

When he came over the next night I asked him about Iris. "She's freaking out. She doesn't want me to do this."

"Well," I asked. "What do *you* want?" And the next thing I knew his fingers were so deep inside of me I kept screaming I was going to pee and he kept whispering, "No, you won't. Trust me."

When it was over, we lay there on my loft bed together, both sorta balled up with nerves in the newness of our intimacy. I wanted to reach out and hold him. He jumped up and off of the bed saying something about Iris.

"Wait, you're leaving? Are you fucking serious?"

"Yeah. I have to call her."

"Now? It's midnight. Just stay with me tonight."

"No, I broke our agreement, and I have to call her right now to process."

"I thought you guys had an open relationship and you could sleep with whoever you want so long as you told her first."

"Yeah, but I didn't know I was going to sleep with you tonight. I just told her I was coming over but I wouldn't sleep with you unless she knew about it first."

"Jesus. How does that even work? That sounds controlling as fuck."

"It's about accountability and integrity, Tash."

"You're seriously just gonna fuck me and leave? Just stay a little bit longer. Please."

"I have to go. I'll call you in the morning to process."

A few months later my friends June and Eloise were married in the Berkeley Botanical Gardens. Mickey invited me to spend the weekend at his place while I was in town. "It'll give us a good chance to talk," he said.

The first morning I arrived I met Iris and when she saw me, she and Mickey shared an awkward we're-both-totally-cool-with-this exchange. On Iris's way out she must have forgotten her keys or something because she came back in a semi-panic attack. She and Mickey ended up at the top of the stairs having a conversation in front of me about how they can support one another's shortcomings as a couple, and whether or not Mickey needed to preemptively remind Iris to slow down throughout the day so she would remember whatever the fuck. The damn conversation lasted nearly forty minutes and was so meta and theoretical I didn't know if it was awe or bile I was filled with. When Iris finally did leave, Mickey and I went out on the balcony to have tea.

"I've been thinking about you a lot," I confessed.

"I have too," he said. "You go first."

"That night we shared was intense and I've sort of been nervous about you since. I mean, I obviously love our friendship and want to protect it, but finding out you felt this way too all this time kinda shifted things for me, but I'm nervous about what to do."

"Okay. Well, I've been thinking a lot about it too, and I really want us to just focus on our friendship right now and fortify that before we do anything else."

"Fortify our friendship?" *You've gotta be fucking kidding me.*

"Yeah, like take time to be with each other as friends and grow stronger in that way before we do anything else."

"Mickey, you've been one of my best friends for going on four years now. We just had a long-ass conversation about how this has been there for the both of us all along. Are you not actually attracted to me anymore?"

"No, it's not that. I just have a lot of stuff that I am processing, and I think you and I need to process a lot more about our friendship before we become lovers."

"Okay, sure, yeah, whatever. Whatever you think is best."

We spent the rest of the afternoon traipsing all over the city with Mickey's roommate Marlo, who taught queer studies at the community college. Over matcha almond milk lattes and curried egg salad tartines with sliced fuji apples, the two of them talked about the underground world of boy's clubs and the politics of transgender admittance. They kept going back and forth on if they were boi enough. Mickey reveled in the freedom top surgery allowed, but Marlo was sure that binding would be enough to get him in. I burned with jealousy as they made plans to formally get fucked by strangers in a relatively safe environment. It's a man's world. No amount of binding was gonna get me in.

"They have straight sex clubs too, Tash. I'm sure you could find some in LA."

"Wow. Way to assume I'm straight. Also, ew. I don't want to go to a straight sex club. My whole life is a straight sex club. I miss this. I miss the Bay. These conversations. Nobody talks like this in LA, or at least not out in public over tea and expensive sandwiches. All fools talk about is their ambition. It's really fucking dull."

"Come back, Tash."

"I don't know, Mick. The economy is still shit and San Francisco is getting more and more expensive. What would I even do here?"

"You could do anything, Tash."

"Yeesh," Marlo piped up. "What would you wanna do if you could do anything?"

"Truthfully? I would do this. I wanna spend all day sitting in coffee shops just talking to people, being in deep conversation over gender politics, or intimate relationships, or theological discourse. Coffee by day and good food and wine by night. When you hear of someone hiring for that position, holler."

We walked to BART together before parting ways. Them to boy's clubs in the Tenderloin and me to the lesbian marriage across the bay. As the subway doors closed, Mickey looked at me from across the platform, held my gaze, bit his lip, and gave me a wink just as the doors shut. *Just friends, huh?*

I wouldn't say I rushed back to the city after what was one of the most touching ceremonial displays of love I'd ever seen. I'd probably just say that I was really really looking forward to seeing Mickey again before the night was out. Maybe I could break through all that "deepening our friendship" bullshit he'd dished out earlier and we could get back to the wink and the lip bite.

I showed up to his two-floor Mission apartment in my pink tutu strapless dress with the black satin sash and three-inch stiletto heels after sundown hoping that I was just precisely adorable enough that we'd stay up all night long, deepening our friendship or whatever. When I got there, Iris and I met awkwardly in the hallway on her way to the bathroom. When she came out again we met at the door and she hardly looked at me. *Was she crying in there?*

"I'm just gonna walk Iris to her car," Mickey said. "I'll be right back and we can make some food or something."

I waited in my dress so that when he got back he could have a better look at me. A few minutes became ten, so I took off the heels. Ten became thirty, and the dress became pajamas. Thirty became forty-five and I washed all the makeup off and brushed my teeth. Forty-five became ninety and the old Jewish lady in me started screaming that he was lying dead in a ditch somewhere. When his phone lit up on the table beside me with my *Are you okay?* text message I really started to worry.

Two hours later Mickey came back up the stairs.

"Dude! Are you okay? What happened? I was really worried."

"Yeah, sorry, dude. Iris is really freaking out and we had to process."

"You said you'd be right back and you were gone for over two hours! At what fucking point does this shit become a little self-indulgent? I thought something happened to you."

"I know. It's just Iris is my partner and I'm committed to being in conversation when shit comes up. And she's really having a hard time with you being here."

"Should I leave? I can always stay with Petra."

"No. She knows who I am and knows what she got into, and sooner or later she's gonna have to face it. But this is part of having an open relationship. You process shit. A lot. "

Before they married Mickey would lock himself in his room and call me to process their fights while Iris banged on the door to get in. Whenever I'd come to the Bay, I'd stop in his shop to see him and try to make plans to hang. At first he'd at least try to meet up. But then there was always something more important to do—or to process—or he was too exhausted and too stressed out to make plans. Eventually my calls stopped being returned.

# CHAPTER 45

I ALWAYS THOUGHT ABOUT writing to Boone when he was in prison, but never did. When he got out and I told him as much, to my deep shame and regret, he hugged me and thanked me as if I had. As if we'd become the very best of pen pals in the five years he was locked up and my letters had anchored him.

"You don't understand, Tash. Just knowing you thought about me, you thought about writing, that's enough."

He was right. I didn't understand.

I knew Boone when we were kids. My brother started middle school in Santa Monica before I did. In his first year at Lincoln and through basketball at the Boys and Girls Club, Boone and my brother conducted what seemed to be a promising friendship. He'd come over after school and we'd watch *Gargoyles*, or *Fresh Prince of Bel-Air* while eating butterscotch candies from the bulk bins at Pavilions. Boone, my brother, and whatever other dudes were around on any given day would tease me to no end whenever they'd get bored. I'd distract myself with these elaborate romantic fantasies involving any number of these boys, and I'd more or less take whatever they'd dole out as tribute for inclusion. My brother hated it when I was enjoying myself with his friends, and if the teasing didn't break me down he'd eventually get annoyed and rally everyone to leave to go play basketball, or walk around the neighborhood, or some such thing twelve-year-old boys do when their little sisters aren't looking.

Eventually the wide net my brother cast when we moved into a new district was pulled in, and along with a number of other friends, Boone was returned to sea. By the time we were in high school together, Boone and Dahlia became whatever the fuck they were. Friends? Lovers? Siblings? I liked having Boone around despite how annoying Dahlia insisted he was.

At a time when my brother was a stranger to me, hanging out with Boone at Dali's house felt like home. Like nothing bad would happen to me if he were around. Boone had my back.

Dali and Boone carried on for a while, then I didn't hear anything about him until he was convicted. Boone would call Dahlia from prison periodically, and who knows what they talked about when I wasn't around, but when I was, she'd put on this big show of being annoyed. Of not wanting to talk. Of not wanting to make calls on his behalf. Like Boone's love was some big nuisance. I wasn't buying it. They relied on each other in a way I'll probably never understand. An energetic contract their spirits made before they were born. A motherless boy and a fatherless girl longing for the constant betrayal of the other.

When he was up in Susanville there was talk of us driving up to visit. I was studying poverty, race, and the prison industrial complex at Mills during this time, volunteering for Critical Resistance and arguing prison abolition instead of reform in my papers. Dali was still in Venice and using pretty heavily, but she'd always been flaky and aloof so I could never really tell that she was getting high with any regularity. We never made it to Susanville. My mind was so filled with PIC rhetoric I was afraid I'd turn him into a class project if I wrote him a letter. So I never did. I just held onto his address, prisoner number and all, and looked at it in my notebook daily, opting for the immense guilt of inaction.

When he got out Dali picked him up downtown and they came to Santa Monica to see me on their way home. He was nothing like I remembered him, at least not in appearance. Boone sported an out-of-the-package crisp white XXL T-shirt, jean shorts that went way past his knees, and stark white socks pulled all way up with a couple of white Nikes that looked like they came fresh out of the factory and onto the Swap Meet floor. All of this gripping a body that had five years of nothing to do but protect itself twenty-four seven. He looked at me with that deep, all-over, no-sunscreen yard tan and his face lit up like he was seeing me for the first time. I must've looked dumb because I just stared at him, mouth agape. The next day we went to Café 50's on Lincoln for breakfast. Boone ordered pancakes, hash browns, eggs, bacon, sausage, toast, coffee, orange juice, and a coke, then ate it all with a spoon in about ten minutes flat as he scanned the perimeter. He was ready for the check before I even had a chance to crack my yolks.

I had a million questions for him, and they all started with "why don't you just use the fork?"

"We didn't have forks, Tash. We weren't allowed to use them"

"Yeah...but...we have them now...so..."

He shrugged. "It's just easier this way."

"Well, what are you going to do now, Boone? Like, is there anything you want to do that you've been dreaming about?"

"I don't know, Tash. I can't really be out for too long. All these people are freaking me out. I need to get a phone, apparently. And then I'd like to drink some beer."

Dali chimed in: "Yeah, Tash. I've gotta get him home."

"Wait. Have you had a steak yet?"

"No."

"Let me buy you your first steak then."

"Oh, my God. You'd do that for me?"

"It would be my honor."

A couple of nights later I showed up in a blue strapless dress and red hoop earrings. Boone wore a navy blue T-shirt with creased khakis and those same white shoes. Dali slapped on a skirt, and whatever else might have fit over her belly bump, yelled at her mom, and snuck out without saying goodbye to Logan like she always did. Poor little dude.

There's this beautiful picture of the three of us on the back patio at The Galley that night. Surrounded by half-eaten steaks, spinach, mashed potatoes, and beer bottles. Before Lacey was born, before her dad Roberto got locked up, before Dante came on the scene, before Dali hid their daughter Laura from everyone, before she stopped being able to hide her addiction, before the State took all three kids away, before all I became to her was a stuck-up, judgmental bitch, before we were strangers on the streets we grew up in, before Boone and I consummated our friendship, before Tonya meant anything to him, before Dahlia was fitted for a bridesmaid dress, before she last-minute ditched his wedding, before we knew how sick Tonya was, before Boone had to move to Washington, before Dali stopped showing up for her court dates, before the girls were adopted by that couple in Van Nuys, before that couple barred us from ever seeing them again, before all of this the waitress at The Galley snapped a picture of the three of us at the table with a disposable camera. Boone still has it up in his house.

A few days later I was laying in Dali's little sister's bed with Boone in deep conversation. "Have you had sex yet?" I asked him.

"Yeah."

"With Dali?"

"No way! That's over with. She's like my sister and I love her, but she's pregnant and...." He made a face. "She's not who she used to be. I love her, but I could never sleep with her now."

"Well, who was it then?"

He pulled out his new phone with the 424 number he hated having to have. "Well, I can totally show you because apparently these things have cameras on them now!" It was some girl who is one of those obviously good-looking people who also looks about as interesting as a bag of rocks. He told me how she used to write to him when he was locked up.

"So, how'd it happen?"

"Well, I drove out to meet her and we had sex, but I don't know. She just disappeared after that."

"Ah," I remarked sympathetically. "That must be hard."

"Yeah. It's been so long since I've held a woman, and don't get me wrong—sex was amazing—but I don't know. I can't exactly go out looking for it. Not yet. I don't know. What if. I don't know."

"Boone, look at me. You are gorgeous. I mean, really. I don't think you're gonna have any problems."

"Yeah, but, I don't know. I just want someone who will be sweet to me."

"I can be sweet to you," I said as both of our faces filled with blood and we giggled. "I mean, I have to talk to Dali, but I can be sweet to you—if you want."

Dahlia gave me the go-ahead and then Boone and I were sweet to each other all summer. I knew he would see other women, and I knew it would be good for him. He must have known I was seeing other men, and I think he wanted to be upset about it, but he wasn't. We spent a lot of time together, grilling carne asada and drinking beers, working out and listening to country music all in the confines of Dali's house on Indiana and the garage that had been converted into his room. Boone still wasn't going out, but all his friends were coming in and some nights they'd fill up the recycling bin with empty bottles of Miller High Life.

One particular night he and Anthony thought it would be a really good idea to hop in Boone's car and drive to God knows where. I pleaded for them to stay, but Boone was headstrong. Fifteen minutes later this fool comes running back through the alley in a panic. His car was still on the corner two blocks away in the brick wall he'd smashed.

"Dude! Where's Anthony?"

"I don't know, Tash! He took off running!"

"Are you guys okay?"

"No! I can't go back, Tash! Tash! I can't go back."

"Boone, look at me. It's gonna be okay."

"You don't know that!"

"Did anyone see you?"

"I don't know I don't know I don't know. No. I don't know. I can't go back. But my car is still there. It was so loud."

"Look, if no one saw you then it doesn't matter. Your car is still there. Someone could have stolen it."

"But I have the keys!"

"That doesn't matter."

"No! No! No! I can't go back! You don't understand! I won't go back!"

"Boone! Look at me. Just try to stay calm. We'll deal with this in the morning."

"Don't tell Dali! Don't tell anyone!"

"Okay. Okay. I'll go back inside. Just stay calm. I'll be here in the morning."

I don't know why I walked away. Why I didn't just stay in his room with him. And three minutes later I don't know what brought me back, pounding on the garage door for him to let me in. When he finally opened it he was holding a steak knife, bits of carne asada still gripping its teeth. His wrists were a mess. I thanked God for Dahlia's cheap-ass Pic 'n Save silverware. "No! No! No! Give me that," I screamed as I snatched the plastic handle away from him. He was sobbing. Tearless. Drunk.

"I can't go back!"

"Goddamnit, look at me! You're not going back! Not over this! Look at me! Boone, calm the fuck down! You're not going back!"

We stood by the garage door. His giant body on mine. Two hundred and fifty pounds of pure muscle shaking as I held him. I'd never felt so small in my life. "We're gonna get through this." I didn't really know for sure, but I promised him anyway. We made a plan as we laid on his twin bed together.

The next day we woke up and went into the house about as gingerly as we could. When Wanda saw us she said, "Boone? You're here? Your car is gone!"

The game was afoot. What a big show we put on. By the time we'd gotten dressed to go to the police station, Dali wandered back to the garage, staring at us through folded arms. "You guys are full of shit," she scoffed.

I shot her a look.

"You fucking knew, Tash? Why would you lie to me?"

"I don't know. He made me promise."

"You guys are assholes." She didn't talk to us for three whole days after that. Boone and I piled into the Chevy in our most sensible attire. He was sweating bullets.

"Look at me, Boone. You did nothing wrong. You woke up with me this morning and your car was gone. You don't know anything else. And you're there to file a report. You're the victim. That is all."

"Tash, they're gonna look me up and see I'm on parole. You don't understand these people. I'm nothing to these people."

"Dude. Take a breath. You have to pretend that you are the world's greatest actor right now. You're playing the part of a law-abiding citizen who is afraid his car was stolen. I'm playing the part of the supportive girlfriend who was beside you all night. Put your fear and your panic on a shelf. Somewhere deep inside you. The moment we leave you can take it back out. But for now you have to bury it."

"I need a Coke."

I pulled over at the Curious Palette on Venice Boulevard and bought us two Mexican Cokes in glass bottles. "I don't need a fancy Coke, Tash. Just a Coke."

"No, Boone. If you're gonna drink this shit, then you're gonna drink the best version of it."

We pulled into the police station. I looked at him and said, "Just a couple of Christians holding prayer books." He tried to laugh, and we took a holy trinity of deep breaths. Boone okey-doked his way through filing the report, and when the cops took his picture for the witness they allegedly had he gave them the goofiest smile he could muster. He may have even done a thumbs up.

"Apparently, Natascia," he spoke within earshot of the officers as if he had his hand over his heart in disbelief, "they found my car a few blocks away smashed into a wall. We have to pick it up out of the impound, and as the vehicle owner I may be responsible for the property damage someone else caused!"

"What?" I did my very best version of entitled white girl in response. "That's ludicrous! I'm glad they found your car, babe, but surely you can't be held responsible for what was done when it was stolen!"

"It's the law, babe. What can we do?"

Three blocks away from the station we broke open. "See, Boonie. It's gonna be okay."

"I don't have the money to get it out of the impound and my pop is gonna be pissed."

"Dude. Last night you tried to turn yourself into carne asada you were so worried about getting locked up over this, and now you're worried about the car and your pop? It's just a car and your dad will get over it."

"They took my picture, Tash."

"It was dark. You'll be fine," I promised. He did lose his car, he did have to pay for the property damages, and his dad was pissed, but to date he still hasn't gone back in.

# CHAPTER 46

WHEN THE OTHEROOM AND the short-lived uptown gourmet deli opened on Abbot Kinney, our little ghetto beach town started to become a place where you could safely walk down the street for beer at night, or grab a ten-dollar sandwich in during the day. I don't know how everyone felt about these changes, but in 2006 one or two joints that weren't total dives were a welcome shift for this girl. Talk of restoration and the historical significance of dear old Abbot Kinney (the visionary) was on everyone's tongue.

Venice pride began to swell in a corporate sort of way. "Where Art Meets Crime" T-shirts were selling in shops for forty bucks, and the words "yuppie douchebag" were the dividing line between those of us who'd always been here and those who were looking to invest. The fancy gourmet deli got a pass because even though its proprietor fit the yuppie douchebag bill to a T, he'd married into a well-established family that had been instrumental in changing that portion of Washington to be named Abbot Kinney Boulevard in the first place. And also the owner gave me my first job in a kitchen, so he was a douche, but he got a pass. The Otheroom got a pass too because delicious beer in a cool setting down the street was a rainbow Pegasus at the time.

In those early years before the fall, before GQ named Abbot Kinney one of the coolest streets in the country, Isabella and I were regulars at The Otheroom. We'd pool our tips from working the breakfast shift at The Brickhouse and throw down Belgian beers into the wee hours of the night. Before I left for Mills College, she threw me a surprise party there, and the place was wall-to-wall packed with everyone I knew. The bartenders wouldn't let us pay for a single drink.

A few months later on a weekend trip back to LA I pulled over on Rose Avenue jaw-dropped, staring at the twinkling candlelit place called "Venice

Beach Wines" where Isabella's extended family used to own property. I mean, I already knew that Venice was changing, but it's only when you leave her for a while that you really notice how much weight she's lost. My shock that night as I read the menu was an equal combination of delight and trepidation. I've always been of the mind that you don't have to eat crap food and smoke crack to have an authentic Venice experience, but by the time I was on summer break after my first semester in the Bay, the Big Lots on Lincoln and Rose had become a flagship Whole Foods and I was like, hold the fuck on, everybody! I'm not sure we should be celebrating all these changes just yet!

I stayed away from that one about as long as I could, making a point to go to The Co-op in Santa Monica for all my organic needs on principle alone. But when Mom suggested ginger for an oncoming cold and pulled into the former Pick 'n Save parking lot, she didn't hesitate to tell me how ridiculous I was being when I refused to go inside. "Besides," she said, "the most beautiful man in the world works there, and if you stay in the car, arms crossed, muttering 'yuppie douchebags' until you're blue in the face, you'll never see what he looks like."

Avery bagged my ginger, lemon, cayenne, and oscillococcinum, and looked at me through the blackest eyes. "Not feeling so good?" he asked in deep bassoon.

"Um...what? Who...me? Uh...no, not re—not really."

"Yeah, me too," he pronounced. "Does this stuff really help?" I nodded with my jaw on the floor. "Well, I hope you feel better!"

I just nodded again like a dum-dum.

"Jesus Christ, mother! You weren't kidding!" I admitted back in the car, and for the next couple of years I stopped into the Whole Foods on Lincoln and Rose every chance I got. Of course, I never said anything to him in all that time. I sorta liked it that way, especially in the early mornings right after opening. I'd slowly sip a tall cup of fresh-squeezed OJ on ice and try to catch a glimpse of the statuesque dark man whose muscles clung to his black T-shirt, and whose dreadlocks cascaded down his strong back. Dreamily, through hungover eyes, I'd wonder dumb things like what sort of music he listened to, how comfortable his couch was, or what his exes looked like. I never bothered even trying. It didn't take a mathematician to calculate how far out of my league he was. Still, I would spend hours wandering the aisles, wondering what it felt like to walk down the street holding the hand of a man like that. I like to think that I'm so progressive and above it all, but I clearly fetishized the shit out of him. In the end, everything I invented about that man turned out to be dead wrong. Of course, I would have never known that if it weren't for Isabella and her eternal impatience for me. She was a good sport most of the time—watching me struggle nervously for years, turning into a pink ball of goo every time he came near.

"Just talk to him, Tash. It's not that hard."

"Whatever, Izzy. Maybe I don't want to. Maybe I just wanna come in here year after year and fantasize about what I would say."

"Dog, don't be stupid. Just talk to him, or I'm going to."

"Goddamnit, Isabella. I don't need you to talk to boys for me. Don't ruin this. I'll do it, okay? I'll fucking do it on my own."

A week later she informed me that he was from Venice and his name was Avery. Some things never change. "Oh, God, Iz! What did you say?!"

"Nothing. I just said hi like a normal person and told him you were obsessed with him. It's fine, Tash. He said he was flattered."

"What the fuck is wrong with you?"

"With me? Dude...you...I just get tired of watching you struggle. You make up that people are out of your league and I have to watch my beautiful confident Tatti turn into an absolute moron. So I help."

"Fuck you, Izzy."

"You're welcome."

"Well?"

"Well, what?"

"Well, what did he say? Like word for word."

"I don't remember."

"Oh, you've gotta be fucking kidding me!"

"I don't know...I just asked him if he knew the girl I always come in here with and he said yeah and then I told him that we always come in to see if he's working because you're fucking obsessed with him and he smiled and asked why you never said anything and I told him you're stupid and he said he was flattered and that was more or less that."

It took me a solid month to go back, and when I did, I tried to just hide through the aisles and get in and out. He found me one day by the kombucha and said, "Excuse me, beautiful," as he pushed past me with boxes of inventory, and I choked on fermented tea. A week later Isabella had given him my number, he called, and we went out on one of the five *date* dates I've ever been on.

We met at the Cinema Bar on Sepulveda. I ordered a Makers rocks double. He did the same. We smoked cigarettes on the back patio and giggled over our mutual feelings. I wore a transparent long-sleeved white lace shirt under the jacket I eventually had to zip up against the November air. He wore all black and told me he liked death metal and showed me a picture of his ex. Turns out I wasn't out of his league in the slightest. Dude had no idea what league he was in, and based on the picture he'd just shown me, as far as he was concerned, I was in the running for MVP.

We went back to his tiny bedroom in Inglewood in the apartment he was renting from some dude he would occasionally share a booth with on the boardwalk. Avery built these incredibly elaborate sculptures and figurines out of wire, bits of metal, scraps of plastic, deconstructed VCRs, and anything else he could get his giant hands on. He transformed garbage into post-apocalyptic insects, mythical creatures, and little characters he dreamt up.

His studio/bedroom was a mess. Flecks of aluminum alloy mingled with sand and dust in every corner. Half-finished sculptures with wire guts glared under Ikea lamplight. I'd already known he was an artist thanks to my hours of stalking. Whole Foods had commissioned a seven-foot mythical creature from him in their early attempts to fit into the neighborhood by featuring local artists. That first night I spent at his house I got to see her up close and in the dark, curled in slumber in the shared and otherwise unused kitchen. It was supposed to be permanently installed over the sushi bar, but in the end she was the sort of thing that weighed more than Whole Foods cared to spend on reinforcing the roof over, so she lived with him in hiding.

Back in his room he turned on a TV set with a built-in VCR that sat on the folding metal chair and popped in a kung-fu movie. We sat on his pleather loveseat/fold-out futon as I listened to my heart thunder like a rainstorm on a tin roof. Above the television on a crinkled scrap of paper, tacked to the wall with a safety-pin were the handwritten words, "She's out there somewhere." Between dubbed "kee-yahs!" Avery talked about his quest for his other half, his queen, a woman to partner with against the world, a ride or die "I swear he was with me that night, officer," forever until the end of days chick.

Between the dust, the safety-pinned words, the steel-toed boots thrown beside the tiny futon bed, the eclipse of shadows in his eyes, and the boy I'd fantasized for more than a year over, I was in a panic. I looked up at the words on the wall and looked back at him. *She's not me.* But I didn't tell him that. Not yet. Instead I stayed and fucked him on that tiny futon his legs hung off of and fell asleep tangled in breath and dreadlocks until the early morning dawning. I dropped him off at Whole Foods the next day so he wouldn't have to take the bus. As I watched him wrap the apron around his waist, I knew I shouldn't see him again, but I also knew I would.

The next time we went out he met me at my mom's and we walked down to the shitty Thai spot that took over the Taco Bell on Washington and Redwood. He ordered a beef pad Thai and ate nervously. I ordered something with tofu and tried to distract him with charm. It wasn't working. We split the bill with his shoulders slumped like he had the weight of a seven-foot wire creature on them.

"Let's go for a walk," I suggested.

As we rounded the corner by the park my Montessori class used to walk to, he confessed he felt he'd never be good enough for me. He was too poor. On the swings I learned to pump on, I just laughed at the thought. I couldn't help myself. Oh, how the merry-go-round turns. "Avery," I took his hand. "You're an incredible man. You are deep and dark and passionately artistic. And fuck me if you're not the most beautiful boy I've ever seen. I don't care about money or things. I care about people. I don't know if I'm the one for you, but I know I sure as shit am not better than you. You don't have to make a ton of money to be good enough for me. You just have to be you, and you just have to let me be me. Everything else is secondary."

I could see he wanted to believe me. He was really trying to believe me.

"Come on," I told him. "My friends are having a birthday party downtown. You'll like them—they're artists too." I drove us to Villain's Tavern thinking if I couldn't put him at ease, maybe my friends and a little booze could. They did their best, but the more they talked about the business side of art, the quieter Avery got, and the quieter Avery got the more whiskey I drank, and the more whiskey I drank, the more I started buying into the idea that despite growing up in the same neighborhood he and I truly were from different worlds, and maybe, just maybe, that did matter.

Driving back to the Westside in the Chevy, one eye open, I slurred out the following star-studded gem: "I don't know. Maybe you should get out while you still can. I'm not good at this stuff. This whole monogamy thing. I mean, I'll try really hard, or whatever—I will—but I'll probably end up just breaking your heart. I can already tell."

We did some version of whiskey-spiked coitus that night, but mostly just collapsed in a heavy slumber. He woke up too early the next morning with a start. Jumped right out of the loft bed Skylar'd made me. "I have to get the fuck out of here," he proclaimed. "I must be a fucking idiot," he muttered as he strapped on his black steel-toed boots.

"Wait...what?"

"I mean, you spent the night telling me you were going to break my heart. Do you remember that?"

"I..."

"Do you?!"

"I...yes."

"I'd have to be a fucking idiot to stay here with you."

All I could think to say was "okay."

"Okay?" he scoffed. "Okay!" and he stormed out of my sliding glass door and into the morning. I just lay there for a while, nude on my stomach, frozen, stunned. I should have just let him leave like that. It was a good ending. But I started to feel bad and the nagging voice in my head that is in charge of making me feel like a piece of human garbage came over the loud speaker: "Get up, Natascia! What are you doing? Get up!"

I tore on whatever clothing was closest and took off barefoot down the block. He'd made it all the way to the alley by then and stopped to take a piss. "Hey!" I called out. He looked up and exhaled deeply. I waited for him to put his dick away before walking over and taking his hulking body in my arms.

"You came after me," he whispered.

"Don't leave like this," I answered, holding his face. "Come back and let's talk and if at the end of that you still want to go I'll drive you home. Just don't leave like this."

"You came after me," was all he said, and then he kissed me, the night before still ripe on his breath.

We made it through conversation and glasses of water that morning; through the drive to his house and the next few weeks. But, I don't know.

I just didn't think I could be what he needed and deserved. If I'm being really honest, I didn't think I even wanted to be. Us against the world? No fucking way. I didn't want to spend my whole life thinking the world was against me and I had to find a partner to fight it. It just kinda fizzled out, and I stopped resisting anytime he'd get upset. He sent me a couple of ultra-midnight voicemails filled with venom and vinegar. I didn't respond. I didn't get it. His emotions about me didn't seem to match the actuality of us. He eventually moved to Brooklyn.

•••

WE RECONNECTED ON ONE of my trips out to New York to visit Mary Jane a year later. We talked about our past and offered whatever amends we could to each other. We spent hours walking around that city together in deep conversation. I talked to him about Samson and the Intimacy Project. Before I was willing to admit I was involved in a cult I would launch into long-winded diatribes about what I was involved in and how it was definitely not a cult. About how I was learning to become an adult and be accountable for my choices. How I was trying to erase my personal history and address what was actual versus what my mind was making up. How to be with people as they were to themselves rather than behaving as if everyone I encountered was just a character in my story. The irony of that last sentence is not lost on me, guys.

Avery listened with an open heart and mind and talked about the projects he was working on. The pieces he was being commissioned to create. How he struggled as a street vendor. As an artist. We discussed the constant philosophical economic quandary of pricing artwork and how at the end of the day it didn't really matter if he'd put a hundred-plus hours into a piece, if someone wanted to give him thirty bucks for it he'd be eating canned salmon for a week. Starving artist was not an exaggeration. He was struggling to make it in New York like so many who have come before him. But for a while, at least, he wouldn't let it defeat him.

The next two nights passed with us in each other's arms. Avery told me about the self-induced scars all over his body. How he'd heat up pieces of iron and take it to his skin to remind him to never forget something. A person. A feeling. A moment. A thought. He pointed out the one he gave himself when we stopped talking before he left Venice for Brooklyn.

It was an emotional goodbye over a taxicab door the morning I left. Neither of us knowing when we'd see the other again, nor how time and distance would have its way with us. We spoke every day when I got back to Los Angeles. I'd think about him trying to survive on tinned fish and I'd send him surprise care packages from Whole Foods with bars of soap and chocolates and crackers and whatever graphic novel I'd just finished. When he asked for a picture of me, I immediately drove to CVS and had prints made of the portraits Mary Jane had taken on my last trip. He put them up on his empty refrigerator, said he kissed them good morning and goodnight every day. I mean, honestly, friends…what could possibly go wrong?

These days I like to blame everything that happened back then on the cult. Whether it was a direct result of the Intimacy Project, or some backroad roundabout effect, just going ahead and throwing a blanket of nonchalant blame on Samson and the rest of those assholes has been incredibly healing. But fuck it. Let's get into the nitty-gritty. Here's the story I've been telling myself about how it ended since 2012.

So, you get that Avery was struggling out there, yes? And you get that he was a phenomenal artist, right? Well, one of the things we often spoke about was how to place monetary value on one's artwork. He constantly felt like he had to undervalue himself just so he could eat, and the minute he'd drop the price of one of his pieces was the very same minute public perception of his work would drop exponentially. I'd been encouraging him for some time to hold steadfast to the value of his work and to demand what his pieces were actually worth. Still, there was always the problem of food, and it turns out that it takes more than a bodega sandwich every other day to sustain a six foot four, 250-pound man.

Logan's tenth birthday was on the horizon and his favorite thing at the time was praying mantises. Avery just so happened to be building a set of three such sculptures so I thought, oh! Perfect. I told him to take some time to think about a fair price for one of them—a price that included its actual worth—and I'd buy it off of him for Logan.

*Five hundred dollars.* Five hundred dollars is what he came up with. Five hundred dollars for a twelve-inch sculpture of a praying mantis for a ten-year-old boy. I mean, really, people. I brought that shit on myself. He said it like that too when I answered the phone. "Five hundred dollars."

"Um, okay. So, I know I told you to tell me what it is actually worth, and I have no doubt that that is precisely the number, but in my excitement to be useful to you I overshot my actual capacity to do so. I'm sorry. I just… don't…have…five hundred dollars."

"Well, what seems fair to you?" he asked. "What could you spend on it?"

*Oh, Christ. One hundred, maximum. I don't have more than one hundred fucking dollars for a gift for a ten-year-old.* "Um…I don't…uh…maybe like three hundred?"

"Okay. I'll sell it to you for three hundred then."

*Fuck fuck fuck shit fuck.* "I…uh…well…I don't have it…all…right now. I mean, I could give you a hundred now and then the rest in a month when I get paid again?"

"Sure. That's fine," he agreed, and then he started telling me about how he was faring as if nothing major had just happened.

"Um, Avery? I have to go. I have to get ready for work. Let's talk later?"

"Okay. I'll text you my bank account number so you can deposit the money today."

"Oh, okay."

I got off the phone and immediately into the shower. My skin was crawling. Like ill. I went to the bank and deposited the hundred bucks because I said I would, but from then on I'd cringe when I saw his name on my phone. I'd tell myself that I was just being silly and that I'd brought this shit on to myself, but I couldn't shake this nasty feeling about him. So I told Samson, the leader of the cult, about it.

"What's really there for you about this, Natascia?" he asked.

"I don't know, Sam."

"Yes, you do, goddamnit. Trust your knowledge."

"Okay! Fine! I don't want to talk to Avery anymore. I don't know what this feeling is or how to explain it. I mean, I know what I did. I know what my part in this was, but I still feel sick about how it went down and I don't want to talk to him ever again."

"You are under no obligation to do so."

"Yeah, but aren't I just abandoning him because shit got hard? I mean, if I'm his friend and his lover, don't I have some obligation to him?"

"I'll never understand you people," Samson told me. And by "you people," he just meant everyone in the whole world who wasn't him. "You all get so caught up in what you feel you should do, and then you sit there in turmoil and angst doing things you don't want to do out of some invented sense of honor. And if that wasn't stupid enough then you want people to feel bad for you because of what you've done to yourself. Poor Natascia. Trapped in a conditioned sense of duty to the men around her who are equally living out their version of the invention of humanity. Boohoo."

Like so many moments with Samson before and after that one, I didn't know whether to cry or laugh so I did both. "Well, shit. What do I do now?"

"What is actual, Natascia?"

"What is actual is that I have a bad taste in my mouth and I don't have an explanation for it, but I don't ever want to talk to this fool again."

"Good."

"What's actual is that we made an agreement and I still owe him two hundred fucking dollars for this stupid fucking sculpture he's already sent."

"You do."

"But I don't want to spend another minute on the phone with him, or ever answer his calls again."

"So don't."

"But do I have to let him know that things have shifted for me?"

"That would be the right order of things."

I called Avery and did exactly that, and I can't tell you how relieved I felt getting off that phone call and knowing there wouldn't be another one for a good while. A month later I got a call from him telling me I needed to deposit the rest of the money. I did, and we didn't speak again for some time. That didn't stop him, however, from periodically leaving angry voicemails about how I'd abandoned him.

A year or so before I properly left the Intimacy Project, but right around the time I stopped trusting Samson, I got a call from Avery and answered it just to be rebellious. He had moved back to LA and asked if we could talk about what happened. I went to his mom's house on Washington Place, where he'd been living in the garage in the alleyway since he'd moved back from Brooklyn. When I showed up, the door was cracked inches from the pavement. I crouched down to announce my arrival and what opened the door took me by absolute surprise. Gone was the straight-backed, ripped man I'd known, and in his place was a slumped-shouldered doughy thing surrounded by darkness. Putting on weight is one thing, but Avery didn't have just a couple of extra pounds on him. He looked like someone who'd crawled out from living in a swamp.

He was swollen and darker, like he'd spent the last few years under a permanent rain cloud. His eyes were vacant as fuck and I had an immediate feeling like I should turn tail. I had to actually will myself across the threshold. There was a cheap air mattress on the pavement, a desk littered with metal scraps, and a solitary lamp that provided the only white glow in that small single car garage except for that same TV set with the built-in VCR. Despite asking him to keep it open, Avery shut the garage door, said he preferred the privacy. Didn't want people looking in and seeing us. I looked on the floor by his desk and overflowing from a milk crate were empty bottles of cheap booze. I leaned against the wall asking him how he'd been even though the answer was apparent AF.

"Come here," he demanded, pulling me down on his lap. I kept trying to have a regular conversation as he held me reeking of inexpensive whiskey.

"Are you drunk?" I asked him, knowing the answer.

"No! Why would you even ask me that!?"

"Avery, I'm uncomfortable. I don't want to sit on your lap."

"Don't go, Natascia! You always do this!"

"This isn't what I came here for. I just thought we'd go out or something and catch up as friends."

"Don't go! Please!"

"Avery...I..."

"No! Come on! We'll talk. I promise. Let's talk!"

But I was already at the door. He grabbed my hand. "Sit with me on the bed. Please! I just need someone to be nice to me. Please. Just give me a hug!"

"Okay, okay, relax. You're scaring me!" He grabbed me like he was dying and wouldn't let go. I started crying and then he kissed me. I pushed him off. "Open the door! Now!" I screamed. It took some fighting and some more screaming and he told me to be quiet or his mom would hear. He kept insisting that I was making a big deal out of nothing as I ran down the alley shaking back to my car. Then came the barrage of calls and text messages about how I don't ever let anyone love me. How true love could be staring me right in the face and I'd never know because I'd be too busy running away from it.

# CHAPTER 47

RIGHT AROUND THE TIME I started hanging with Helena, but right before she insisted I attend these meetings with a group of people who called themselves the Intimacy Project, I was introduced to a wide circle of artists and musicians that came out of the Afro-Brazilian community in Los Angeles. Drummers, capoeiristas, dancers, painters, and Sonny. He was impossible to miss on a Thursday night at the Santa Monica Pier Twilight Concerts. When he told me he was a carpenter, I practically threw my number at him.

Sonny must have asked me a dozen questions in the first fifteen minutes of meeting, and before the night was even over, he called. Like on the actual telephone. And we had a conversation over the wire like girls and boys used to do. No "hey" text message. No "sup." No sideways smiley face. No obscure emoji. Just two voices talking for hours on a telephone line like it was 1997 all over again.

We had our first date over breakfast on a Saturday morning at The Wood café on Ingelwood and Washington. Breakfast was his idea and I'd altogether forgotten our plans when I woke up to my phone chiming "on my way." I jumped out of the disheveled loft bed shaking, the room spinning around me, the wine from my after-hours Gjelina party with Jay the night before doing somersaults in my stomach. I ran into the house, splashed cold water on my face, brushed my disgusting mouth, and ran back to the garage to throw actual clothes on. On my way in I stepped on the used condom Jay had thrown carelessly on the floor. "Oh, thank God" was my first thought as I picked it up, and "you're a real piece of work, Tash" was my second as I buried it in the trash right before letting Sonny in. I ordered fruit and bacon to be polite, praying with every slow bite of watered-down icebox melon that I wouldn't hurl. I didn't want him to think that I was one of those girls who wouldn't eat in front of men, but I was hanging on by the skin of my teeth that morning and really had no choice in the matter. Sonny ate a huge breakfast and we had a pleasant, mostly not awkward first-date conversation. After he paid the bill, I didn't even try to protest, and he took me to his apartment to show me his woodshop.

The garage door rolled up from the alley to reveal a studio with just about everything Sonny could ever want. A drum set, a table saw, a drill press, a tool chest, a box full of permanent markers and paint pens, a jar full of ganja, and half a dozen road bikes in varying degrees of repair hanging from the ceiling. There was a sink and a kitchen against the back wall and personally handcrafted steps that led up to a perfectly adorable little studio apartment filled with custom-built furniture. *Um, yes...I could 100P get used to this.* He finished out the tour with all the projects he was in the middle of working on and complained that it was hard to motivate himself to finish when he got home from work exhausted every night. Then, like a perfect gentleman, he drove me home and said goodbye. It was only noon. I crashed hard.

We kept seeing each other that summer and it was always like it was that first time. Pleasant, warm, perfectly civilized. We'd ride bikes to art shows in the neighborhood, or I'd go over to his workshop, smoke ganja, and doodle on the table while he played roots reggae, or he'd come over to my garage after work and pass out on my couch mid-conversation. When he wasn't sleeping, Sonny would talk about Juliet. About what an amazing artist she was. About how toxic their relationship had been. About how he wanted the best for her and hoped she was well but from a distance because she was fucking crazy. I don't remember the things I talked to him about, likely because I was doing most of the listening. I'd spend hours talking him through his heartache wondering what on Earth he wanted with me, and if we were just friends, or if not, how did I miss out on the fun passionate sexy beginning and skip right ahead to being his stand-in girlfriend?

I didn't know what the fuck Sonny and I were supposed to be. I don't think he really cared all that much about me. He was just lonely and wanted the girlfriend experience. He'd come over to my house and have dinner with me and my mom, or he'd stop by on his way home from work to spend time with me passed out on my couch all night, or he'd fix my bike and we'd get lunch and shit, but we were definitely not a couple. A couple of assholes, maybe. But not a couple. Still, sometimes Sonny would do or say certain things and I'd think, wait—are we?

Like this one night I came over to his house. We were watching *Rockers* for the hundredth time together and Bridget kept texting me. She'd just been dumped by that stupid boy who was the brother of one of her coworkers at Top 2 Top and she kept begging me to come have a drink with her. I half-joked to Sonny that I'd just wait for him to fall asleep before sneaking out of the house to meet B. He took both my hands and got really serious and said, "Please don't leave me tonight. I'll stay awake this time. I promise. Just please don't leave me." Caught me way off guard, so I promised. As soon as I did, he sighed a breath of relief and turned back to watching our favorite Rasta saunter down the streets of Trenchtown. But by the time Horsemouth buys the bike from Gregory Isaacs, this fool Sonny was in full opened-mouth sawmill. It was 8:30. I left the front door unlocked and took the Chevy to Bigfoot West praying that the sound of my engine turning over didn't wake him up.

Bigfoot West used to serve this drink called The Bourberry, which is nothing like the watered-down version of the thing they still have on the menu today. They used to take a mason jar, fill it about a quarter of the way with fresh blackberries and mint, muddle them, pour Buffalo Trace over a few ice cubes, top it off with a splash of Reed's Ginger Brew, and put a whole mint stem in to garnish. I was never one to really mix bourbon with anything more than a little soda water, but The Bourberry was the exception. You know when you go to an annoying mixology-forward bar and you ask the bartender to level with you on whether or not the "Sweep the Leg" is sweet, and he adjusts his bow-tie, brushes the sides of his pencil-thin mustache, and assures you with smug tongue that everything on the menu is designed to be perfectly "well-balanced," and that you should just trust him and not change the recipe even though you think your pallet is a little more suited to bitterness. So instead of arguing the finer points of flavor profiles you just get the damn thing because his attitude made you realized how badly you actually need a drink, and it ends up tasting like you just took down a shot of Maraschino brine and now you have to send it back with your apologies like you're the one who did something wrong by not just ordering four fingers of whiskey in the first place? Well, the premade candy piss that's on the menu of Bigfoot

West today is just like that. About as well-balanced as my ass. But that old shit? That muddled, tart, juicy, fresh, effervescent broad? That bitch was like sweet Justice herself, blind in cascading marbled robes, scales in hand. Balanced AF.

Bridget and I had about seven each that night, and we shoved the mason jars into her oversized purse when we were finished. I can't really explain that last part. We just used to steal random shit from bars and restaurants sometimes. A candle from La Cabaña here, a wine glass from Gjelina there, a bottle of soap from the bathroom at Petit Trois. I don't know why. It was just our thing and the night that dumb boy broke up with her I thought going overboard and taking as many glasses as we could without getting caught would cheer her up.

When I got back to Sonny's, the sun had started to rise. He was in the precise position I'd left him in hours earlier. The *Rockers* DVD home menu still played on the TV. I curled up next to him in the early morning light reeking of blackberries and bourbon and wondering what the fuck I was doing with this boy. He woke up an hour later and kissed me on the forehead before he left for work. When I left his house closer to 3:00 p.m., I looked at the bag of mason jars by his sink and felt bad about leaving the night before, so I left them for him as an offering. He was totally indifferent when he found them, and I confessed that I'd broken my promise.

I don't remember the first time Sonny and I kissed. I just remember it feeling detached and desultory, like a shrug. Like we might as well. Sex with Sonny was like that too. Infrequent, impassionate, and just like, yeah, sure, okay, whatever. Might as well. I'm sure we had sex more than once, but I only really remember this one time.

He came over to my garage in the afternoon and instead of falling asleep or talking about Juliet, he climbed into the loft bed that Skylar'd made me and I climbed up on top of him in what folks like to refer to as the reverse cowgirl. I couldn't see his face, which felt like way too intimate a position to be in for what we actually were to each other, and all of a sudden I was in the throws of a panic attack. "I just need a minute," was all I could manage to say. Sonny lay there silently. Waiting. Fifteen minutes passed, and after some very deep breaths I turned to him and said, "Okay. I'm back."

"What was that, Tash?"

"You know, Sonny, that was something old. Something that used to happen to me that hasn't happened in a long time. Something that used to take me out from whatever I was doing and launch me into the past. But I'm not going to let it do that anymore. I'm okay now. Really, I am." I kissed him and smiled.

"Oh, I get it. You were just being a Debbie."

"A what?"

"A Debbie Downer."

# CHAPTER 48

IDON'T REMEMBER A ton from my parents' divorce. The screaming. The broken glass. My brother slamming on the piano keys to distract me from all the noise they made. The picture book called *Mommy and Daddy Still Love You*. The role-playing games in the therapist's office. My brother's fits of rage getting hosed off of him in the backyard. Packing a hobo bag and tying it to a stick to run away and live my life in peace like a normal person. Making it all the way to the front door before my mom saw the bag tied on a stick and asked me in Italian if I was an idiot. My dad taking me to a restaurant and interrupting my mom's date to drop me off because it was "her night with the kids." I don't remember much from my parents' divorce except bearing witness to the raw, unfiltered pettiness and pain of two grown-ass people. But after my parents' divorce, after my pop moved out, I remember that. All of it.

The Lunchables and Pink Lemonade Snapple that waited for us in my pop's car after school. The straws he would make us use so we wouldn't chip our teeth on the glass bottle rim. The swim lessons at the Y. The piano lessons in Santa Monica. The art classes in West LA. Nick Van Axel, Vlade Devac, and James Worthy on the big screen at the bachelor pad my pop shared with his pal. Ace of Base and Beck on MTV. *The Harder They Come* soundtrack playing in the Bronco on the way to Burton Chase Park after school. Taking turns reading *Charlotte's Web* and *Stuart Little* to each other. Me and my brother holding hands rolling down the green grass hill. The voices of Maria Bethânia. João Gilberto. Gilberto Gil. Caetano Veloso. Jorge Ben. Gal Costa. Jobim. I remember the hot Passarinho served at Zabumba while the boys on stage played mostly pagode, and learning how to samba holding my dad's hands as the sun set on Venice Boulevard. The insanely hot, late-night, all-age parties at Café Dança on Pico Boulevard. Running around the back alley with all the Brazilian kids hopped up on cans of Guaraná. The sound of the whistles during the capoeira demonstrations. Watching *Only the Strong Survive* on loop at my pop's house and trying to ginga when no one was looking. Feeling like I would never be happier than I was when my pop and I were singing "LlêAiyê" to each other in the car. Fast forwarding the tape through "O Leãoziho" because it always made me cry. Climbing into the limo at Fats' house with the rest of the Brazilian kids as he'd regale us with stories of the famous people he'd get to drive, and what Sade is like in person. (Yes, she really is that beautiful.) Bringing over a bottle of wine and flowers to Fernanda's party and spending most of the night chatting with Astrid, who would sip caçasa and spontaneously break into song. Spending World Cup '94 in Italy with Nonna and watching Roberto Baggio blow the final penalty shot against Brazil, and thinking as all of Italy fell silent, I wish I were three Guaranás deep with my pop at Zabumba back home. That was the week Nonna slapped me clean on my face because I told her I thought the divorce was the best thing that ever happened to my parents.

"Disgrasiata," she called me. "How could you betray your mother like that?" Those first few years after the divorce, before Café Dança closed down, before one of the owners was murdered by her husband and Zabumba fell into disrepair, before they found Fats alone in his apartment a week after he'd died, before Astrid moved to San Diego and took her kids with her. Those first few years after the divorce between '92 and '95 when my dad became an honorary Brazilian were the best years of my life. They were also the years I first knew João.

•••

IT'S 2010 AND I'M hanging around with a new crowd of girls who don't do meth and don't have kids. Young girls who are into art and poetry, African dance and drumming. Live music and restaurants. Writers, thinkers, talkers. Girls who speak of true intimacy. New girls who hang out with new boys who are carpenters, musicians, artists, and architects. I throw a small dinner party in July and Vera asks if she can bring a date. She shows up with this boy who looks really familiar but doesn't talk much. After dinner we all hang out on the couch drinking wine. I take a risk and put on some Tropicália. The boy starts singing along with me. "Wait, you know this stuff?" I ask him incredulously. "Oh, yeah, sure," he dismisses. "I grew up on this stuff. These guys are the best."

It wasn't until October and I was invited to him and his sister's birthday party that I put it all together and called my pop. "Hey, Poppy. Did Astrid have a son named João?"

"Of course, Tatti. You don't remember João and Lorena?"

"I remembered Lorena for sure, but I guess I forgot about João. Anyway, I got invited to their birthday party. Astrid is gonna be there! You should come!"

Our families had a sweet little reunion that night as we danced to the rhythms of samba and pagode that Sonny and a dozen other men on drums banged out until the cops came. Twice. Astrid pulled me aside in the middle of the party when João was getting me another caipirinha and asked me what I thought of her son. I shrugged, "He's nice."

"No, what do you think of the two of you?"

"Oh. I don't know. I don't really think anything yet."

"Okay," she said. "Maybe you should think of it."

I danced with João all night and gave him my number while Sonny mostly ignored me. João called me a week later and invited me to a dinner party at his house in Mid City. This was right around the time when Sonny started calling me to do these random check-ins that stopped leading to plans. Sonny phoned while I was on my way to João's, and called me "cosmopolitan" when I told him what I was doing. The dinner party was sort of cosmopolitan, filled with a bunch of really interesting people from all over the world like Nepal, India, Brazil, and Mexico. After we ate, everyone performed, and João sang Caetano Veloso off-key but genuinely. When he walked me to my car he didn't even try to kiss me.

Another couple of weeks went by and he posted something on Facebook about having an extra ticket to a performance at the Dub Club in Echo Park. I wrote "I'm down" in the comments and by the end of the first set, João and I were behind the Echoplex full tongue and mouth to the rhythms of the one and three. But by that point in 2010 I'd just started with the Intimacy Project and even though it felt wildly out of character, I stopped us, pulled back, and said, "Shit, we should probably have a conversation or something first. I mean, at the very least I should have discussed this with Vera."

"Vera? We were nothing," he promised. "I'd be surprised if she even cared."

"Still, she's my friend, and we're in this…group…thing together, and it wouldn't be right…I don't think."

But it was too late and there was too much magnetism. I came twice in the car parked out in front of my mom's house that night, and once more in the loft bed Skylar'd made me. When I called Vera the next morning to apologize and tell her how bad I felt, "I don't know what to tell you about feeling bad, but I don't care if you fuck João. There's nothing there with us and never really was," is what she said. But before long she'd start calling me every day to emotionally dump on me, and whenever I was hanging out with João she would find some way to insert herself right before proclaiming she had to get away from us because we were being "weird" and were "really in it"—whatever the fuck that meant. The next Sunday I'd be chastised for doing some version of conditioned romantic relating when she told them about me and João in the Intimacy Project meeting. I got so confused during that time period that I eventually invited João to join the group just so I could make sense of everything.

Big. Fucking. Mistake.

•••

AT THE GREAT URGING of Helena, I finally and reluctantly attended one of the earliest meetings of the Intimacy Project. Vera had been meeting with this old white man named Samson since she was a kid. The Intimacy Project was dreamed up as an extension of their meetings and was supposed to be a place where a group of people could come together to practice and discuss the notion of "true intimacy." A distinction was immediately made between what Samson described as intimacy and the act of sex itself. He argued that sex and intimacy do not actually go hand in hand. "Especially," he would add, "the way you conditioned folks do it. You people go around fucking anything that walks and calling it 'being intimate,' but you wouldn't know true intimacy if it slapped you in the face."

He'd say things like, "True intimacy begins by stating what is actual. For example, if someone is unloading on you about their day and you're not really listening because you're so distracted by how bored you are hearing the same old story from them day in and day out but you go on pretending to listen, then you are not being actual or intimate." Contrary to what the socially conditioned response to something like that might be, Samson would argue that not saying what is going on with you would be ruder than actually stopping the person and telling them that they are boring the hell out of you. Sharing precisely what is coming up for you when it comes up for you instead of filtering the "actual" through your thoughts, beliefs, and ideas of how one is supposed to behave, or what manners dictate, is true intimacy.

Okay. Stick with me.

So intimacy then is about being with people as they are to themselves, not as they are to you. People are not just characters in our script. They aren't the roles we give them with our minds. Your mother is not just your mother. Your best friend is not just your best friend. Your boyfriend is not just your boyfriend. To relate to these people with true intimacy is to engage them as they are to themselves, and to in turn engage as you truly are to yourself. Not with the version of yourself society or the relationship dictates you are supposed to be.

We live in a socially conditioned world, Samson would preach. We live in the invention of humanity. Your ideas about family, your ideas about work, your ideas about friendship and love and sex and health are all just that—ideas. If you are willing to take a close look at how you came to those ideas, and you are willing to unravel the tangled web they've weaved in your mind, you are likely going to discover that many, most, or even all of your ideas are not yours. The great discord you carry, the angst, and the pain of the generations that came before you are all energetic indications that you aren't living from your true authentic self; your true nature. You are living from the notions, beliefs, and constructs of your mind, and guess what? You are not your mind and your mind is not real. Okay, okay, that's pretty straightforward basic shit, right? So you may be wondering as I did, how do I discern between my true nature and my mind? How do I go about telling the difference between an authentic response and a conditioned one? And then once I'm able to discern between the two, how do I practice living only from my authentic self when I'm so conditioned not to?

You erase your personal history.

You take all of your experiences, your ideas, your traumas, all the thoughts you've ever had about them, all the things you've ever done because of them, how you've chosen to feel about them, the contracts you've made with yourself as a result, the stories you tell yourself, and you systematically process them through deliberate reverse recapitulation until every molecule, every minute, every relic, every thought, every feeling, every breath is unpacked and you don't stop until all the debris is cleared. Until what you are left with is not your mother's daughter. Not your boyfriend's girlfriend. Not a fourteen-year-old girl trapped in a woman's body. Not the sum of your life's experiences. Not a person confined and defined by the stories she tells herself. Not a person subject to the ideas of others. What you are left with is your true self. Your core erotic nature. No longer Natascia, but the name you were given before you were born. The self you were before your parents fucked you into existence.

That's how he got me. Samson Stone. The sixty-eight-year-old white man from Milan, Tennessee, who looked like Santa Claus, talked like Carlos Castaneda, and had the presence, the knowledge, the stoicism, and the stern concern of the grandfather I never had. "I know how to do this work," he promised. "I won't abandon you while you break apart. I won't bail on you when the storm rages around us. I'll sit by your side as we stare into the great void together. I'll maintain the tether as you dive into the abyss. I will never leave you."

In the Intimacy Project, an interaction that took place over the course of five minutes could easily be discussed over the course of six hours. Twelve people in varying stages of "the work," mostly young beautiful women and Samson, taking an idea, a phrase, something implied, a palpable shift in the room, and breaking it down to the movements of energy, until what was actual was no longer obscured by what was thought (or, God forbid, felt). This wasn't a place for feelings. This was a place for sensations. For knowing. For seeing. Emotions were thrown out unless they were deemed authentic, unless they were congruous with what was actually taking place right in front of you.

"How do you feel?" was replaced with "what are you doing?" and "how did you come to that?" "What are you thinking?" was replaced by "what is coming to you?" Identification, the tendency to define one's self, and to associate or disassociate were all greatly discouraged. Where you are became tantamount over who you are. Samson would say it does no good to be enlightened if you aren't connected to the worlds outside of you. You could be the most enlightened individual on the planet and it wouldn't mean dick if you crossed the street in front of a bus you didn't see coming because you were so busy being enlightened. How you identify yourself, what you feel about something you've done, and what your supposed intentions were are all meaningless pursuits of an untrained mind. All we have is what we do, and intent isn't a feeling. It is an agreement with Power. A force one can either harness or succumb to. And the ultimate responsibility of adulthood was to *intend for others*. To Samson, we were simultaneously the most dedicated and the stupidest group of people he'd ever encountered, and he never shied away from telling us so. In the same meeting we could be chastised for our lack of imagination and discipline, and in the next breath celebrated for our intelligence. And João? João is the poor sucker who fell in love with me after I met Samson.

He first came to the group because I asked him to. Because I couldn't keep trying to explain. Because if he wanted to be with me then he should at least know what I was involved in. But the Intimacy Project wasn't the sort of place you could stay in unless you were in alignment with what was being practiced. If you were just there because you were in love with one of the members, not only were you gonna be found out lickety-split, but your whole concept of love was gonna be dissected to such an extent that when it got handed back to you it would be virtually unrecognizable.

I dove right in and didn't look back. For the first few years nothing was hidden, unspeakable, unshared. This charismatic dude was like, "I'll show you how to be free from the prison of your small mind," and I was like, "I've been looking for you my whole life! LET'S DO THIS!"

João and I didn't stand a chance. Not like a normal relationship. Not like anything remotely familiar. Relationships (like feelings) were strictly taboo, and if you were caught hiding out in one you'd be shamed and ridiculed to no end. That's not a gross exaggeration, either. We used to do this exercise when someone was "stuck in their mind." We'd place them in the center of the circle and surround them, adopting the various voices of the dark mirrors of their mind. We were allowed to be as vicious, as cruel, and as unrelenting as a mind could be. To say whatever "came to us" to say. Externally personifying their inner turmoil sometimes for hours until their defenses would drop. Being the most zealous of the bunch, yours truly more often than not found herself in the center, and more often than not João would end up in there too, right beside me.

Every interaction, every conversation, every thought exchanged between the two of us would occupy some, or all, of the six-hour meeting those first few months after João joined, until we'd be chastised for taking up everyone's time with our self-importance. For all his feigned equality, all his insistence that there were no leaders in this group, no hierarchy, that this was "our" group, Samson never went in the middle. Not once. And when João or I would meet with him for individual sessions we'd get a whole lot more of all this shit, but it wasn't until we started meeting with him together that we had to call it. Whatever kind of love we shared for one another, whatever kind of attraction, we were but pitiful humans who broke under the onslaught of groupthink and a charismatic leader.

We just stopped trying, stopped trying to justify it, stopped trying to make it work within that framework. It kills me to remember how histrionic it all was. One week we'd be screaming "go fuck yourself" to each other at the top of our lungs, and the next week he'd push me up against the neighbor's wall and wrap my legs around his head. What made things worse was that João and I shared the same fetish for shame and punishment. We knew we'd be chastised in the group for coming together in passion, we knew it would have consequences after the fact, we knew those closest to us would lose trust in our word, our discipline, our dedication to "the work," but fuck me if it didn't just turn us on more. Sex was explosive, magical, otherworldly. What's that thing that Alan Watts says about the Christian repression of sex? That the secret intent of it was to make people more interested in sex because if it is so easy it is in danger of becoming a bore? Something like that. Anyway, I don't suggest it or anything, but becoming a part of a cult that valued abstinence was the most powerful fucking aphrodisiac in the world.

João worshipped me at his core. And at my core I need to be worshipped. The fucked-up part was that we were supposed to be doing "the work" to discover what was at the core in the first place. Only once we had, no one believed us, and what we "thought we saw" was deemed dangerous, deranged, and subsequently ridiculed.

You know, it is easy now that I'm out to see all the contradictions; all of the obvious way in which we were being manipulated. But this shit is mad stealthy. Cults work incrementally. By the time you even start to get the faintest inkling that you may be involved in one it's too late. I mean, this shit was so insidious we even held meetings where we discussed our concerns as to whether or not we technically were a cult. And here's the kicker, folks.

As we took a deep and sober look at the definition of the word we all sort of had to agree that that was precisely what we were. *But we're not a cult cult. This isn't a religious thing. Hell, it's not even a spiritual thing. It doesn't cost any money* (at least it didn't at first). *This isn't the cult of Samson because he keeps insisting that it is "our" group. We formed it, and we dictated the terms of engagement.* It was total bullshit, but the egos that we were supposed to be destroying, or whatever, ate that shit up like, yum, yum, yum. Can I have some more, please!

When I finally broke free, when I finally turned my back and closed the door on all the hypnotic hypocrisy, I was sitting with my pop at the old Panini Café in the Marina, tears rolling down my cheeks with the shame of how I'd turned my back on my family and friends because of the Intimacy Project. How I had been so depressed and hungover from bourbon and Vicodin one morning that I'd nearly killed myself in a car accident speeding to a 7:30 a.m. meeting in Pasadena with Samson so he wouldn't yell at me for being late and I wouldn't have to confess how much of a mess I'd become doing "the work." I cried to my pop about how the people I trusted with all of my darkest secrets and truths had turned their backs on me the moment I left the group. Like I didn't exist. Ghosted in reverse. Like, I'm the ghost but I have to continue to exist without a trace of acknowledgment. I was full of confusion at the pride I had because the work I did on myself in that group was actually very real, but I was so ashamed of all the things I did in the four years with them. My dad took my hand and said, "Tash, you graduated. In four years if all you learned was to trust yourself enough to say no to those people, then you graduated. You got the diploma. You don't need them anymore because everything that was being taught there you learned the moment you saw it for what it really was. And you walked away. They have no power over you any longer. You took your power back, and no one will ever be able to take it away from you again. You should be proud."

You know, João and I spent almost four years together. Four years in love and lust, doing the dance of attraction and repulsion. I was made to share everything about us. Every little intimate detail every other Sunday and privately on Tuesday mornings. Four years' worth of stories of our time together of friendship and sex, of growing and drifting apart. There are so many little stories that I could share with you now, but I'm not going to. For once, I'm keeping those just for us.

# CHAPTER 49

I BEGAN MEETING SAMSON privately about a month after the Intimacy Project formed. I'd wake up before the sun rose and drive to Pasadena by seven thirty sharp. Anything after seven thirty would earn me a tortuous conversation about how I decided to have a total lack of regard for his time, talent, and will. How I imagined my time as more important than his. God forbid. So seven thirty sharp I'd meet him at whatever coffeehouse he'd be conducting business in that morning and buy him breakfast as an offering for our sessions. His other "clients" had to shell out something close to a hundred bucks minimum if they wanted to meet, but Samson never charged me a dime. He used to say the kind of conversation I brought didn't bore him to death and that breakfast was payment enough. Boy, did my ego love that. He'd sit there all morning eating muffins, doughnuts, eggs scrambled with cheese, toast with butter and jam, potatoes, bacon, coffee, and some combination of soda that usually looked like one-third Pepsi, one-third Dr. Pepper, and one-third root beer. I'd sit across from him with a cup of black coffee and sleep in my eyes, and I'd tell him everything. No one can listen like a sociopath.

About a year after Samson died from complications with colon cancer, I was walking with my brother in the Lafayette Cemetery across from Commander's Palace in New Orleans. The sky cracked with heat and precipitation. Dark, balmy bayou clouds snuffed out the sun, and globules of water like plague frogs fell from the sky, thick as molasses. I hadn't seen or spoken to Samson for at least two years and hadn't cried a lick when I found out he died. I hadn't felt a goddamned thing except maybe relief. But that afternoon, with a belly full of twenty-five-cent apple martinis and turtle soup, surrounded by marble and iron tombs, the Louisiana lightning and thunder synced up with my heart and drummed like a second line in the sweltering July heat. "Joyo," I wept, "you don't understand. I hate that man. I really fucking do. But those conversations. No one ever listened to me like that before. No one I've ever met before or after could hear all of the layers simultaneously. No one could jump from New Testament theology, to Gnosticism, to emotional complexities, to platonic philosophies, back to Talmudic theologies, to theories of mobile devices as artificial limbs, to the historical significance of spaghetti westerns, to the six explanatory propositions of the Eagle's gift, the mastery of awareness, the art of stalking, the mastery of intent, and then back to something that Mom did when we were kids, and how that all related to the pursuit of true freedom and communion with Power. Never, Joyo. I fucking hate him, but I will never ever get to have conversations like that again."

Oh, my darling readers! If you have never had the chance to dance the seductively treacherous tango of love between an empath and a narcissist, and you don't have the fortitude of a cockroach, I offer you this morsel of unsolicited advice: stay away from its provocative allure for the rest of your days. Just because I made it out alive doesn't guarantee you will, and even though he is dead now, this trace of him will always be inside of me and I'll have to walk the rest of my days with the mark of Cain.

"You've lived your life in folly," Samson used to say to me. "Which is okay for the average person, Tash, but you are not an average person so it is extra dangerous for you to live this way. I'm going to teach you how to contain your energy. How to have command over it. If you're any good, your encounters with Power will be calculated, and if you die in them it won't be because you were subject to your own folly, but because you chose the life of a warrior."

"Sam," I'd say. "Sometimes I feel like I'm a sea anemone. Like I'm taking in everything around me. Subject to the movements of the ocean, the tides, the fish, the sun. But my stinging cells are all turned inward, and everything I take in stings and I'm in such a state of constant pain. But it isn't even my pain, and I don't know what to do or how to move or how to go on like this when everything hurts all the time."

"I'm going to teach you how to not take everything in. You see, your problem is that you take in things that don't belong to you and you hold onto them. I'm going to show you how to discern between what is yours and what is someone else's. Between what is necessary and what is unnecessary.

How to have autonomy over your body and sovereignty over your energy. How to let things pass right through you."

"But that's just the thing, Sam. We don't choose what touches us. And I feel like all my circuits are open all of the time, and being open like that is who I actually am and what I love about being alive, but there is so much electricity passing through my system all the time that my circuits keep getting fried, and I've fixed this shit with duct tape and super glue so many times that my motherboard is going to go up in flames any minute."

"Well, of course. Your problem is that when you built the motherboard you had no idea what you were doing in the first place, so you crossed and jumbled all the wires. Once we've gone about untangling them we can be about the business of rewiring the circuit board, and once we rewire the circuit board you can reprogram the operating system so certain energies do not pass through."

"But I don't know how to do any of that!"

"I do."

"But I don't even know if I *can* do any of that."

"You can."

"How do you know that about me? How do you know that about me when I don't even know that about myself?"

"You just have to be willing to trust my knowledge of you. Trust that sometimes there will be things I see about you that your mind or your feelings won't let you see about yourself. Sometimes your mind and your feelings will even tell you that the exact opposite is true. But you have to trust me. We can't do this work if you don't. If you can't put your trust in me fully, then you won't be able to see what I can show you."

•••

I FIRST MET HELENA when she was dating Avi. You remember him? Chapter 32? Best All Around? He brought her to one of Jude's shows at Zabumba, of all places. You remember Jude, right? Chapter 29? That *Love In The Time of Cholera* shit? When Helena and I met briefly in the parking lot next to Zabumba I remember thinking, Ah, intelligence! Good for Avi! They didn't last, however, and the next time I saw her at Avi, Spencer, and Ford's housewarming party, she and Avi were already on their way out of whatever they were in. Helena and I spent much of that night in conversation.

Someone snapped a Polaroid of the two of us like that, facing each other, captivated by each other's intellect, oblivious to the photographer. She put that picture up on the dashboard of her car and there it remained for all the time I knew her.

When I asked Avi after her he'd always wince. His face would distort, like, "I can't even begin to tell you what that was about but I'm sure glad it's over." How strange, I'd wonder quietly. She seems like such a lovely, reasonable, strong, discerning kind of woman. Just the sort of woman I'd imagine for a man like you. Huh. What am I not seeing? In our developing friendship when I'd ask her about Avi she'd usually scoff and roll her eyes before weaving a tale of boyish stupidity in the bedroom, which, when held up to my own experience with him, I'd think, okay, I could see that. And yet, what became ever apparent in my early dealings with Helena was that in all her lamentations, her struggles with herself and other people, a single truth rang out clear as day: she had no idea who the fuck she actually was.

"You need to get your heart broken," I told her. "To learn the things you want to learn about yourself, about your life, about who you are in relation to other people, to love, to know true love, you have to get your heart broken. It's as simple as that. You'll never know what you're made of if you don't break apart."

We had that conversation in front of her parents' house in Venice. She had begun flirting with me on the drive over. I called her on it and flat out asked if she wanted to fuck me. "I don't know," she kept saying. "I'm not gay," she kept insisting. "And yet," she relented. "There's this thing with you, Tash. I'm drawn to you physically. I've never felt that way about a woman. Like I want to possess you." She started to cry. "I have to tell you something. I'm sorry I've kept this from you for so long. I fucked Jay." You remember him? Chapter 40? The one she'd been friends with for years without any attraction? "I got drunk one night after the two of you had slept together, after I knew how you felt about him, and I fucked him. I don't even like him, not like that, and I know being drunk is not an excuse, but I guess if I'm being really honest, I did it to be close to you. I wanted to touch what you touched. I'm sorry, Tash. And I'm not gay. But maybe I'm gay for you? Is that a thing?"

I laughed. "It's okay, Helena. You don't have to be sorry. I understand."

"You're not upset?"

"No, I get it. And trust me, I've done worse. As far as you being attracted to me—gay, straight, or whatever—it sounds like you have a lot of things to sort out, so let's just table that for now and not act on anything. We can just keep the conversation open. You don't have to hold all your feelings in. I won't hold them against you."

It wasn't more than a year of knowing each other before she insisted I come to a meeting of something called the Intimacy Project.

"You belong there, Tash. They sound like you," she'd say.

Sexually, the thought of her was interesting enough, I guess, but I wasn't desirous of her in any way. My affection for her as a friend increased exponentially the more she revealed herself to us, but there was definitely something lost in all that. The more I learned about who she was to herself, the more I became impervious to the charm she relied so heavily upon to keep people interested. The Helena she was willing to allow and the Helena she actually was were at odds with one another, and once the veil lifted even the smallest inch I couldn't not see the masks for what they were. The more she revealed about her true self, the more her haughty persona looked like a little lamb bleating for the protection of the flock. To the ultimate detriment of our friendship, once I saw the lamb, my response was nothing short of laughter. Helena, who spent so much of her life being told she was too intense and too intimidating, couldn't scare me if she tried. She and I had another mutual lover (who didn't make the cut for volume one of this book), and he summed her up pretty perfectly. "The problem with Helena is that she takes herself so fucking seriously it is absolutely impossible for anyone else to."

The things that initially attracted me to Helena were the very same things that hooked me to the Intimacy Project. The willingness to confront what was actual. The determination to strip away one's conditioning. The discipline to train the mind. The practice of living from one's true nature. The sovereignty of being responsible for everything that takes place in one's life. The freedom of self-determination. The communion with Power once you can harness intent. Yet these very same things deployed through the persona of the Intimacy Project, and the caricature of its leader, Samson, ultimately faltered behind the mirror of their own true nature. Despite whatever principals were held as truths, when taught without kindness by a man who was in the end incapable of empathy, these truths were immediately falsified. Samson and the Intimacy Project just took themselves too fucking seriously that they made it impossible for anyone else to.

Helena and I spent a solid three years developing a friendship in and out of the cult before we revisited any physical attraction to one another. Right around the time when Namazzi (Helena's self-proclaimed non-romantic wife and roommate) moved to the Netherlands, I told Helena she could move into my tiny apartment in Santa Monica with me. At that time she was dating this young thing named Grayson we'd met in the early days of going to Deus Ex Machina. She seemed happy enough in that I-have-enough-sexual-power-over-this-one-to-be-satisfied-for-now sort of way.

Namazzi and I took a road trip to Oregon right before she moved to Europe. The night before we left I had all the Deus boys over to my tiny apartment in Santa Monica for a goodbye dinner of tagliatelle with lamb ragù. Twelve of them showed up, mostly uninvited, and we squeezed into my living room until pasta with wine eventually turned into whiskey with suggestion. At the end of the night it was just Helena, Grayson, and me, and I was all, "Yeah, sure. You guys can totally spend the night here…on the couch, or with me in the bed. I'm game for whatever."

Grayson, who'd just lost his virginity to Helena not a month before, and Helena, who was "not gay," got in my bed like they had their hands tied behind their backs. I had to do all the work. Poor Grayson. I had an intense affection for him that was not at all sexual. Helena was way too busy with me to pay him any mind. He kinda just sat there and watched, trying to figure out how to insert himself, denied at every turn. Helena just sort of lay there timidly asking me if we could try all the things she thought lesbians did. When it was all over, she asked Grayson and I to hold her and made us promise—made us swear—that we wouldn't tell Namazzi. That we wouldn't tell anyone, but especially not Namazzi. I didn't really care either way, but she seemed so scared, so earnest in her request. "I have an agreement with Samson and João to disclose any sexual encounters," I told her. "But beyond them, I won't tell a soul."

When Helena moved in after the road trip and we finally had a chance to talk about what happened, I told her that it had been a lark for me. That our friendship was more important than sex. She told me that she was confused about her passion and her curiosity. Ultimately, she said she didn't know what she wanted with me. She didn't know what any of it meant and didn't know if she could sleep with me like that without wanting more. I told her that we should just keep the conversation open because now that we were living together, if we weren't careful, all of this confusion could very easily give rise to tension.

The months that followed from May to October were different. We'd check in about rent, and utility bills, or the next IP meeting, but then she'd insist that she'd have to go to sleep early and wake up for CrossFit or hop on a conference call for work. Any time I'd ask her how she was faring in the house she'd just say "fine." Any time I'd ask how she was with what had taken place between us before she moved in, she'd just say "fine." Grayson stopped calling her when he started at Cal State Northridge and that was fine too, but Grayson and I were still hanging out, and she was fine with that. Just fine. "I'm practicing nonmonogamy," she'd remind me. "I don't claim any ownership over him. It's fine."

By October I couldn't take it anymore. I decided we were going to have a party. "We'll celebrate your birthday and Día de los Muertos and Halloween all in one." It was a fine idea. We spent the whole month preparing. By the night of the party we'd spent so much time together that I thought it was all in my head. Helena was fine. Our friendship was fine. Everything was fine. Even Grayson came to the party and they were fine too! By the end of the night the three of us were in a tangle in my bed again "practicing non-monogamy," and the next morning everything was fine. So fucking fine. An onslaught of fine.

From that point on, the hostility of "I'm fine" would explode about once a month. I'd usually corner her in the kitchen and she'd try to "I'm fine" her way out of it. "Come on, lady. Out with it already," I'd demand when she would broadcast her obvious discontent with one too many sighs and bangs of the pot. After a few minutes the salt water would brim and I'd hear this month's version of how precisely not fine she was. How she felt like I didn't take her seriously, or how she was sure I hated her, or how she felt like she was my annoying little sister, or how some nights it was so hard to not crawl into bed with me, or how she wanted to know what it was like to have a girlfriend, or how she wasn't gay, or how she needed me to make concessions for her—to not call her on her shit, or to call her on it more. She didn't know.

I guess I could have been nicer to her about it. The Intimacy Project was supposed to be about taking people as they are to themselves, not as you imagine them to be. Helena's just about the gayest monogamist person I've ever met, but there she was insisting she was straight, insisting she was polyamorous, and insisting on her dedication to our friendship as she went about ensuring its fall. What was I supposed to do? Tell her I didn't believe her? Tell her I knew who she was even though she hadn't fully discovered it yet? I didn't even really believe that myself. I didn't really believe I could know a person more than they knew themselves. That is the ultimate betrayal. To take what someone has shown you through the grace of your closeness and to use it against them like you're some kind of expert in who they are. That, I wouldn't do. Not with Helena. Not ever.

I'd let her air her grievances. Tell me all the things she just knew I thought of her. Tell me all the ways she just knew I felt about her. Then, when she was done and she couldn't fight anymore I'd slowly walk her through what I actually thought about her. How I actually felt about her. It was always an exhausting process. "We have to talk to each other, Helena. If you don't tell me the effect I have on you, I won't know until your hostility is fucking overflowing. I can't be responsible for your feelings about me, and you can't keep expecting me to know what is going on for you if you don't tell me. It's not my fucking job to drag this shit out of you once a month." She'd nod in agreement, say she'd try harder to be open in the future.

We only ever hooked up one time after that at a strip club in Thessaloniki when we were visiting Namazzi and her Greek boyfriend the next summer. Helena made Kappa swear he wouldn't tell Namazzi, who had stormed off earlier in the night in a drunken rage. Actually, Namazzi's utter belligerence in Thessaloniki nearly brought Helena and I closer together, but by the time we got to the beaches of Khalkidhiki a few days after we hooked up, I decided to take the single bedroom in our rented apartment instead of opting to share a room with her, and all our closeness flew out the fucking window. It wasn't long before she began broadcasting her discontent in scoffs and sighs. Helena began behaving as though I was the most ridiculous person she'd ever met and telling me to shut the fuck up any chance she got. I cornered her one last time in our apartment by the beach and asked her what her fucking problem was. She told me that she couldn't believe that I could hook up with her without wanting anything more, and she was pissed off that she didn't have a hold on me. That sex didn't hook me emotionally. That I wasn't beguiled by her sexual energy. Word for word, people. I can't make this shit up. Too fucking serious.

I was having a beer with Namazzi at Kappa's bar in Utrecht two weeks later when Boone texted me that DCFS had taken all of Dahlia's children away. I cut the rest of my trip short and returned home in haste to do what I could to help. I met Samson the day after I returned from Europe for what ended up being our final meeting together.

At our final meeting in Pasadena all Samson could still talk about was the fucking suckling pig party months earlier. I'd been completely away from his influence for the longest time since we'd first met four years earlier. He brought out all the big guns. Every horrible, deep, dark secret I'd ever shared with him and every fear I'd ever had were his ammunition. He took all my dark mirrors and held them in front of me, hoping to break me down to the desperate girl I was when we first met. It was so absurd. I mean, sure, all the things he was saying about me were true at some point, but he only knew these things about me through the grace of the intimacy we shared. The whole premise of the Intimacy Project was to take people as they are to themselves, not as you imagine them to be, and here I was, actually different than the person he'd met four years ago, and he refused to see it. He refused to acknowledge me as anyone other than the character of Natascia in his mind. He did the very thing he'd been training us not to do. Samson's whole life was built around him being the smartest person in the room at any given moment, but he never banked on the fact that I might have actually learned anything from him. That morning, his attempts to keep me under his thumb were as plain as they were pathetic. I left the Intimacy Project and their bag of lies for good.

When Helena found out, she told me she didn't know how to relate to me anymore if I wasn't in the group. I told her how shitty that sounded but that she could go on living in my apartment until the end of the year. We barely spoke and by January she moved out. We threw a last party in a final attempt at friendship. She showed up hungover and late the day of the party asking me if there was any coffee and did approximately zero work to help prepare. When I asked her if she would at least do the dishes before she left, she banged around in the kitchen huffing and puffing for an hour. I didn't care why. I knew the Intimacy Project would meet the next day and she'd spend six hours telling everyone what a villain I was and they'd all agree because that was what they did to people who got out of the cult. They took everything they'd ever learned about them and used it to distort their memories into something monstrous. People who left were seen as weak, resigned to their conditioning and self-indulgence. And I was the worst of them all. I had hoodwinked the group for four years, pretended to be so dedicated to "the work" because I was obsessed with attention and admiration. Conned them out of their money and used their energy to build myself up like I used everyone in my life. I was a thief.

Two days after the party, Helena called to inform me she was "resigning from our friendship," and then a murder of lies, winged black and gnarled, flew through the ether from her mouth to my ear. A murder of lies structured in Samson syntax and worded from the Intimacy Project lexicon. A murder of lies intended to break me into unrecognizable pieces and return me to the forge of the IP fire. I know this, I thought. This was me when I was under his spell too. There's no arguing with this. She didn't call to have a conversation. She has lost the ability to think for herself and so she's hiding behind him. "Sounds good, Helena," was all I said. She hung up the phone and we never spoke again.

# CHAPTER 50

LUKE ONCE REFERRED TO himself as the Original Hipster when he showed me a photograph yellowed with age of him on his first motorcycle. I used to see him around Deus all the time, mostly in his gear, quietly waiting in line for a cup of coffee or slipping into the shop in back.

"Your tires are low" was his opening line.

*Fuck this dude* was my opening thought. *My tires aren't low and I'm not really in the mood to have PSI mansplained to me by some rider who thinks I'm hot.* I gave him a thumbs up. He shrugged and walked away.

About an hour later, as I was getting ready to leave the coffee shop, I had to laugh. My tires were noticeably low. *Shit. I'd better take care of this before I see that dude again and give him a reason to talk to me.* I drove away and got busy with my day and didn't remember that the tires were low until I pulled back into Deus the next morning. He kinda looked at me, looked at my tires, and looked back at me. "Don't give me any shit," I told him. "I didn't have time to fill them up."

"Want me to fill them for you?" he asked. I scoffed, waiting for the rest of the pickup line that never came.

"You mean, like, now?"

He walked over to the shop in the back and leaned in through the top of the open Dutch door. The mechanic fed him a hose and I stood around looking like a girl while he filled all four of my tires. That was it. He didn't use it as an opportunity to talk to me. Didn't try to hit on me. Didn't mansplain shit. When he was done, I asked him if I could buy him a cup of coffee for his troubles, and he said, "Nah. I'm good," and got on his bike and rode away.

Weeks carried on with mornings at Deus. We would just say hi to each other after that. Weeks turned to months and "hi" turned in to "how are you?" More months, and then "I'm fine" bloomed into real answers with real details. Luke had a motorcycle apparel shop down the street that specialized in racing gear made from the finest Japanese leather. He was very quiet, which made him very easy to talk to. By the time I finally made it to one of the monthly Sunday motorcycle rallies they used to have in the Deus parking lot, we were friendly enough for him to feel perfectly comfortable stumbling onto the couch with an extra beer in hand for me. He handed me a Corona, barely asking if I wanted it, and put his tired head on my shoulder like we were pals. By the time he handed me his phone so he could friend me on Facebook it was a no-brainer, and that night when he slid into my DMs and asked if I rode, I responded right away because it just felt like the natural thing to do. We carried on a conversation about motorcycles for the next ten minutes before he wrote "we should go for a ride sometime."

It was a Tuesday evening when we went out. I remember that because I used to meet with Samson on Tuesday mornings and at that particular meeting I made a conscious choice to not disclose that I was going out later with a dude. Well, that and some of the Deus boys were throwing a Taco Tuesday party at their apartment that night. Luke picked me up at my place in Santa Monica and we met up with this big group of riders somewhere near Griffith Park. We rode through Los Feliz, Glendale, Eagle Rock, Highland Park, and when we got to Pasadena and passed by the very same café I'd spent the morning thoroughly deconditioning myself in with the cult leader, I wondered what Samson would say about all of this. *How's he gonna spin this moment of absolute joy into self-indulgence? What egregious error is he going to tell me I'm making by going out with this dude? What will he see about this ride that I'm not seeing?* Luke pulled on the throttle as Arroyo Seco became the 110 South, and all my thoughts disappeared.

We pulled into some biker bar downtown, and I drank bourbon and soda while he sipped on a beer and asked me questions about myself. *Here it comes.* "Uh, listen, Luke. I'm happy to answer your questions, and I'm happy to get to know you and have you get to know me, and I really enjoyed this ride, but this isn't a date for me. I'm not interested in fucking you."

I think he just laughed and said "okay" as I hit him with the whole Intimacy Project one-two. About how I was learning to reshape the energy of my existence through true intimacy, through proper regard, proper distance, and the right order of things. How I was practicing abstinence in order to maintain my erotic fortitude and repair the hole in my dreaming womb. Abstinence was Samson's latest prescription for me to gain some discipline and stop blowing my energy out all over town. He'd more or less convinced me that I was a monster at that point. A beautiful powerful monster. Like Rogue or Mystique or at the very least Jubilee, and if I didn't start taking this shit seriously and learn to harness and properly deploy my energy I was just as dangerous to myself as any hormonal teenage mutant before they found Xavier's School For Gifted Youngsters.

On that first date that I swore wasn't a date, I told Luke things I'd been taught to say. "I don't date, I don't hang out. I don't hook up. I don't get involved in implicitly casual relationships." Shit Samson would applaud me for saying in our next meeting.

Luke just rolled with it. Told me he didn't need anything from me, asked me how I learned about all of this. Talked to me about studying Aikido. Just kept being himself and letting me be me. We had a really great time.

"I can't have another beer," he said at the end of our second drink. "Not if I wanna get us both back safe." He paid the bill.

On the freeway, I held onto him tight. The cold April air cutting through my nylon black catsuit. He reached back and held the bottom of my leg. When we pulled up to the party I was already late for, Grayson was hanging off the balcony, rushing me through goodbye. Luke was already back on his bike with a "see ya!"

Upstairs, Grayson met me in the hallway, grabbed me, and spun me around. "I did it, Tash! I lost my V-card to Helena! Don't go in yet," he pleaded. "I need you out here with me." He gave me all the details and we celebrated the fact that he no longer had the look of a virgin. "So are you dating that old dude, Luke?"

"Nah, G. That's not what that was."

Luke and I stayed friends after that, seeing each other at Deus or texting random thoughts throughout the day. We went on a couple more rides, grabbed lunch a few times and a drink here or there. By the time we were driving through Mt. Shasta on our way to Oregon I remember telling Namazzi how much I liked him. A few days later we were piling into the car after a long hike in Eugene and Luke hit me with a text asking if I missed him. I surprised the hell out of both of us when I texted him back yes.

We went out for drinks when I got back. A month of making out went by until we had our first fight. It wasn't the first time he tried to turn kissing into something else, but this time when I stopped him he just got up and put his boots on. He didn't want to talk about it and walked out the door to the sound of "please don't just leave like this."

I didn't understand anything anymore. I didn't understand what was happening to me or who I was becoming. I didn't understand how having sex with someone had become such a bad thing. I liked Luke, and I couldn't even explain why I liked him without getting all tangled up in Intimacy Project rhetoric. So much of what we learned in the Intimacy Project was taught to us through psychological punishment, and any two-bit psychologist will tell you that memory retention and punishment do not go hand in hand. Samson's lessons never included kindness or compassion or love. Love, as far as he was concerned, was about what sort of agreements could be made. I didn't love Luke, but I knew I didn't want him to leave. I knew I was unwilling to let him fuck me to stay, and above all I knew that the intensity through which I was experiencing his departure had very little to do with him. Maybe fifteen minutes passed and I got a text: "Meet me outside in ten. Dress warm."

I got into Luke's convertible Z3, puffy-eyed and heavy. We drove north on PCH in silence and I thought of Clay. Of all the long drives on dark nights we took through this city when we were kids. It'd only been a year since he'd died. Luke and I pushed through the Palisades, sped past Sunset, wound through the glory of Topanga and Tuna Canyon, and ended up at the Mulholland overlook with the glittering neon valley below. He shut the engine off and turned to me.

"Do you like me?"

"Yes."

"Why?"

"I don't know."

"But you like me?"

"Yes, Luke. I do."

"Okay."

"You can't do that again. You can't just leave like that without a word."

"I know. I'm sorry."

There's a reason most cults use sexuality as a mean to control their members. Whether it's abstinence or sexual subservience, the goal is to isolate members from any outside influence. After four years of spilling my guts to him three to four times a week, Samson knew me well enough to know that even if I wasn't saying anything I was most likely seeing someone. The next morning at our breakfast meeting he looked at my puffy eyes and accused me of hiding out. I broke down and confessed the whole thing. He immediately launched into a diatribe about Luke's fragile masculinity. "He's trying to get you to sign the Man/Woman contract, Natascia. Don't you see? That way he can dictate the terms of your engagement from the broken conditioned male in him while abandoning his true masculinity and rejecting the true feminine in you. How do you not see that?"

I thought of Clay again. I thought of the way he'd smile and shake his head at me, "Naughty, I've been watching you do this for years. You deliberately do things to make yourself feel bad about having sex with people." I thought of him holding my hand as we listened to "Enjoy the Silence" in his black Honda accord with the flashing blue neon lights coming from his stereo. "Vows are spoken / To be broken / Feelings are intense / Words are trivial / Pleasures remain / So does the pain / Words are meaningless / And forgettable." As Samson droned on and on, chastising me for my stupidity and the misuse of my Dreaming Womb, I saw the ghost of Clayton sitting next to him, laughing, *"Oh, I don't know you?"*

In that moment I decided I would never tell Samson about another man or woman ever again. I was done disclosing. Feeling guilty. Being punished. Pushing back. Explaining myself. "Yeah, you're totally right, Sam," I said in private resignation. "I totally see that." We spent the rest of the morning discussing other matters, but Luke, my vagina, my dreaming womb, and my core erotic nature? Henceforth that fool would only get lies. Omissions and lies.

I slept with Luke the next time I saw him. Gave it to him whatever way he wanted, whenever he wanted, and I relished every moment of it. He paid for everything and I cheerfully let him. Every rendezvous over bourbon, dinners, and long rides up the coast. His bed, my bed, blowjobs in the back of the truck. Drinks, lunches, a spontaneous trip to Vegas. No discipline. Sex was fun and frequent, but most of the time we just talked for hours. We'd pass whole nights like that. Him at a two-drink maximum, me no-holds-barred, gabbing away. Or sometimes I'd go to his shop and we'd order tonkatsu chicken curry from Fresh in the Box and he'd put on a motorcycle movie and work while I just sat there until afternoon turned to evening in the office chair beside him.

As much time as we spent together, Luke had rules of his own to maintain a proper distance. He was very against getting attached. Something about a crazy ex-girlfriend and years of therapy. He showered immediately after sex. Like immediately. And other than the nights in Vegas, there were no sleepovers. They made it easier to get attached. I remember cutting through Barstow in the Z3 on the way back from Vegas.

"So, do you feel like we got closer on this trip?" he asked as "Purple Rain" looped for the seventeenth time on the mix he'd made.

"Huh?"

"Like, do you feel closer to me now, or something?"

"No. Not really, Luke. Why, do you?"

"Do I what?"

"Do you feel closer to *me* now?"

"Nope."

My preparations to leave for Europe and the opportunity it gave me to rethink my position in the cult took up most of my time in May of 2014. As a result, Luke and I were seeing each other less and less. One afternoon in the back of his shop over chicken tonkatsu curry he very uncharacteristically asked me if when I left it would be over between us. When I asked him where this was coming from, he shrugged his shoulders and said, "I'm sure you'll sleep with other people out there because we're not exclusive, or whatever."

"I don't know, Luke." I shrugged back. "I'm not planning on it, or anything. I don't know what's out there or when I'm coming back, but that doesn't mean I won't remain connected to you."

A couple months later in a little café in Piazza Santo Spirito sitting across from Aegir's old flat, I realized that Luke had already blocked me from everything without a word. The telephone, Facebook, Instagram, email. It was two years before we spoke again, and by that time the Intimacy Project was just another thing in my personal history to erase. We haven't slept together since before I left for Europe back in 2014. It's not there for us anymore. We are just friends now. You know, lunches, dinners, drinks, the occasional long ride up the coast.

I'm inclined to write something trite, like, *I'm sure that Luke and I will be lifelong friends*—but I certainly thought that of Helena, of Mary Jane, of Dahlia, for God's sake, and just look where that got me. I never thought Bridget and I wouldn't be on speaking terms, or that Sonny would call me seven years later to apologize for telling me I was being a "Debbie," or that Jude and I would be as close as we are now. And if you would have asked me to wager who out of all the fifty would still be around today, I'd have cheerfully and wholeheartedly put all my money on Skylar. But so it goes. Time and the Great Mystery hold no prisoners and have their own tales to tell. We are mere matter in the Great Matter, comprised mostly of wishful thinking. I'm sure ten years from now Luke and I will not be on speaking terms for one reason or another, and I'll have a different story to tell.

# ACKNOWLEDGMENTS

Nᴏᴛ ɪɴᴄʟᴜᴅɪɴɢ ᴛʜᴇ ꜰɪꜰᴛʏ that lie within, there are several people without whom this book would have never been possible. To my high school teachers, David Herrera, Peter Sawaya, and Cindy Milwe. I would have never made it to adulthood had it not been for your small encouragements. To my dear friend Bernadette Bolan, who read every single chapter in its rawest form the moment it was written, and who in the purest act of friendship spared me any criticism. To her wonderful husband, Jed Smith, who would let me crash his workspace at Soho House Malibu to finish the book because he said I belonged there, even if I didn't have a membership yet. To my new friend Scott Caan, who casually mentioned he knew a publisher and would pass my book along if he thought it was good as though it were no big deal. It was a VERY big deal, Scott. You have changed my life forever. To the unnaturally talented Conner Marx, whose enthusiasm for this project was a powerful antidote to my inner saboteur. To Casey Jackson, who may be the only person to truly see me, and who has never asked me to be anything other than exactly who the fuck I am. To my good friends Mercel Chambers and Kevin Shattuck, who read the earliest versions and took the time to really tell me what they thought. In intimate detail. To the ever present, supportive powerhouse that is Doselle Young whose answer to a horribly written essay is a three-page outline on what it *could* be, and whose response to a good essay is an hour-long phone call on how we can tour this book in a post-pandemic world. To my beautiful, sensitive, talented brother and best friend, who reminded me that I am the only person in the world who will believe in my own dreams, so I'd better be courageous enough to dream big. To my mom, who has supported and encouraged me to never sell myself short. To my pop, whose kindness and diplomacy kept me connected to the rest of my family when the cult tried to pull me away. A mio zio. Siamo piu simili di quanto tu sappia e spero che tu lo riconoscerai leggendo queste pagine. To my publisher, Tyson, who took a chance on a total ingénue, and to my editor, Guy, who had about a million opportunities to condescend to me and didn't take a single one. Finally, to the coffee shops that never asked me to leave: Menottis, Superba, and Quentin. Without you and your dedication to those magic beans this book would have remained a list for eternity.

CPSIA information can be obtained
at www.ICGtesting.com
Printed in the USA
LVHW030555260721
693443LV00002B/4